THE
TESTAMENT
OF CALIBAN

"DEFIANT LUCIFER"

This Edstrom fragment is found in several art collections, including that of
Iowa City

THE TESTAMENT OF CALIBAN

BY

DAVID EDSTROM

FUNK & WAGNALLS COMPANY

NEW YORK AND LONDON

1937

FOREWORD

MOVE over, Benvenuto Cellini, and make room on the narrow shelf of great autobiographies for this self-life of David Edstrom, a rival of your genius in sculpture, as in the revelation of himself and of the amazingly various people he has met.

A lover of beauty, a philosopher, a poet, a great sculptor, a seer of vast conceptions, a struggler with the most sordid, cruel, and the most luxurious evils, he tells with shameless honesty the story of a life of extraordinary richness.

This autobiography is as enthralling as a novel with the added power of authenticity unafraid either of beauty or its opposites.

RUPERT HUGHES

CONTENTS

CHAPTER   PAGE

	FOREWORD	V
I	CHRIST VERSUS ODIN	I
II	THE TRIUMPH OF SKAM	13
III	FAITH STORMS A CITADEL	21
IV	THE RETURN OF SKAM	29
V	BLACK LOAM	35
VI	THE BRIDGE TO LONDON FALLS DOWN	40
VII	I STUDY FOR THE MINISTRY	47
VIII	STOICISM	52
IX	A HOBO	59
X	ALONE	67
XI	HATE	77
XII	I VISIT THE ROYAL ACADEMY	83
XIII	I OUTRIDE THE STORM	91
XIV	THE BAND BEGINS TO PLAY	94
XV	I FINISH WITH THE TECHNICAL SCHOOL	102
XVI	THE BEAUTY OF BONES	110
XVII	ELIZABETH	120
XVIII	ROARING WATERS	128
XIX	NEGLINGE	146
XX	THROUGH THE CITY OF LIFE AND DEATH TO THE CITY OF FLOWERS	157
XXI	CALIBAN	163
XXII	BRIEF FREEDOM	175
XXIII	BONDAGE	183

CHAPTER   PAGE

XXIV   DESPAIR 195

XXV   PARIS 203

XXVI   THE END OF AN EPISODE 206

XXVII   CUBA 213

XXVIII   CONQUEST 218

XXIX   NOW BEFORE I DIE 225

XXX   TERROR 233

XXXI   PARIS IS KIND 238

XXXII   THE FOURTH DIMENSION 244

XXXIII   PALLAS ATHENE 256

XXXIV   HIS ROYAL HIGHNESS 267

XXXV   IN SWEDEN WITH CORA 272

XXXVI   PRINCESS PAT 278

XXXVII   THE BATTLEGROUND OF LIFE 288

XXXVIII   I REFUSE A QUEEN 303

XXXIX   IN A MAN'S HEART 307

XL   LOVE AND TANGO 309

XLI   NEW YORK CITY 315

XLII   SING SING 318

XLIII   SAINT IGNATIUS 320

XLIV   NEW YORK—1917 325

XLV   WHERE THE WEST BEGINS 327

XLVI   OPINIONS 336

ILLUSTRATIONS

	FACING PAGE
"Defiant Lucifer" . . . . . *Frontispiece*	
"A Country Girl"	44
Michelangelo's Delphian Sibyl	45
The Sculptor and "The Eternal Triangle" . . .	92
David Edstrom at Work on a Bust of Gloria Swanson .	93
Ernest Thiel, Patron of Art	148
"Christ and Medusa"	149
"Hunger"	196
"Protecting the Flame of Life"	197
"Ophelia"	276
"The Hunchback"	277
Proposed Memorial to John Ericsson	308
Margaret, Late Crown Princess of Sweden . . .	309
"Childhood"	332
Harry Chandler	333

THE
TESTAMENT
OF CALIBAN

I

CHRIST VERSUS ODIN

THE brilliant, beautiful snow of winter had gone, and the chill bleakness of March was upon the land, when I burst, in angry protest, from the warm seclusion of my mother's womb to the harshness of a world which was not fashioned to my specifications, on the estate of Dalsheda, in the province of Smaland, Sweden. It was midnight, March 27, 1873.

The room was lit only by the uncertain light of flickering candles. Beyond their little gleam, in a corner the darkness of which better suited the character of her supplication, hovered my grandmother, rapidly muttering Runic incantations against the piercing screams of my mother's agony, while above both sounds rose the stentorian prayers of my father whose Christian voice thundered hoarsely, that it might frighten away the Devil and reach the ears of sweet Jesus.

Seldom have three such strangely assorted and antagonistic persons gathered in one room as those three who waited for my birth—Mother, Father, and Grandmother.

The eldest of them was an illiterate peasant woman of tremendous and often frightening vitality, living still in the pagan beliefs of her Viking ancestors, worshiping gods which were anathema to the infant religion of Jesus, her dark mind brooding on witches' sabbaths, on the austerity of Heimdal standing guard over the way to the abode of the gods, fearing the coming of another "no-dar," concocting potent "Troll-skott" (magic formulas) during my mother's pregnancy that I might "jell" into the kind of person who would rank high by the standards of her ancient beliefs and personal ambitions.

In direct contrast to her beliefs were those of my father who, at the age of thirty, had been converted to the beliefs of the "Readers," a Protestant Christian sect of very positive beliefs, given to expounding them vigorously.

He had been born in circumstances of great hardship, and at an early age was thrown out to shift for himself as apprentice to an itinerant tailor. He used to tell me that during the first years of his apprenticeship he was fed so little that he often robbed the farmers' hogs, beating them off with a strong club while he ate ravenously of their swill. He told me, too, of long weary marches from place to place with his master, the boy carrying the heavy pressing irons, his growing, undernourished body shivering beneath too scanty clothing.

At the time that he was converted to the creed of the "Readers," he could neither read nor write. But with his conversion came an awakening of the imagination, and a vision of life which had never before entered his narrow world. The element of mystery in religion acts as a strong mental stimulus to primitive minds, and Father was prodded into an intellectual activity far beyond any that he had known before. He applied himself with tremendous passion to the task of getting an education. At first his objective was the reading of the Bible, but soon he extended his study to other fields and even became a teacher in a theological seminary founded by his sect. Meanwhile he was also studying advanced methods of agriculture and cattle raising.

I suppose it was a combination of his religious zeal, which always includes a certain desire to proselytize, to "save others," and his interest in farming, which made him find his way into the superintendency of Dalsheda, which had been converted into a "reform farm" for delinquent boys from the cities. It was to Dalsheda that he brought his third wife, a fragile, nervous woman who had hoped for a better marriage, a strange companion for his robust and often grim vigor, my mother.

Mother had been reared in cultured surroundings and been taught to expect the delicacies of life which she never found with my father. Among her ancestors were Poles and Italians, as well as Swedes. She had been driven by economic necessity into marrying my father. Her hope for a son was based upon a need for something, some one, who would save her from the ghastly gloom of her marriage.

As a girl Mother had danced with "the King" (as she always said—though he was not king then), and she never tired of telling me about it. It was when Charles XV, then Crown Prince, had been entertaining the Prince of Wales who was visiting Sweden. Young and handsome and gay, the two princes had tired of their escorts and, escaping them, had ridden to Motala, where Mother was visiting. At first overcome with embarrassment, her aunts and uncles had turned to stare with amazement at the two royal scions whose familiarity with complete strangers to them, and commoners at that, so upset the old people that they became speechless and scarcely fit for their duties as hosts and hostesses.

But the girls had suffered no such handicap. The two princes, riding their horses up to Mother's uncle's house in the rain, had been drenched to the skin, and, gaily removing their soaked clothing, had put on other garments much too big for them while their own dried. Then, after they had eaten supper, they insisted upon dancing with the girls. One of them would play the piano—not too well, apparently—while the other danced, and then they would change about. Mother used to show me some of the quaint old steps and sing the strange little songs which dancing partners had sung to each other in those days. Caught by a marriage which did not bring her happiness, she lived in other days when hope had burned more brightly.

Thus was I thrown into a world ruled by three persons almost as completely out of sympathy with one another as three persons might be. Between Mother and Father was the resentment which hovers over every unsatisfactory marriage. Between Grandmother and Father was the fear and distrust which marks a relationship between any two persons who hold deeply felt, but opposing, religious beliefs.

During my earliest years Odin, in the person of his dour and vociferous protestant, my grandmother, and Christ, through the equally noisy declarations of his servant, my father, fought a battle for my soul.

My father's intense interest in his work and my mother's illness left me to the care of my grandmother during my babyhood. It was on her knees, snuggled close to her wrinkled old cheeks, that my baby eyes commenced to focus on the fascinating material things of the world, that my ears learned to listen to and grasp a word for the first time and that my gradually awakening mind came to seize and ponder on hazy conceptions. How ample, how protecting, seemed the great lap between her powerful legs where I reposed before the immense fireplace in the long common room, while the hot flames from mighty logs darted like hissing dragon tongues up the dark mysterious chimney and out into the inky void where the northern storms hissed and roared.

Even now every thought I have of my grandmother is associated with fire and storm, the angry flash and flare of lightning, the crashing roar of thunder, and the weird tales of the other world with which she filled my mind at its first awakening. So naturally and at such an early age did she give me her conception of life and nature, as it had come down to her from the inland tribes of pagan Sweden, that today it seems as if some of the tales she told me are things through which I have lived myself.

When it thundered loudly she muttered darkly to me that Thor was riding too recklessly and, if he were not careful, would drop a "Vigg" (a bolt of lightning). At a loud clap in the sky she would screech:

"Now he hit a giant on the head!"

Every storm told her a story; in fact every mood of nature had a special significance to her. A big Troll lurked behind the blue hills, and might, at any time, emerge like a great shadow before the sun and slip ominously down into our valley.

Mysterious little creatures rode the air and made plaintive sighing noises, which we heard when the wind passed over our heads. The darkness was filled with monstrous shapes which she described for me, disembodied spirits who took what forms they could in which to roam the lonely moors at night and dance in nefarious rites.

Long before I knew anything of the meaning of Christmas, I learned from my grandmother of the older Swedish holy day which has been replaced by a celebration of the birth of Jesus. The history of the feast called "Midwinter's Blood" I learned later—how the northerners of long ago, feeling the inclemency of the Arctic gods in midwinter, offered a great sacrifice of human blood, killing off many of their people that the others might live—but from Grandmother I learned only of the celebration held at various meeting places of the spirits which roamed the night.

The most terrible of these assembling places, and the only one which I ever saw, was on a low meadow near the highway to Hvetlands, where seven children had been buried alive at one such "Midwinter's Blood" feast. Every time we drove by this place I would tremblingly hide myself behind some one, but so loyal was I to my grandmother's repeated admonition never to reveal her secrets to any one, that I never told why I was afraid.

Carl Larson, the celebrated modern Swedish painter, has made a magnificent painting, showing how, long ago, the King himself offered his body to burn and bleed as a sacrifice to the great Odin at the feast of high winter.

No one knows how much of the old religion is left in the northland. But that some still cling to it is certain. Only a few years ago travelers in an out-of-the-way region in Lapland found a secret place in which there were altars and sacred stones. It had obviously been in recent use and a definite effort had been made to conceal the place and guard it against profanation.

Charmed and terrorized in turn, I gazed wide-eyed into the leaping flames of the fireplace, my head against my grandmother's shriveled breast while she told me of such things as the sacrifice of horses to Odin, and how they talked like human beings before they died on the altar and started on their journey to Valhalla. So vivid was her telling that I could see their flowing manes streaming down the wind and hear their gradually diminishing human words floating back to earth as their spirits, still bearing the shadowy impress of equine bodies, rode the air on their way to the hill of the gods. I could see them as they paused uncertainly, hovering before the entrance to the rainbow bridge leading directly to the gods' own abode, where Heimdal stood guard and announced their coming, as he did the advent of friend or foe, by a blast of his trumpet, challenging them and determining their fitness before they could come even to the foot of the heavenly bridge.

Dalsheda, at the time of my childhood, was a fitting background for instruction in the religion of Pagan or Christian. The estate consisted of some two or three thousand acres of land, most of which was covered by dark spruce forests stretching from a long, narrow valley, up the sides of blue hills. Passing these on a windy night I could hear the voices of such creatures as I dared not envision.

Nearby was a craggy waterfall called "The Fall of the Seven." Grandmother told me how seven brothers had tried here to jump the gorge and how all except the youngest, the seventh to jump, had perished. She told me how you could still hear the brothers crying out there, as they tried, over and over, through eternity, to make that dreadful leap.

Every sound in nature had a hidden meaning which it revealed to her. The wind in the trees, the sound of running water, the thunder, the echoes which rumbled distantly from the surrounding hills, the plaintive cry of two branches rubbing together in the night, the crackling of the fire—all were voices which spoke to her and which she translated for me while I sought security within her surrounding arms and the soft monotony of her tireless voice.

But there was one horror from which I could find no surcease, an ultimate terror which made the skin creep on my flesh—her own fear of a coming "no-dar" and her memory of destruction in other no-dars through which she had lived. A no-dar is a year of famine so great that, in the olden days, it was alleviated by killing off the old people. Grandmother told me that the church warden kept clubs in the sacristy of the church that they might always be ready to help the aged and the weak over the dark flood to the land of death, when famine came. Again and again she made me promise not to let my father club her to death when no-dar came.

It was my grandmother who taught me to smoke. While I was still a small child sitting on her knee she let me suck at her pipe. It was at such an early age that I can no more remember my first smoke than I can my first mouthful of solid food. As soon as I was able to walk I found my father's collection of fine carved pipes carefully kept in a polished wooden box, and from this I took, whenever I wanted to and Father was not around, one of the smaller pipes, loaded and lit it, and enjoyed the ravishing delights of wicked indulgence.

My father was a man of extremely simple habits, an enemy of all luxury (in contrast to my mother, who loved and longed for luxurious living which her marriage denied her), but he insisted that the materials of his few indulgences be of the best quality. As a result of this attitude the tobacco which I learned to smoke as a toddling child was so excellent that, wherever I have gone as a man, I have had difficulty finding any so good.

At last I was caught; a terrible inquisition took place, in which both my smoking and my thorough tutelage in northern magic and pagan mysteries were revealed, and I was completely separated from my dear grandmother.

Father now set out avidly to undo the work his mother had begun. It was as though the religion of Jesus, having lost the first round in the battle with Odin, now entered the second round with a fierce zeal tripled in strength by temporary defeat. Having lost six children in his two former marriages, he had counted greatly on his son and was determined that I should reap the blessed harvest of his own conversion. But the mind of a race of people so recently carefree savages as had been the Swedes, raiding the seas, seeking rather than avoiding danger, filled with the dramatic pagan blackness of Scandinavian folklore and a religion based upon the fury of the elements, does not easily accomplish the long journey from terror and bloodshed to the gentle kindliness of the New Testament. The creed of the "Readers," at least as it was interpreted by Father, was a strange mixture of Christianity and Paganism, taking more of the spirit of the Old Testament than that of the New.

Father's terror of sin and the Devil was magnificently jumbled with the picturesque tales of Revelation. Through his primitive imagination the Lamb and the Beast roamed as tangible, living creations, and as he told me of them, my grandmother's tales became as weak as water in comparison with the fury and vividness of his descriptive narratives. The climax of horror which my grandmother had been able to produce had been her fear of no-dar, in which she might be killed. But Father managed to personify horror to me, to bring it into my own life, to make it a part of myself, by warning me that, in the last days of the world, I might become affiliated with the Beast and have his number, 666, marked on my forehead.

His visualization of the Bible was undoubtedly influenced by the art of Swedish peasants, to whom sin was a person synonymous with the Devil. He—it—was often called "Skam." Used as a verb the word means "shame," but as a noun it means the Devil or the Evil One. Skam, in Swedish peasant art, is black, awful, and shameful. But in this art it is a bit difficult to distinguish between the good and the bad, if visual presentation alone is to be considered. The Lion of Judah, for instance, may be seen with the face of a dog, the body of a horse, the horns of a ram, and the claws of a cat.

But in my father's Christianity blackness and evil were not always predominant. When he was worrying about my future and the basis for it which my grandmother's paganism had furnished, terror and black violence thronged his thoughts and words as he searched in my childish mind for sins of which I hadn't the faintest conception. At other times he gave me a shining picture of the New Jerusalem which even Tasso in his poem, "Jerusalem Delivered," did not surpass.

Born of his eloquence a new force seemed to enter the estate of Dalsheda, in conflict with the evil powers which had lurked over it in my grandmother's tales—the shining wonder of the Christian God.

Around the main buildings in the middle of the valley was a strong echo which, in my earliest conceptions, had thrown back the burdened moaning of the evil ones' hurrying to their pagan trysts. But now in the springtime it reverberated for me with the pleasant resonant "hoo-hoo" of the cuckoo which seemed to tell of the gentleness of God. Hundreds of swallows lived about the roofs of the buildings, eternally fluttering under the eaves, only to shoot out again like arrows and skim through the air, all the while chirping and twittering their praises to the infant Christ. By a little brook running through the grove hundreds of Pentecost lilies bloomed. The frail, watery texture of their petals, the pale yellow at their hearts, and their ethereal perfume made them take highest rank with the profusion of lilies of the valley and pussy willows near them, as symbols of sweet Jesus.

But so thoroughly had my mind already become conditioned by pagan theology, so expectant of horror had it become, and so confused was my father's mind about the frequent identifi-

cation of beauty and evil, that I found myself constantly turning to the conceptions of horror in his teachings, and rejecting
those things which told of kindliness and gentleness and peace.
I was less interested in the New Jerusalem than in the ever-
present drama of evil. That hope to which the weary hearts of
men turn, that remote city not built with hands, the perfect gift
of God, was much less vivid to me than Valhalla and the low
meadow on the highway to Hvetlands where seven children had
been buried alive at the feast of "Midwinter's Blood." Flowers,
birds, and pussy willows were beautiful, but they were not
exciting. They were nice and good, but their beauty was not
comparable to that which the Devil, Loke, and the Troll used
in their conquests of mankind.

This most awful and exquisite beauty against which my father
warned me became an obsession with me. To discover and meet
it face to face became my most fervent hope. I took on the
habit of conducting secret definite expeditions in an attempt to
find it. Most of them centered in the vastness of a great spider-
webbed attic. Here, in a chaotic clutter of broken furniture,
books, bundles of old paper, clothing, pictures, rusty guns,
powder horns, bullet molds, and hundreds of other things long
since forgotten, I pushed my fevered search.

One day I came across an old book. It was lying neglected
and out of sight behind a piece of furniture. It was covered
with dust, its leaves yellowed with age. Opening it, I found
it filled with colored pictures of the Christian martyrs. Some
of them, with their beautiful bodies in elegant postures, were
being boiled in great kettles. Others, in apparent ecstasy, were
slowly roasting on elaborate piles of burning cordwood.

And it was within the pages of this book that I suddenly
found the Evil One. It was not a picture, but a tangible form,
surely one of the most magnificent he had ever assumed. Thin
and long and shining, it had been easy for him to slip in between the pages of the book, where he lay in wait in resplendent
glory, flaunting green and golden rings which wavered around

the perfect beauty of a purple eye. Granny had first told me of Loke, but in her version he had been chained to a rock by the other gods, so that he was harmless. But the Loke of the Bible could be anything, from a fish to a man, could change himself at will into forms so ravishingly beautiful that weak, sin-ridden man could not resist him. And it was this Loke who had crept in between two pages of the book of Christian martyrs and lay there, a wary trap for my enchanted eyes.

After one ecstatic look I slammed the book tight shut and quickly sat on it, so that he could not get away, my heart beating thunderously against my breast in rapturous terror. Then, clutching it fiercely in both hands, holding it shut so tightly that even the Devil himself could not escape, I rushed to my mother.

I was too modest, too overcome with the magnitude of the event, to say outright that I had found the Devil. Instead I held the book tremblingly toward her, still clutching it tightly, and when I finally spoke, it was in a choked whisper.

"Mother," I said, "I have caught something wicked."

She reached out to take the book from me, but I, fearing that he might have got out after all, withheld it while, bit by bit, I opened it a tiny crack and peered in. Yes, he was still there, and so, with a shuddering "Oh," I pushed the book under her eyes.

What she told me then made me suddenly bitterly ashamed, agonizingly aware of my own inadequacy to recognize and sift the good from the evil, convinced me of the uselessness of my little knowledge. I hung my head, dropping my eyes to avoid hers, as I thought how silly I must seem to her. Yet, looked back at now, it seems to me that the depth and intensity of my feeling that day were simply a forecast of the power visual beauty was to have on me during my entire life.

"Why, David," she said, in gentle surprise, "that's a peacock feather."

But even as I walked away in hurt silence, grasping the lovely thing in my hand, even with my newly acquired knowledge that it was but a feather after all, taken from a bird which was neither good nor bad in itself, but only beautiful, that which I clutched in my hand, that which I had run down to its hiding place in the garret, was still something deliciously wicked, terrible, dangerous, and desirable.

II

THE TRIUMPH OF SKAM

O UT of these terrific currents of emotion which swayed my
infancy, out of the conflicting streams of paganism and
militant, dramatic, horror-producing Christianity, out of the
burdened, overwrought attempts which my secret heart and
mind made to analyze and synthesize all the magic and mysticism and glamor and terror which had been poured into
them, I emerged, a child who, doubtless in defense against his
own confusion and lack of inner assurance, developed a growing
aloofness and self-assertiveness. In later years my sister has
told me that in any group everything had to be done my way
or I wouldn't play, and that I acquired such a bad reputation
that the other children on the estate would drop what they were
doing and walk away whenever I came strutting among them.

One story of my childhood tells how a neighbor lifted me
over a stile without asking my leave, and how I, furious, faced
him on the other side with clenched fist.

"If I had my knife with me," I screamed, "I'd plunge it
into your heart!"

This fierce repugnance against familiarity which I was developing then has been a dominant factor in my entire life.
Because of the arrogance which it has produced in me it has
made many enemies, some of them persons whose friendship I
would have liked to gain. But in those days I was conscious
of few implications. I knew only that I did not want others to
touch me, that for most of the time I would rather be alone
than with another. I went my own way, studying out, in a

gradually deepening solitude, the glamorous mysteries of life, more and more aware of the puzzles which tortured my mind and the cross-currents of emotion which swept through my heart, less and less aware of others about me.

And thus it was that when the Evil One did at last come to Dalsheda I had felt no prescience of his coming, nor did I recognize him when he arrived. I was scarcely aware even that the sedate, orderly life of the estate had been torn to shreds, and have had to reconstruct most of that cataclysmic episode from information I have gained during my adult life.

Mother had invited a friend, a beautiful and ardent girl much younger than herself, to our home, and Father, gazing upon her, forgot his duties as master of a pious institution, forgot his position as an elder among the holy ones, forgot how long and difficult had been his struggle out of poverty and ignorance, and how precipitate might be his fall back into the pit. Mother and my sister were sent off to a resort while Father and the newly-found object of his adoration threw themselves into the consuming vortex of ecstatic love.

The violent blood of a mighty, barbaric race flowed in his vigorous and supple body, and for the first time he met another capable of boundless, fearless passion as violent and limitless as his own. What of it if the heavens fell? What if the Devil himself were the boatman as they rode the tide of lust? They lived defiant, careless of where the rushing flood might carry them.

Not until his beloved had borne him a son did my father fall back into the professional groove of an ordained child of God. Love and passion may reign for a time, but training, convention, lifelong habits of thought and action, take charge at last. The woman and her child were sent away, after Father had eased his conscience as much as he could by making ample financial provision for them, and Mother came home again.

I did not, at the time, realize that she had been away so long, nor do I think I was aware of having missed her much. I remember only the keen joy I felt when she alighted from a carriage one day beside my father. Such simple things as that I remember; the dramatic intensity behind them was lost to me.

None so great that he is not also a pigmy, or so small that he is not at the same time a giant; there is always something beneath us and above us which we cannot grasp. The terrible noise of the laboring ant, or the thunderous murmuring of Earth as she turns herself round and round before the sun, we cannot hear.

I know that, before this time, my grandmother died, but I have no memory of her death nor of any impact it had on me. No more was I aware of the tension and heartache brought about by this interlude of love in my father's life.

But others were aware of it, others upon whom Father's position in the community and the church itself depended. Social and financial ruin were the aftermath of his whirlwind. Harassed from within by his conscience, from without by accusation, he held an auction which lasted for days, at which cattle, horses, farm equipment, household furniture—everything we owned—was sold. Yet even though the prices were those of a forced sale, all his debts were paid and there was a surplus of several thousand crowns—enough to take us to America and let us start with a clean slate in the place Father called "the Promised Land."

With what mingled excitement and pain he must have looked for the last time at the forests and fields of Dalsheda, a place which by now was woven deeply into the fabric of his life! What bitterness, if any, he felt toward those whose intolerance of his lust was driving him away, I do not know. It is likely that his own intolerance was as great as theirs, and that he would not have had them treat him differently. What stentorian pleas for forgiveness and help born in his tortured soul flung themselves from his lips upward seeking the ears of sweet Jesus, I did not hear.

In the midst of his pain at least one thing must have comforted him. For there was a group who had not joined his accusers, a group who felt only affection and gratitude for him, and these indeed he must have left with difficulty. Both as an important figure in the affairs of Dalsheda and as an elder in his church Father had come in constant contact with the poor of the region as their benefactor, and these remembered only his kindnesses and closed their ears to tales of his wrongdoing. On the day that we left to begin our long journey to America they came from miles around to tell him good-by.

It was in the springtime; the sun was shining and the birds singing. These unfortunate ones, these who had so little, were weeping bitterly because Father was leaving them. He had been their champion, their protector, their comforter. They kissed his hands and clung to him and cried out that there would never be another like him there.

But I did not weep, as I looked for the last time at those lovely hills and smelt the fresh green of the new grass and the delicate fragrance of wildflowers mingled with the breath of the snow still lying in compact drifts where the sun could, not reach it. I laughed aloud with joy, my heart beating with such feverish intensity as it had never known before, while my lungs filled themselves lustily with the precious air of imminent adventure, and my legs rushed madly about carrying me from place to place so that I might share in every detail of the final packing.

And why should I have wept? I was a child, and a child's world is another world. His joy and sorrow are as real as ever those of man or woman, but they are different; a day is like a week, a week like a month, a month like a year, and a year a lifetime, which is to say, eternity. I could not see the wave of destiny on whose crest we were being carried out into the world, any more than adults can see or comprehend at the moments of their greatest force, the catastrophic waves which, century after century, carry the human race from the trough to the crest, only to hurl it again into some dark, unforeseen abyss. When Father, Mother, my sister and I embarked for America, I could see no tragedy before or behind, was aware only of an accelerated sense of resplendent, glorious adventure.

First we went to Gothenburg, then across the North Sea to England, then on over the Atlantic and through the old Castle Garden of New York as immigrants, then westward to join relatives living at Paxton, Illinois. We were in a new world, facing a new life, and Skam was left behind with the forests and fields of Dalsheda, but I can remember chiefly only how hot it was in Paxton.

Mother had seemingly become quite well and (whether because of the advantage my father's guilty conscience and repentance gave her, I do not know) definitely rose to a position as head of the house, while Father, his emasculation becoming complete through violent, bitter quarrels with Mother, gradually settled down meekly into second place.

He had never done manual labor in his adult life, and, although he possessed tremendous vitality, his effort to do farm work ended disastrously with a sunstroke and a severe illness. Unable to stay longer with our relatives, we went our way, and I remember dimly and unpleasantly the shock I received when I looked for the first time at the dilapidated shanty which was to be our next home at Rankin, Illinois.

Winter was imminent, but we cheered ourselves with the belief that a country in which summers were so hot would surely have mild winters. I really think we dreamed that there would be no snow, that from fall to spring the grass would grow green, and that we could go hatless and coatless the year round without discomfort.

But our dream was soon shattered by a stormy, wet autumn, which dragged on desolately, each day seemingly more dreary than the last. The bitter chilling rain drove in through the cracks in our shanty despite all that we could do to stop them up with newspapers and rags. As December came upon us the nights grew bitterly cold. Day by day the temperatures descended to new low levels, and the wind, darting like knife-blades through the cracks in our flimsy shelter, struck into our flesh and seemed to rasp against the coverings of our bones.

We picked up enough coal along the railroad tracks to keep our little stove glowing red during the daytime, but once we failed to attend it the shanty would not stay warm for five minutes. All night long all four of us huddled together in a heap on the floor, covering ourselves with every bit of bedding and clothing we had, trying to draw warmth from each other as we shivered through more bitter nights than we had ever known in Sweden.

But nightly, before we crept under our poor covers, there was a chore to be done, a degrading bit of scavenging, in which we all joined. Hundreds of chickens and turkeys froze to death that winter and were, in the careless, wasteful American fashion prevalent in those days, thrown out into the back yards, the alleys, and the fields. Late at night, long after our neighbors were asleep, Mother, Sister, Father and I crept out with sacks and gathered the dead fowl. Bringing them home, we stripped them of their feathers, which we secretly sold. The carcasses we buried in holes chopped with difficulty into the frozen earth.

Both pride and fear of punishment as trespassers, and perhaps as thieves, made the whole business one of awe-inspiring secrecy, the intensity of which rivaled for me that of my search for Loke in Sweden. We were strangers and had an Old-World fear of the authorities. We were constantly haunted by vague misgivings about what might happen to us if we were discovered.

Often I thought I saw our neighbors looking at us suspiciously. More than once I hid when some one who seemed especially fierce to my fear-ridden eyes came near while I was at play.

And sure enough, we were being watched. I imagine that the man who bought our feathers and saw how eagerly we

grasped at the few miserable cents he gave us, had let his imagination fill in details of our story which we had not supplied,
and talked about us.

For one night, as we sat silently in our shanty waiting for
the time to pass so that we could go forth stealthily to strip the
poor cold coverings from the dead who no longer needed them,
we heard a mumble of voices outside, followed by a violent kick
at the door. Father rose, his face a mixture of questioning
surprise and apprehension, while the rest of us looked from one
to the other in terror. The mumbling voices, the staccato kick—
they seemed the voice of accusation itself. We waited, breathless, while Father opened the door.

Nor was our fear appeased by the enigmatic sight which
greeted our eyes. A man came in, grasping with both hands a
huge sack slung over his shoulder. Looking up at him from
my position on the floor, he seemed the biggest man I had ever
seen in my life. Tall, broad-shouldered, his face a solemn
mask, the mysterious sack pendent from his shoulder, he seemed
terrible, yet magnificent too. A few years before, I could have
named him Loke with as great ease as I had the peacock
feather. Now I could only stare, and wait, and wonder fear-
fully.

Behind him were perhaps a dozen other men, each carrying
a sack or a bundle. Silently, unhesitatingly, they poured in
through the door, as though a flood had been released and we
were in its path. First the leader, then the rest, dropped bags
and bundles on the floor, each with such a thud that it shook
the shanty. When they stood back the little space was so
crowded that no one had room in which to turn around. Then
the leader cleared his voice and spoke gruffly, as if in embarrassment.

"We don't aim for any one to be hungry or cold in Rankin,"
he said.

Then, without greater elaboration, silently, they filed out.

Speechless with surprise and pleasure we began to examine

the treasures they had brought. There was food of all kinds—potatoes, beef, hams, bread, prunes, flour—and bedding and clothing, and, for Mother and my sister, many of the little things peculiarly dear to the heart of every woman.

Thus did we celebrate, during our first year in America, the time of the feast of "Midwinter's Blood." Thus did we discover, during our darkest days, the kindness which can dwell in the heart of man.

I was not yet ten years old.

III

FAITH STORMS A CITADEL

PERHAPS it was the impetus given us by that act of kindness on the part of our neighbors; perhaps it was the natural outcome of settling into life in the new land—whatever it was, our fortunes began to increase slightly after that startling night when we experienced the beneficence of Rankin, Illinois. Plenty of hard years were still ahead of us, and for a time we continued as we had been doing, supporting ourselves by such things as selling the feathers of dead fowl. But Father, meanwhile, had resumed his occupation as a preacher, taking occasional pulpits in churches of his sect made up of poor congregations. Knowledge of the scandal in Sweden had not yet come to America, and to the simple impoverished people whom he addressed he was a man of God with no blot on his record.

My next clear memory of a home is of a neat little three-room cottage where we lived in Ottumwa, Iowa, during the winter of 1882 and '83. The house itself was charming, set as though to furnish a contrast to the other houses, all of which made up a group called "Smoky Row" in one of the toughest and filthiest parts of the city. Our only view from the front of the house was the dingy, barren embankment leading to the Wabash Railway bridge. Thinking of Smoky Row now, I have the impression that we lived directly under the great steel structure over which smoke-belching trains thundered throughout the days and nights. Yet, for all its dirt and the thunderous noise of the trains and the filthy surroundings, I remember it chiefly for its drama for the continuous pulse and throb of human life which surged through and out of it, and were I to choose another existence on this earth, and were I able to arrange it all to my own choice, I should insist on living again, at least during a part of my childhood, close to some great moving vein of life such as a railway, where people and goods from other parts of the world would thunder past me, or by the side of a great river, where mighty waters come rushing down from far-away mountains, to destroy the deadly contentment of insularity. I should want, also, to live in a place where the tragedies of life are evident and close to the surface, so that I might not grow up with any illusion of human perfection. I should want, as I did, to come to close terms with filth and vermin and germs, so that in later life fear of all of these unsavory minions of the lords of life and death might hold no terrors for me.

Such a place was Smoky Row. It had almost all the undesirable qualities one could imagine. But it also possessed something only kings and the high and mighty of the earth possess —freedom. Smoky Row was as free as the jungle. It was a place where things grew wild in untrammeled profusion, not a narrow, puritanic, meager, thin, dreamy little place like Dalsheda in far-away Smaland. I reveled in glorious squalor, dirt and freedom as soon as I was outside the paternal roof.

Spring came with a rush on Smoky Row that year. The sun poured down its flood of heat; night and day the river groaned and boomed with millions of tons of ice that filled it from shore to shore, many layers thick. Although seemingly a solid mass, it crunched and roared past on the spring flood with tremendous speed. Houses with cackling, terrified chickens on the roofs, pianos, dead cattle, and all manner of articles whirled past on the turbulent waters.

The wet and muddy months were soon past and June came with its rich vegetation and flaring heat. The alleys and railway embankments were luxurious with strong-smelling weeds.

In the river hundreds of spoiled oranges and rotten eggs bobbed and circled like some strange flora of yellow and white on a moving field of brown. To the east a large slaughter-house sent forth its foul stench. Heat, blazing tropical heat, with strong odors in the daytime; cool nights with resplendent moonlight and the passionate sputterings and yowlings of stray cats, made a background for the glories of June in 1883 in Smoky Row on the banks of the Des Moines River in Ottumwa, Iowa.

For weeks the city had been ablaze with the colored posters of P. T. Barnum's Greatest Show on Earth. The boys talked of nothing else, and of how they were going to gain entrance. Some had money saved, some would get it from their parents, aunts or uncles, while others were going to work for the circus men, carrying water, in order to get in.

For me there was no hope. My father's attitude was absolutely beyond any such worldliness as a circus. Yet that morning toward the middle of June, a hot, stifling, windless day, with the streets thick with powdered dust which burned my feet, I found myself at the circus instead of school. I do not know how I got there. I made no criminal decision, had no evil intent, there had been no moral struggle. I just remember I found myself carrying water for the men, that my hands were blistered and that my arms ached as I staggered on with bucket after bucket long beyond the point at which I felt like giving up. From eight-thirty in the morning until way into the afternoon I never stopped a moment. I awoke as from a dream when a gruff voice said: "Hey there, kid, hain't ye goin' into the circus?" In the hurry and bustle they had forgotten to let me in with the other boys, and I, afraid of losing my supreme reward, was not asking any questions, slow-witted, stupid Swedish kid that I was. The man lifted up the side of the tent for me to crawl in.

In one hungry glance I drank in the glory of it all. The band was playing; it looked cool and high inside; a white clown jumped from a colored barrel, and in the dim light I saw the

manifold wonders being performed. But, like Moses, I was
doomed to see the Promised Land only to intensify my loss of
it. As my eager child's body was about to hurl itself forward,
a hard hand grasped my collar from behind. It was my father.
I had not come home for lunch and through some strange intuition he had found me at the divine moment, both from his
point of view and mine.

Yes, it happened just so. And then when I had received my
whipping, far less bitter than the loss of the circus, I was com-
pelled to thank God for the punishment and also thank God
that I had a father who shielded me from sin.

But there was a better show than that put on by P. T.
Barnum, a show even more suited to a country which has mixed
quackery and idealism so often and in such gigantic proportions
as America. Its producer was Dr. Lamereux, the hero of that
part of my childhood spent in Ottumwa, the man among all
men for all the boys of the town. He could never have happened, save in "the land of the free and the home of the brave."
Only America, daring to experiment, daring to challenge the
great taboos of history and orthodoxy, could produce such
spectacular variants as Billy Sunday and John D. Rockefeller,
Ralph Waldo Emerson and Mormonism, Father Divine and
Dr. Lamereux.

Today I can smile at the half-forgotten idol of my boyhood
—"the world-renowned Indian fighter, scout and medicine-
man," Dr. Lamereux. Yet I am unceasingly grateful that it
was my fortune to be caught in one of those mysterious migra-
tory currents which since the beginning of time have swayed
the human race, and carried to America where I could find
outlet for the need of hero-worship every boy feels in con-
templation of a Dr. Lamereux instead of some little local
dignitary such as I would have found in the blind alley of
Smaland, Sweden, where I was born.

Dr. Lamereux combined the mystery of magic with all the

delights of a circus, the romance of savagery and the ecstasy
of religion. He traveled around the country with a large
troupe of Indians and wild mustangs, a splendid company of
minstrels, selling patent Indian medicines. He dressed in shim-
mering black velvet, his raven locks fell in ringlets around his
shoulders and his beard swept down almost to his waist. This,
together with his dark, large, solemn eyes, brought out the
milky whiteness of his thin, hard face. Every button on his
coat was a twenty-dollar gold piece, and every button on his
vest a ten-dollar gold piece. Around his splendid sombrero
was wound a delicately woven lariat that almost gave the impression of a coiled snake, and when he chose to demonstrate
his skill, the snake became alive as truly as any blacksnake
speeding its flashing way through the grass, as it whirled in
flashing arcs about his magnificently clothed body and his shining riding boots, which were supple and soft and the especial
envy of every boy in town.

When Dr. Lamereux operated in Ottumwa he followed the
practise of circuses by giving a parade. First came his Indians,
riding on beautiful ponies, togged up in savage finery; then
came the minstrels with their black faces and comic costumes;
and lastly came the great master himself. Four prancing, coal-
black steeds (which one would never think of calling horses)
pulled his magnificent carriage, and the doctor gave an impression of dignified splendor in his black, gold and white color
scheme. Bowing seriously to the right and left, he threw with
great skill handfuls of money to a host of boys and men scram-
bling in the rear of the cavalcade. These gifts ranged from
five cents to a dollar, and sometimes even a bit of gold slipped
in. Indeed there were rumors that some boys had grabbed
up twenty-dollar pieces! What a visible proof of real munifi-
cence—a man who had come to give, not take!

When we all had filled the vast tent, the show began. The
Indians danced and, swayed by the rhythmic, ominous thud of
their drums, every sensitive soul there found his way, in imag-

ination, back to the time of our prehistoric forebears when we were ourselves free, fierce, and terrible. At the very height of the savage noise and fury the Indians stopped and disappeared.

In their place on the stage came the Negro minstrels who relaxed the strain of martial tension and sent everybody into roars of laughter. Like a soothing purge the ludicrous antics and comic rhythm of the minstrels made us feel at home and all defenses were let down.

Then the doctor began his spiel.

"You laughing, happy audience; you mother, you father, you young man, woman and child, every one of you—within you are developing the seeds of death! Is it cancer? Is it consumption? Or is it, perhaps, one of those unknown maladies that are not yet named or recognized by medical science?"

Fear is a queer force. It always acts the same; just as the "bugs" which make pneumonia always have a certain number of tails or humps, so fear has a certain characteristic. In fear the blood rushes to the heart and the arms or legs are pushed out to protect. Fear is always a contraction. In fear every atom contracts, every blood corpuscle contracts. All that is vital tries to rush in, in, in, and sometimes this movement inward is so great it produces death itself.

By the savage Indian dances the doctor had created a painful tension. Then he relaxed his audience with humor, purged every heart with laughter and opened thus the gates of the soul to his suggestion of fear. After he had everybody frightened, feeling and thinking about symptoms, digging into their memories for recollections of every cold and fever they had ever had, or the symptoms of diseases some dear one had suffered or died from, the doctor made his master stroke—gave his *coup de grâce*—put his net under the sprawling trout.

"But why should I talk to you of my skill, of my years with the noble red men you have seen with us here tonight, and of the knowledge that preserves them in health far beyond their hundredth year? My friends, I will show you here now before your eyes, and demonstrate these remedies. They are not mine. They are the property and inheritance of these noble red men. Come closer! Let me help you!"

With that everybody who had a pain, or a tooth that needed pulling, came up to the platform. In those days the poor did not go to dentists and have their teeth filled, and the extraction of teeth cost fifty cents apiece. Sometimes he would have ten or fifteen people on the platform at once. With swift deftness he would smear some pain-killer in a mouth, snatch from a tray held by an assistant the proper instrument, and in a second a tooth was tossed high in the air. All the time he kept up a flow of assurance that they would not feel a thing. Sometimes he would pick out a whole mouthful of teeth from some old man or woman so gracefully, easily and happily that it all became a sort of joy feast at which pain ceased. Rheumatics were rubbed and coughs were doped. To see poor creatures one minute tearing themselves to pieces, coughing, and the next smiling beatifically and relieved from all suffering was wonderful. As soon as the audience had no more teeth to be pulled and all who cared had come up and had aching limbs rubbed or their coughs soothed, the selling began.

Liver and kidney pills cost three dollars, pain-killer five dollars, blood purifier ten dollars, and consumption cures twenty dollars. Everybody who had money hastened, yes, scrambled to buy as if afraid the supply would run out. A limited number of bottles was promised for a reduced price to those who could not afford the regular price. A score of young men rushed through the audience with great baskets full of packages, containing the remedies, which were distributed with professional skill. All the time now the Indians kept chanting monotonously and beating their tom-toms, the doctor himself roaring like a bull while some of the minstrels kept up a furious ragtime dancing until the sweat rolled down their black faces and they were relieved by other members of the company.

Not for a moment did the savage noise abate until everybody who could buy had done so, and the will of the necromancer had been achieved.

I was so convinced of the marvelous potency of Dr. Lamereux's remedies that after one session at his show I ran to the shanty of a poor washerwoman of our acquaintance who had tuberculosis, and persuaded her to get a bottle of consumption medicine. By borrowing from her customers she managed to scrape together the necessary twenty dollars for the cure. When I told Mother of my kind deed, she upbraided me as she never had before for being a fool, a sucker and a cruel meddler.

Barnum said that the public likes to be humbugged, and had he known Dr. Lamereux and attended one of his shows he would doubtless have felt that here was an excellent example in evidence of his thesis. But his thesis is false. We do not love mystery; we hate it. We all live in terror; a gnawing fear of the darkness around consumes us. In fear we have always turned to men who have penetrated the gloom and brought us some light, and close behind them, surrounding them on the fringe of their prophecies, have come the great fakers, the men who, adopting a technique composed essentially of self-confidence and an outward assurance of knowledge, have been able to take advantage of our fear and our need for light, because they have claimed mastership over the mysteries.

That people believe in them, that they have faith, is neither surprising nor ridiculous. On the contrary, it is the most beautiful thing in life, for it is as pure an expression as is possible to us of the essential faith of the soul of man without which we perish. It is from such faith that we gather courage for our furious charges up the holy mountain to take the citadel where Nature keeps her secrets of life and death. And in these assaults mankind betrays his divinity—whether he takes the citadel or not.

IV

THE RETURN OF SKAM

IF only Father had been able to forgive himself for what had
happened in Sweden, God undoubtedly would have for-
given him also, and perhaps even the "Readers" of Ottumwa,
Iowa, might have done so after they had heard the story. For
they did hear it—how, I never knew—and when they called
Father before them and accused him, instead of making any
defense, he meekly accepted their accusation and the punishment which followed. In a sense I think that he rather wel-
comed it as something to which he had looked forward. Indeed, had it not been for Mother's good sense he would probably long before this have proclaimed his sin publicly. Now
he accepted the loss of his license to preach in his own church
in an attitude of resignation which seemed fairly to shout "Thy
will be done."

However, the law of supply and demand in nature is exquisitely balanced. A pound of slightly moldy cherries, or a
preacher with a somewhat tainted reputation may, if properly
marketed, find buyers among the discerning with slim purses.
The Readers of Burlington, Iowa, needed a minister, and
Father won the post over the other applicants by his superior
oratory. To be sure, the official national synod of the Readers
had taken away his license and with it the coveted privilege of
free passes granted by the railways to ministers of the gospel
in those days. But friends secured a license for him from the
American Congregational Church without too great delay and
so he got his passes again.

Before we had reached Burlington it had already become a town in full development, which had apparently achieved its growth and then settled down to remain the same, year in and year out. It had considerable wealth which came from the lumber industry, and had already spent some time learning how to use its money in quiet cultural pursuits, in contrast to the blatancy and rawness and noise of Ottumwa. Father's salary was very small—I think eighteen dollars a month—and we were very poor. But the compensations of life in Burlington were so great, after having lived in Ottumwa and Rankin, that I cannot remember having worried about our poverty.

It was here that I was first actively conscious of that love for, and the desire to create, beauty in form, which later made me choose that which I would do for the rest of my life. On our written examination papers in school we were obliged to make simple decorations copied from patterns given to us by the teacher. But the teacher's designs did not please me, so I originated one of my own and used it, even though I had to argue and almost fight to be allowed to do so. My design, repeated with infinite variations, was a sailing ship on an ocean which in one place was blue, in another green and in another red. The picture itself I encircled with a banner in bright colors, green and crimson mostly, on which I might print the splendid mystery of my name. I remember that I chose gold for the name itself as the only thing which seemed to me capable of reflecting the glory of that mystery.

Fired with the delight which my own drawing gave me, I began drawing maps and made scores of them in a few months. Delighted by the effects of color which I found I could get by steeping old dyed rags in hot water, boiling weeds of various kinds, and mixing inks and water colors, in a passionate effort to make tints which would be exactly what I wanted, mountains, rivers, lakes and oceans came into being under my hand and I worked feverishly, often far into the night, carefully tracing the boundaries of states and later their names and even those of counties and cities, all in fabulous combinations of shading and color harmony.

My teacher, Miss Gunnison, scolded me because I became so untidy and messed up my books and desk so terribly with what she called my daubing. But when her scoldings had no effect she finally appealed to Mr. Thomas, the principal, telling him what was true, that I was neglecting my studies in my color madness.

One day he came to my desk, asking to look at the things I had been drawing, and I, rather grudgingly, pulled some of them out to show him, in a mixture of apprehension and resentment. But when I saw how long and carefully he looked at them and how kind and thoughtful his face was as he did so, I took new hope, so that it seemed quite the natural thing when he told me that he thought they were very good and said that he would ask Miss Gunnison to let me continue with them. Then he asked me very gently, as though it were a personal favor to him, not to neglect my other studies. He took the best of my maps and hung them in the high school. After this I worked so hard at my studies that I became the leader in my class in all subjects, including mathematics, which I never liked, and, of course, I continued my drawing.

There was a business college in Burlington, in which a Mr. Pierson taught penmanship, including figure drawing in long flowing lines. When I saw specimens of Mr. Pierson's elaborate work, I thought I would rather be able to draw as he did than do anything else in the world. But I am afraid that not even this desire was strong enough to make me go to work in order to earn money to achieve it. It took a much more powerful urge than that, and this urge was furnished by my first sweetheart, a golden blonde Swedish girl, eight years old, a year younger than myself, named Lilly Lorine. She had eyes like forget-me-nots, cheeks as fresh as pink roses, and she was as dainty as a fairy. To my worshiping heart she was not a creature that ate or walked or possessed any of the crude realities of ordinary beings. There was no precedent for her in the history of the world. I adored her, and if I had been able to pick the stars out of the sky one at a time for her, they would have seemed none too good a present. But far from being able to do this, I could give her little more than my adoration, since I had no money.

One day in our Swedish Chicago newspaper I came across an advertisement for agents to sell elaborate visiting cards popular in the Eighties. They were magnificent and terrible things. The name was covered with a flap on which were embossed beautifully colored pictures of flowers and little birds. I wrote and secured an agency and worked so energetically and successfully that not only did I get funds to buy Lilly presents but saved enough to enable me to take a course in Elliott's Business College in penmanship and arithmetic when vacation came. I even could afford to take a private lesson once a week from Mr. Pierson, the teacher in penmanship. These lessons cost fifty cents an hour. I learned to draw lions and eagles with beautiful long strokes in glossy ink.

There was one picture in particular that he taught me that I did over and over again. It was of a mother bird feeding her young in a nest, while the head of the family with swelling throat and mouth wide open, turned upward, was singing with joy.

An annoying situation developed when school commenced; because of my open adoration of Lilly, the boys commenced to call me Pickalilly. At last their attitude became so aggressive that one day I came running home with a whole mob after me. Father had forbidden me to fight and my only escape from their torture was superior leg work. This fatal day my mother happened to stand on the back porch and saw my humiliating flight. As I rushed up the stage she cried at me:

"Are you running from those boys?"

"Yes, Father has forbidden me to fight," I replied.

"Go right out and fight them now," she continued in a low, husky, commanding tone.

I needed no second urging, and at my cry of defiance they turned back and soon the fun began. For weeks the battle continued, with varying results, first with one boy, then another. Our code did not allow more than one boy to engage another in an actual fight at one time. In vociferous attacks, yes; but with fists, no. Finally I fought my way into a standing as a regular fellow in spite of my awful degrading love affair with Lilly. After that I enjoyed my darling in peace and contentment, and she was so prim, so silent and so shy that she did nothing to mar my perfect dream of love.

But a new, unique and quite unexpected development in Father's church commenced to endanger our position. A stranger, a man coming directly from Sweden, joined the flock. Over in Sweden a group of the Readers had discovered a new wrinkle in theology. The Readers originally had split with the Lutheran Church on the interpretation of the atonement. The old orthodox church held to the belief that God was angry with man and that Jesus, by his suffering and death, atoned for the sins of man. The Readers asserted that God was not angry with man and that he could not be atoned for by the death of his son. Man atoned for himself by following Jesus' example. Now the new revelation which this stranger brought with him was that no one was a Christian at all until he became perfect. A true Christian could not even commit the smallest of sins. A Christian must be absolutely without sin.

The stranger had received the grace of complete immunity from the flesh and the Devil. In the Blood of the Lamb he had been washed whiter than snow, and through an improved process of conversion received the power forever to remain sinless.

One by one the members of the sheepfold became perfect until the shepherd alone remained obdurate, claiming that sinful man here on earth could not reach perfection. For once in his life Father fought valiantly for himself. Long into the nights I heard the bitter arguments over holiness between Father and various members of his congregation until the air was so charged with rancor and hatred that I trembled with terror as I lay in bed listening to the rise and fall of their impassioned voices.

But for all his valiant defense, for all his impassioned oratory, Father was beaten. He had been able to rise above a scandal, but he could not win, single-handed, a battle against the desire of man to call himself perfect, and, recognizing his defeat, he resigned before the church had time to kick him out.

V

BLACK LOAM

ALL things have two sides to them. Father's disgrace in
Sweden brought us to America. His wrangle over the
perfection of man took us back to the soil. Both were good
moves for us. Father's soul may have belonged to the Lord,
but his heart and body belonged to the earth. Ever since we
had reached America, he had been looking with loving eyes at
the deep rich black loam which makes up the prairies of the
Middle West. Now, as he decided to quit the ministry forever
and become a farmer, I think that, just as Mother had been
secretly glad for the cataclysm which had sent us to America,
Father grasped the falling-out with the church which made it
seem reasonable for him to leave the pulpit in order to minister
to the pregnant soil. His prayers were no shorter nor his read-
ings from Luther's *Postilla* and the Bible less diligent, but there
was a new vigor in his movements, new light in his eyes, new
laughter in his voice.

Father had two wealthy brothers, both Iowa farmers.
Brother John was pious and a Reader, Brother William a
scoffer and a drunkard. Being a godly man, Father wrote first
to Brother John asking for aid, but his very godly brother
turned him down, and he then turned to the despised black
sheep of the family, Uncle William, with better results. The
scoffer, the drunkard, the man who, being fleshly, understood
the needs of the flesh, promptly bought, within the city limits
of Ottumwa, a little truck farm of four acres, with a fine, modern, four-room house on it, and turned it over to Father. Be-

sides this he helped Father to buy two Jersey cows, some pigs, some chickens and necessary farm implements. We paid Uncle William rent for it, to be sure, but the rent was exactly the amount of the interest on the mortgage—about ten dollars a month.

Our place was near the south side of the river, and the soil was black and fertile. I remember watching Father as he took a handful of the fat loam and crumpled it between his fingers, letting it fall gently back to the earth as he murmured to himself: "God is good, God is good." Thus might a prophet of Israel have fondled the soil of Canaan when the Jews at last arrived in the Promised Land.

It was early spring and Father put me to work helping him dig, hoe, and plant. Soon my hands ceased to blister and my back to ache from the hard work, and all my five senses drank in voraciously the earthy things. I sniffed the musky smell of damp soil, of aromatic weed and wildflower, and gloated in the sensuous delight they gave me. I watched the germination of the seeds with a sense of tremendous excitement, and when tender shoots of delicate green pushed themselves through the soil, so gently, yet so irresistibly, I was filled with contentment. So abundant was our first crop of potatoes that we told each other over and over again: "Never again need we go hungry in this wonderful country!"

There was more, though, than just a promise of satisfaction for material needs in the fecundity of the soil. Awe and peace were blended in the close contact with the mystery of creation which I found in the fields. It was only when I encountered for the first time another evidence of creation that I found myself again in the grip of terror which had assailed me when, in Smaland, I had discovered the peacock feather in the attic.

One day I was sent to a farmer named John Baker with a heifer to be covered. As soon as the giddy young thing smelled the bull she gave a bellow, sprang high in the air and jerked me off my feet, carrying me along for quite a way before I could untangle myself from the rope around her neck. Sprawled on the ground, I watched her in the fulfilment of her destiny, and became frozen with terror at what I saw. I seemed unable to move until Baker and his two sons burst into loud guffaws of laughter at the sight of my overawed expression and posture on the ground. They could not know that here, in this new land, I was again seeing the power of Loke made material.

A year or two passed in happy work, school, skating, swimming and fishing. Now and then I would play truant with some chum and roam far away in the hills, seeking adventures, usually ending in a luxurious whipping with a supple rattan, scientifically wielded by my father.

According to reason and common sense, my life should have continued on the farm, but my sister Hannah had a sweetheart who was a clerk in a Jewish clothing store, and somehow he had planted in her heart the vaulting ambition that through his influence I might also some day become a clerk and wear a white collar. Thus, shortly after my twelfth birthday, I became an errand boy and janitor with the Charles Sax and Brother Clothing Emporium on Main Street.

Came days and weeks and months of sweeping floors and cleaning filthy spittoons. But there were new foods to keep my romantic mind from becoming overdepressed through longing for the green fields, the biting fish in the river and the swimming hole down by Baker's grove. First of all there was the lodge room that I swept and dusted once a week. Here there were heavily embroidered robes, golden crowns, swords, magnificent mystical symbols, altars and all the various implements used in the work of secret orders. Whenever I had a chance I would secretly creep up there to dream, and ponder, and live in a world not made by the Sax Brothers nor even the rulers of Ottumwa Masonry. One of the clerks was a Mason, and he, noting my interest, gave me some Masonic literature which filled many an evening with romance and awe for me. But soon a more vivid force entered my life.

Up the street there lived a tall, beautiful lady with painted lips and rouged cheeks. She was a golden blonde, often dressed in blue velvet. I was just approaching the age when a boy ceases day-dreaming about girls as fairies and begins to dream about them at night as physical creatures. My sleep was troubled and my mind brooded in sinful thought.

Boys in those days were told very little or nothing about sex, and I was no exception to the rule. My confusion increased by my ignorance, I could think of little else save the strange impulses which tore at my body. One day I came upon a circular written by a quack doctor and containing information every boy ought to know. I read it with fear and eagerness, and promptly came to the conclusion that my spine was melting away, my brain softening, and that I would soon be locked up in an insane asylum.

An old Scotch doctor had for some time been our family physician, and, having a tiny bit of sense left in my terror, I went to him instead of writing to the quack about my symptoms. Dr. Mackenzie, when I told him myself that I had a terrible disease, didn't look surprised but asked me quietly how I knew. Pulling the thumb-worn circular from my pocket, I shoved it at him.

"It tells all about it here," I said tremblingly.

He gave a snort of disgust and then took me on his knees and told me in a different way what every boy ought to know. Then, being more than a doctor of bodies, he deftly questioned me in general and found out that above everything else I liked flowers and pretty pictures. When I left I had a fine illustrated volume of Scotch landscape painters and a book telling how to raise flowers.

At once I began to cultivate a garden during my spare moments. I became quite an expert with tea roses, and in half barrels sunk into the ground I brought forth some beautiful varieties of water lilies. Pansies, narcissi, goldenrod, tulips, morning glories and many other kinds of flowers were thereafter ever in bloom in their season in my garden. Contentment began to come back to me.

And then I had one of those strange experiences which, in one form or another, have occurred throughout my life and made me wonder about myself and about things unseen by most of us. One night, sitting on the back porch, tired but contented, looking up at the full moon I saw a diamond white cross shining across the silver disk of our sister planet. It was the most beautiful and exciting thing I had ever seen. I reveled in its loveliness and wanted to share it with others. I called Father and Mother out to see it, but they seemed troubled when they could not see that which I saw.

"It's so clear, Mother dear. Can't you see it?" I inquired. But she and Father only looked at each other in troubled silence at my earnestness.

VI

THE BRIDGE TO LONDON FALLS DOWN

NATURE hates a void—in fact there are no voids in nature or in men's lives. My zest for study and school, the thrills of play with congenial chums, the sweaty, healthy toil on the farm—for these I found no substitute in the activities in the store. With the exception of Jake, the junior partner, O. D. Wray, my mentor in Masonry, and Mr. Bullock, the bookkeeper, who helped me play the flute, I despised and hated every one in the store. However, there was none who at one time or another did not curse me with all the holy and unholy words his vocabulary could command. Damn kid, lazy, stupid, stubborn, blankety this and blankety the other.

The moral tone of Main Street was low and sinister. I, a boy of twelve, eager and green, had been suddenly dropped into the bilgewater of a tough town to sink or swim. The revelation of such things as bawdy houses, drunkenness, gambling, crime, and death coming swiftly from gun or knife in this boisterous, tough town that was soul-searing, and the brutal selfishness, the deadly hatred I saw flash forth now and then filled me at times with terror.

But a guiding star was in the offing, in fact just around the corner Fate was awaiting me in the personality of a great man whose influence was to change my whole destiny. But I came very close to blowing up the whole works before this benign influence became tangent with my path.

It was winter and I was in charge of the furnace. I became interested in the mystery of steam and, to test its power, I took a three-inch pipe about three feet long, filled it with water, screwed caps on at both ends, and then threw it into the hot fire of the furnace. For safety I crawled outside the furnace room behind the coal chute and awaited developments. They came with a far more devastating force than I had anticipated. A section of the pipe with terrific power blew the furnace door clear across the room and the pipe imbedded itself in the stone wall. Had I not been so discreet it might quite easily have blown me in two. The furnace walls were shattered and bricks were scattered far and wide. The Sax Brothers themselves, the clerks and bookkeepers, and every one else in the store came rushing into the basement.

Old Charles Sax seemed almost to collapse with anger.

"Py Gott, dis damn David is not only the most damn stupid boy I ever had. He'll kill us all yet. Get out—get! You're fired! Get away quick before I get mad!" he yelled.

I had gathered my things together when Jake, the younger brother, turned up and caught me before I had time to leave.

"You're not fired, David," he said. "Not as long as I am here will you be fired."

With a push he impelled me toward the packing room and told me to stay out of sight for awhile. Sitting in the gloom of the packing room I heard, some minutes later through the elevator shaft, Charley's rumbling voice exploding in violent expletives, getting weaker and weaker, meeting the soothing murmur of Jake's smooth, steely tone that always won.

All that is has ever been, yet each moment is a song that never has been sung before. I mean by that, that whatever happens to us is just a continuation of all our yesterdays, that in fact our today is all our yesterdays.

Primitive minds such as that of my grandmother attribute significant events such as birth, death, fortune or misfortune, to luck. To court luck, only magic, witchcraft and sacrifice have any power. But belief in luck is the fruit of ignorance. To the mind that knows all, there is reason, order, immutable law governing all things in the universe.

Because I know this, it does not seem overstrange to me that I stayed on at Sax Brothers, or that one day, as I walked east on Main Street, I noted a picture in the show window of our leading photographer in Ottumwa. The picture was a large, full-length crayon portrait of the beautiful actress, Mary Anderson. I can thrill to this day in the memory of what I felt at the sight of it. To my untutored eyes the velvety softness of the tones, the perfect expression in the features, was the acme of beauty. There was romance in the somber shadows of the velvet folds of her dress, and to draw silk so well that you wanted to touch it seemed an achievement beyond human skill. Yet there it was—a hand-made picture finer than any print I had ever seen.

That evening I took a sheet of paper and far into the night worked on a drawing of a young girl from my imagination. I sought the most perfect profile I could devise and then shaded face and hair with infinitely patient attention. The next day I slipped away from the store and called on the photographer and, showing him my drawing, asked him:

"Do you think I could ever learn to make something like that thing in the window?"

He scanned my drawing, reflected awhile as if in debate with himself, and at last replied:

"I am a photographer, not an artist. I'll send you to a man who will no doubt take a deep interest in you, my boy."

On a piece of notepaper he then wrote an introduction for me to Mr. Johannes Schiewe, Lincoln Street.

The following Sunday, groomed to shining perfection, I called on Mr. Schiewe. He was a German artist who had married a wealthy American girl. He was a Prix de Rome scholar from the Royal Academy of Berlin, but before he had begun to study painting he had been graduated from the Royal Academy of Music. Later, after his Roman days, he had worked in Vienna with the great Makart. He was a very cultured and able man.

He took, as the photographer had assumed, a spontaneous interest in me. I had read a great deal of poetry. Moore's "Lalla Rookh" had been a special favorite of mine. Besides showing Schiewe my drawing I was not backward about telling of my other achievements—my maps, my penmanship, my flowers, especially the fine points about coaxing tea roses into bloom; keeping the bushes healthy, I made him appreciate, was no mean achievement. I think I really did my selling too well. I was only anxious to get him to help me a little, and I sold myself as a child prodigy. He praised my little drawing and offered to teach me if I at odd times helped him with his garden.

I've known mountaineers in the Cumberlands to feed their babies whisky and cornmeal mush, and now and then babies have survived the diet; but that I survived those first months that Schiewe taught me is a miracle. He had thousands of reproductions of classical art, and the first that struck my interest was Michelangelo's works.

If I had been scatterbrained before, in my work at the store, from then on I became nigh to an idiot. My eyes groggy with strange dreams, I walked as one in a sleep, and a sudden shout of my name would make me jump. Schiewe also played Beethoven to me until at night I dreamt of wonderful fountains of many-colored streams of water rising and falling in strange formations, they being at the same time not only water but tones that moved in rhythmic ideas as I'd heard them on his piano. Sometimes the dream music would suddenly take the form of landscapes where brooks and flower-decked swards formed into mountains, sunshine into rain; where crashing storms and lightning bloomed forth into rippling moonlight murmuring over heavy waters. It might have been the dream of God creating worlds.

In my cellar fastness I modeled, made drawings, and read.

At the store they were content with me if I kept the furnace going. But even over this work Charley Sax growled.

"First this David freezes us to death, then he roasts us alive. And to think my own brother Jake should protect him!"

Perhaps I loved the Sibyl by Michelangelo from the Sistine Chapel more than all his other pictures. One of them in feature and form, in her aged wrinkled power, reminded me of Grandmother. Then the titanic, the overnatural of Michelangelo was in keeping with the imagery from my grandmother's lips of troll giants and mighty forces and power. Thor, the mighty, was just a near brother to the Moses of Michelangelo.

This artist is the creator of the super-mighty in art. His figures juggle worlds in their hands, and among their flying locks stars are lost in vast distances and awful depths. Like the flare of a quick flame, Adam leaps forth into being, perfect in fulness of form and beauty from the index finger of God. Swifter than thought his angels speed from the uttermost to the uttermost. And in their speed they had reached Ottumwa, Iowa, to bring delight and wonder to my youthful soul.

As a result of Schiewe's urging, it was suddenly decided to send me to London to study art. Tickets were bought, letters of introduction to religious, respectable people in London were secured, and I woke one morning to read in the paper that the local genius, David Edstrom, was about to leave town for London.

At once I dramatized myself as the most remarkable boy that had ever lived. Only one thing was lacking now to make the drama perfect. In my superb mood I craved the romance of a sweetheart to leave longingly and sadly behind me. None of my contemporary feminine associates could fill the requirements, so I hit upon the plan of stopping off a day in Burlington to say good-by to Lilly—Lilly, the first sweetheart of my youth, the golden maiden for whom I had fought a dozen boys!

It scarcely occurred to me until the time was upon us how hard it was going to be for me to leave my mother. For, re-

"A COUNTRY GIRL"

The author's first portrait bust, made while working as a farm hand in 1894

MICHELANGELO'S DELPHIAN SIBYL

From a photograph of the engraving which Edstrom carried with him when
he set forth as a tramp in 1894 to study art in Europe

gardless of my desire to say good-by to Lilly, Lilly was only
the symbol, the form for something which I felt should be in
the life of a young artist departing for foreign soil, and it was
Mother who filled in my heart the place reserved for love—
filled it so completely that there was really no place then for
any other woman.   Our attachment had grown deeper and
deeper throughout the years in America.   If I ever allowed
myself to speak a cross word to her in the morning, that day
was one of misery until I could see her again, tell her how
sorry I was, and receive, within her arms, the warm boon of
forgiveness.

We both knew that there would be a scene if she came to the
station to see me off, and so it was decided that she would tell
me good-by at home.   But, just as the train pulled in, just as I
had told my father a solemn good-by, she came running up,
her arms outstretched toward me, bearing one last caress, her
face bathed in tears.   She had been unable to control herself,
and throwing all plans to the winds had rushed after us.   I
gave her one agonized embrace and jumped on the already
moving train in complete bewilderment and misery, while
Father put his arms about her to support her sagging form.

By the time I had arrived in Burlington I was mad with
homesickness and terror of leaving for England.   And when
I saw Lilly the last shred of my resolution melted.   She had
grown up to be a very pretty girl.   Everything about her reminded me of the tenderness and love of my mother which I
was leaving behind me.   I was then sixteen years old and large
for my age, but I was as helpless in the sweep of my childish
emotions as a child of six.   I knew I could not go through with
my trip.   But what could I do?   I could not return to Ottumwa
and face the shame, and I could not put thousands and thousands of miles between me, Mother and Lilly.   I cut the
Gordian knot by sending my traveling money and ticket back
and taking a job in a lumber yard at Burlington, carrying wet
lumber from the Mississippi River.

I was strong as a man but not yet knit tight enough to stand this grueling work, and I became sick and was sent home. I shall never forget my shame as I walked into the door of my home. But no one reproached me. Every one was so kind to me that it broke my heart. I was still dramatizing myself, but as a tragedy now, not a triumph. In some book or another I had read of how degrading it was to be shallow. I decided that I had not continued to London because I was shallow. I was one of whom Jesus had said:

"Because thou art lukewarm, and neither cold nor hot, I will spew thee out of my mouth."

I was too ashamed of myself to go near Schiewe. No excuse could I even dream of that could give me courage to meet this great man. As mortal sinners flee the thought of God when they become enmeshed in evil, so did I flee Schiewe.

And it was fitting that, in this mood of debasement, I should get a job in a slaughter-house.

VII

I STUDY FOR THE MINISTRY

MY work at the slaughter-house was to take a piece of meat from a table on my left side and put it on a spring scale at my right side. This work had to be done so lightly and swiftly that the indicator of the scale did not tremble but immediately registered the weight without losing a second. If the dial wobbled and lost a second, it would mean that every man in the line of twenty-five would lose a second—in other words that twenty-five seconds would be lost! A horrible thought! The labor was so regulated that the men acted like an endless chain, the work of each man fitting precisely that of the next, and the work of each department fitting precisely that of the next department.

Of all the curious and mighty things I have seen, nothing has left such an image of power in my brain as the work of the killing gang in the slaughter-house. Outside, in the pens, were jammed together thousands of pigs driven in an endless stream to the entrance of the killing room. Ten or fifteen pigs were driven at the same time into small pens, where men stood waiting to hurry them to their doom. With amazing regularity and casualness the men slipped a chain around a hind leg of each squealing beast and attached it to a constantly moving hoist which took the terror-stricken animal off its feet and hoisted it into the air, where it was automatically transferred to a constantly moving carriage. In a few seconds after it had left the floor of the pen its frantic squealing was hushed by the thrust of a sharp-pointed knife into its throat. So rapidly

47

did one writhing, squealing pig follow another that the arm of the sticker was in constant motion, back and forth, back and forth, and each time it came forward it released a crimson fountain of blood which covered his arm and ran down into a trough through which it was carried away. Every hour this man sent forty or fifty animals from the bright, if turbulent, realm of life, into the dark oblivion of death.

As soon as the pig was stuck it was started rolling down a rail to be slid with a steaming splash into a huge scalding vat, where it was caught by an endless chain which whirled it round and round into a high scraping machine from which it came out on the other side scraped clean of its bristles, its body as pink and shining as a baby's just out of its bath. Here men stood ready with knives, and cut open the pigs, extracted the entrails, split the carcasses in two. Then each half was again whisked on to a rail swung high from the ground, on which a stream of slaughtered halves rumbled on into the vast chilling room where they were soon frozen stiff.

No words can describe the turmoil, the roaring steam, the shrieking of the terrified animals, the cursing of angry foremen, the flashing of knives, the hoarse laughter of strong men in violent exertion. In the cutting gang there was one mighty Negro armed with a tremendous ax-like cleaver which he swung up and down with the regularity of a machine as the carcasses passed before him on a moving table. At each blow he cut a pig in two.

There was something satisfying to me in the slaughter-house, something which filled a need I could not name or describe. Though it dealt in death, there was a warm sense of life and reality about it that comforted me in my disturbed state of mind.

But I did not stay long. A new friend named Crawford invited me to be his guest and companion on a fishing and hunting trip in the Rocky Mountains, and I accepted his invitation eagerly.

My most vivid memories of this trip are of the Royal Gorge

in Colorado, where the Gunnison River plunges with mad fierceness between perpendicular walls of granite fifteen hundred or two thousand feet high. For weeks we lived in a hunting and fishing lodge at the east mouth of this terrible gap. The river was filled with giant trout, and fishing in this roaring, turbulent stream, at the bottom of a crack in the mountains, so deep that the sky above seemed like a narrow blue ribbon, gave me a never-to-be-forgotten feeling that I was close to the vitals of the universe.

On our trip we went as far west as Cimarron, New Mexico, where I saw hard-faced, weatherbeaten men carry guns on their hips. And so won was I to them, so much did I want to be like them, that without saying anything about it to Crawford I secured the promise of a job on a ranch where we stayed for a few days. But when he found out my plans he was horrified and set up such vigorous opposition that at last I capitulated and agreed to return home first before I became a cowboy.

But I have always wondered why I did it. The tang of this outdoor life, the feel of horseflesh under me, riding wild trails, the fine edge of manhood in the men I met—why did I ever allow Crawford to take it all away from me? My nostrils quivered with delight at the sweaty, horsy smell of the cowboys. Their good-natured chaff and leathery smiles were open invitations for me to stay.

But I was like putty in Crawford's hands. Not only did he pull me like an aching tooth from the roof of the world, but before I was back in Ottumwa he had persuaded me to say that I would go to a Baptist college and study for the ministry.

The place picked out for me was Central University, located about fifty miles from Ottumwa in a sleepy little Dutch town called Pella. Dr. Stewart, the president of the school, was a friend of Crawford's.

And so I went off to school, where I was at once taken in hand in a way that showed me that I was a person of interest to the head of the university. In all studies excepting literature, philosophy and theology, I attended preparatory classes. In philosophy I was established in the senior class under a fiery ex-colonel of the Confederate Army who was a fundamentalist. The involved reasoning which a fundamentalist philosopher needs when he is trying to interpret the Bible literally is as intricate and wonderful as a spider's web and as frail as that bit of gossamer before the assaults of logic. I had long since ceased arguing with my father about these things. But when I met a man who scornfully assailed Darwin, Huxley and Spencer, scrambled the philosophy of Kant in the same bowl with Jonah and the whale, and crammed the time of creation into a period of five thousand years, it angered and disgusted me so that I became argumentative, voluble, truculent, and bullheaded. It is not surprising that I also became unpopular. I told myself that I didn't care, that I scorned the students and their diligence in trying to create a rational fabric out of the woof of the Bible and the warp of modern science.

Studying, as I had been doing, the writings of the great men of the past, in a childlike manner following their leadings, the gross superstitions I met shocked me with their ugly and uncouth absurdities. My father was a fundamentalist, but his naïve peasant's mind reasoned with the sublety of a poet, and poetically anything and everything is truth, if rhythmic, visionary and beautiful. To the poet all things are possible, and most religious men are poets. It is when a scientific method of procedure is used to organize and rationalize poetic products that gross superstitions are created. Poetry and religious mysticism have their own laws of rationality, but they cannot be understood by unimaginative experimental scientists or analyzed by them.

The type of religious man represented by the colonel who had become a teacher of philosophy was that of the Christian who has been vanquished by modern scientific methods of research and criticism. Being gross and stupid, such men have lost the traditions of the poets; Thomas à Kempis, Loyola, St.

Francis, Job and Esaias are not understood by them. Sweden-
borg was a mystic, as fantastic as any that has ever lived, yet a
great scientist. Michelangelo was a great engineer and architect—yet a mystic. Leonardo, one of the world's greatest
geniuses in science, was a mystic.

And it was between their kind of mysticism, of which my
father, with all his fundamentalism, partook, and the stupid
crassness of the colonel and the students with whom I mixed,
that I found my quarrel—not between belief and disbelief.

Had I not by race and habit been a canny Swede, I would
have left school when their dislike of me had come to a head.
But a financial arrangement for my support at school had been
made, and my sense of economy would not let me waste the
money that was being spent, for it gave me a chance to study
and to use the splendid university library. In addition, I even
found that the embittered discussions in which I engaged with
students and professors gave me a grim pleasure.

And so I stayed on until just before commencement, when
I relieved them of my hated society. At bottom I was such an
intense idealist and mystic, with an imagination so catholic, that
had they not used steamroller methods to get factory uniformity in their products, I could, in the course of time, have reached
a compromise between my reason and their faith. I loved Pella
and it broke my heart to be a misfit there.

VIII

STOICISM

CHARLEY DORN, the superintendent of the Johnston Ruffler Company, was a tall, paunchy, quick-tempered Irishman. Ever since the time I had commenced to work at the factory as a boy he had indexed me as a stiff-necked square-head. I had quit the shop several times in anger, but because I could at a moment's notice do almost any job in the place, he had always taken me back when I turned up again. He knew that I'd been away studying for the ministry and it was a shock to him when I now came back interlarding my request for a job with violent cursing. He was profane himself, but the spectacle of a divinity student using his own kind of vocabulary made him look at me in wide-eyed surprise.

"Why swear about it?" he asked. "I'll give you a job. How about the buffing room?"

This was the best-paying work in the whole factory, and I was delighted and went to work again. And deep beneath my desire to get my hands on the machines in the factory was my growing desire to be an artist. The two desires were alike, for art in its more normal expression is just a form of labor. This is especially true of sculpture.

With a hungry heart I looked up Schiewe. At the university I had been drugged to a state of nausea by religious and philosophical speculations, and he gave sympathetic response to my mood of revolt against intellectualism. He knew just how to handle me. I was sick of the goodness of God and the fanatic hatred of the agnostics. Any desire to decide what was or was not the truth I had lost in a yearning to do things with my hands again; to make money with my hands, to model beautiful forms with my hands—and have pretty girls to caress with my hands. These things now seemed enough for me for the rest of my life.

Every dollar I could save I put into a lot I bought on the instalment plan. My hope was that it would increase in value and give me money with which to start again for Europe to study art. I also studied French and German, and through Schiewe's suggestion I read biographies and autobiographies of great men. Having realized too late—after my abortive start for London—that he had overdeveloped my artistic nature at the expense of my character, he inspired me especially to study *Plutarch's Lives,* and talked to me at every opportunity of the strength and virtue of the Stoics. In his discussions he accentuated the privations and hardships of all men who had done the unusual—originated great things in art, literature, music and in practical life. At the time I did not realize his influence on my character; only later on, in the midst of loneliness, sickness and poverty, did it dawn upon me how Schiewe had prepared me to endure and suffer.

Sometime during this period the *Inter Ocean,* a Chicago newspaper, announced a competition for a picture and motto symbolizing Chicago. If I remember truly I gave Schiewe the idea that won the second prize, and although the design was never used, the idea—my idea—has been adopted by Chicago ever since as its motto. It was "I will." Even at this time my "Man Triumphant" monument and the philosophy from which it sprang were germinating.

Schiewe pursued, in his art, beauty in form and color, pure and simple. He considered my philosophical tendency a handicap. He believed in "art for art's sake." Character was a necessary thing, he taught me most vigorously, but he believed that to pursue the beautiful would produce greatness of character.

He tried to impress on me that all great artists had been noble, exalted personalities. Later in life I found this to be a fallacy—many of them have been libertines, weaklings, braggarts and cowards. However, to inspire me with fortitude and courage, to enable me to overcome the obstacles in my way, he had to make me visualize the ideal artist as a strong, persistent and patient person, willing to live in obscurity and rely upon himself for incentive and inspiration. The writings of Epictetus, the Roman, who from being a slave became a great man, was an element in the hardening process of my manhood. Marcus Aurelius I liked not so much, because he was less rugged and somewhat tainted with a softness akin to sweet Jesus.

The summer of 1893 I visited the World's Fair in Chicago, but so thoroughly had Schiewe taught me the classical masters that I did not find much to excite me in the modern art exhibition there. Schiewe had previously visited the Fair, and he asked me particularly to study the exhibit of his teacher—the great Makart—who had five large panels of nude and semi-nude female figures entitled Sight, Hearing, Smell, Touch and Taste. They did not impress me any more than the modern sculpture.

I had already become a dyed-in-the-wool classicist, and although I had no skill or technique at all, my heart was given with all the fervor of my young nature to the Greeks and the pre-Raphaelites, including Michelangelo. Even Schiewe could not influence me to like Raphael, whose art he worshiped. To me Michelangelo, his contemporary, though magnificent, is always naïve and direct, scorning sophisticated effect or trickery in any form, whereas Raphael since my boyhood has seemed to me the archetype of the popular "arrivist" kind of artist— a flatterer of women, an elegant dandy, whose profligate life sent him to an early grave.

The following year, 1894, America passed through a great panic and for the first time in my life I wandered from shop to shop unable to get work. Even Charley Dorn could not give me work any longer. I tried to sell my lot, which was now paid for, but real estate values had been reduced to the vanishing point, and my particular offering to a glutted real estate market lay on the low flats of the south side which were completely flooded that spring. Thus, in my first real estate venture, I was caught in the same net which enmeshed many large financiers that year.

The whole country became afflicted with strikes and labor troubles. It was the year that Coxey's Army marched to Washington to prevail upon the government to set aside one hundred million dollars for the building of roads and thus relieve the poor of the nation and at the same time give us much-needed public thoroughfares. Coxey's plan was considered visionary and dangerous by the wiseacres of that time, and his army of workingmen were hunted and harassed like criminals. Yet his plan was basically that of the WPA, one of the most important factors in the fight for recovery waged by Franklin D. Roosevelt.

At this time I was a member of Company G, Iowa National Guard. One day our company was ordered out by the governor to protect some coal mines about forty miles from Ottumwa. Here about thirteen hundred colored scabs had been imported from the South and the efforts of the strikers to dynamite the mines and mop up the Negroes sent us double quick to the place of violence. The strikers had in some way secured an antiquated cannon which they did not know how to use, but its presence gave us a sense of real war when we were told that we might have to face artillery.

The two weeks in camp were very happy ones. There were good food, danger real or imagined, poker, camp fires and boisterous horseplay. One day we left camp under Sergeant Saunders to relieve the guards at the mine. On the way we came to a bevy of admiring Negro girls hanging over a fence. Seeing their pleasure, the sergeant commanded us to halt, right about, forward march, halt, and present arms to the black, giggling girls. Another thing I remember is how, when little pigs rambled over the deadline of our camp, they were arrested, court-martialed, executed and roasted.

Upon my return from the mines I at last secured a job polishing knife handles at a cutlery factory. By keeping seven automatic machines going constantly, I could make eighty-five cents a day. My average, however, was less than this. By being economical one could in those days live as well on seventy-five cents a day as on five dollars now. Shoes with better leather than is used in the most expensive footwear of our time could be purchased for three dollars, a good suit of clothes for ten dollars, good meat for four or five cents a pound, a standard sack of flour for ninety cents, etc. In a first-class restaurant you could at that time eat a meal for twenty-five cents and your appetite was the only limit to the amount you ate. There were usually half a dozen different kinds of vegetables and all the meat, pie and coffee you could consume. A sandwich of hot ham, pork tenderloin or beef cost a nickel, coffee in big mugs a nickel. Saloons served free lunches, and when you were hard up five cents for a glass of beer would also pay for all you could eat.

The price for unskilled labor in the Nineties ran from a dollar to a dollar and a half a day. The job I held at the cutlery works was a boy's job, which I had taken for lack of something better.

As a whole, this period was the golden age for labor in America. Because of the low purchasing power of the dollar today, wages now are not equal to wages in the early Nineties.

One day the papers proclaimed that Kelly's Army—a unit of the Coxey Army—was coming to Ottumwa. Kelly and his men had come to Des Moines in box cars. In Des Moines they built barges to float down the Des Moines River as far as Keokuk.

It was a glorious summer's morning when, before sunrise, I joined several hundred others on the east side of the town to meet them on their arrival. The placid river and the shores heavy with green foliage made a beautiful picture. Before we could see the boats there came to us over the still water the boom and throb of hundreds of male voices singing in unison. They were the soaring voices of men united in a mighty chorus to inspire and strengthen one another for an ideal.

How many thousand such crusades from age to age have gone down rivers, over deserts or mountains, singing—often to end in shame and oblivion! They've often been wrong, perhaps deluded—more often than right—but onward they've gone, and onward we are bound. There is nothing that can stay the onward surge.

The barges were made from new lumber, and in the light of the rising sun they glinted like bright gold against the dark water. All were decorated in red, white and blue bunting, and as the men on the boats saw a multitude awaiting them, their voices increased in power.

And with them came a man who was to bring my life as a workingman to its close.

One day, on leaving the shop, I met an old friend, Ed Leonard. He was the son of an insurance man of some means, but Ed was a waster and a tramp. He had for years hoboed all over America, coming home now and then for a rest, a new wardrobe and the pleasure of telling us slaves in the mill of labor, stories of his wonderful adventures. He was well educated, a good talker and always cheerful and smiling. I was glad to see him, and when he had pumped my hand for a bit I was in a mood to listen to the stories I felt he was bursting to relate. Ed, however, did not begin to tell me stories, but quite abruptly made me a proposition.

"Say, Dave," he said, "this country has no opportunities for a young man any longer. Africa is the country of the future. The gold fields there are booming. Come on along with me to Africa and we'll make a fortune."

For an hour he talked about Africa, glibly, easily, and I reflected that Ed considered going to Africa more casually than I did going on a week-end Mississippi River excursion from Fort Madison. Ed had never held a job, I mused; he was no good at anything, and yet he roamed over the world at will. I, who had never even been fired from a job—why couldn't I get to Europe in the same way that Ed intended to go to Africa?

"Ed," I said, after we had talked awhile, "I'll tell you what I'll do. I'll go with you as far as New York and you go on to Africa to hunt gold and I'll go on to Europe to study art."

"All right," he said, as easily as though he had agreed to meet me for a walk after dinner.

The next day I told Adams, the superintendent of the Ottumwa Cutlery Works, that I was quitting on Saturday. Instantly he tried to dissuade me.

"For God's sake stick it out, Edstrom," he said. "In a week or so I'll have a good job for you."

"No," I replied. "I am going to Europe to study art."

He was a hard-boiled German-American, and when I explained how I was to tramp my way to Europe, he looked at me as if I'd gone crazy. He got in touch with Dorn and Hunt, the superintendent of the iron works, as well as the owners of the two companies. Although the force of workers had, because of the bad times, been cut down to one-third of normal, Hunt came himself to my home.

"If you will stay, you can come tomorrow and we will sign up a four-year apprenticeship agreement. I guarantee you personally that besides your regular wages you shall have enough contract work to give you a good income."

But I was now thoroughly filled with the heady wine of my plans and dreams, and I hardly heard what he said. Not until later on did I realize what a fine opportuntiy I had left behind me.

But nothing in the world could then have shaken my resolution to go. It was not only art that called me. Ever since I had returned from that first, ill-fated departure for London, it had been necessary for me to go and not come back until I had really been to Europe, in order to regain my lost self-respect.

IX

A HOBO

ON Monday, July 29, all my affairs were settled. I deeded my lot to Father and gave him what cash I had, except four dollars. I wanted to make it this time on my own resources.

Father had as a boy and young man been a tailor and knew good cloth. He bought me a pair of jeans pants. Jeans is a cloth now unknown, made of cotton and wool and impossible to wear out. He also resewed the buttons so they would never come off. We almost quarreled over whether I should wear suspenders or a belt. Father considered a belt unhealthful, like corsets, because it pressed on the liver; but I had to have a belt to strop my razor on when tramping. He at last compromised with me when I agreed to wear both, and I promised to wear the belt loose and let the suspenders do the real work.

My pockets bulged with sandwiches, a brush, soap, razor, a pipe, extra socks, an extra cap in case I should lose my hat, and plenty of horseshoe chewing tobacco. I had chewed a ten-cent plug of horseshoe tobacco every day since I was a boy.

The night before I left I had two remarkable dreams, both of which cheered me many times later on.

In the first dream some unseen being conducted me on a journey toward some unknown but superb ending, something final and infinitely desirable. On the way we came to a beautiful fountain of colored water that made music while the water rose and fell. Delighted, I stopped.

"Here we are," I cried.

"No, not that," said the guide gently, and we went on and came to more wonderful fountains, like clouds, spraying glories of colored mists and water with still more wonderful music.

"Not that," said the guide, as I wanted to stay.

Then we came to still more splendid musical fountains like pillars of fire bursting bubbles and undulating formations of liquid flames, the melody changing constantly as the colors changed. Again I paused, sure that at last we had reached the end of our search. But still my guide urged me on.

"Not this," he said.

Then all became so dark and silent I could hear my own heart beat. It was the most absolute quietude and darkness I have ever known. There was absolute silence and peace, and I thought clearly, and my mind and soul were at peace and very still. My thoughts were free and my heartbeats were free. The guide was not there any more, and as I awoke I knew that this was the journey's ending.

The other dream was more picturesque. I was at a very beautiful river, the water of which was as clear as glass. As I stood on its bank wondering how I could cross it, two men came up. They were young and looked as I have always imagined the angel looked who traveled with the young Tobias in the Bible. They had a large slab of white marble which they tossed into the water, where it floated, as light as cork. Then they plunged in and beckoned me to follow. Without hesitation I plunged into the water and all three of us seized the slab of marble and were supported by it as it moved swiftly through the water. Soon we came to a bend in the river and a high building with a golden dome appeared. Then I woke.

During the last hours of our parting my parents and I spoke in soft, subdued sentences. There was not much to say because the last few years of grinding toil and hard determination had reached a climax and they were as aware of the inevitableness

of my move as I was. Not a tear was shed, not a dramatic gesture or even a question raised as to the wisdom or unwisdom
of my leaving.

The evening of July 29, 1894, was tempered with the mellow coolness peculiar to the Middle West near the rivers. I
can remember the soft, out-of-focus quality of the trees, the
dream-like quality of the sounds which seemed to come slowly
through the evening mists, and the aromatic odors steaming
from the ground, just before the night took over the agitated,
fierce activity of the day.

I remember the afterglow in the western sky, and how the
great cottonwood trees in our grove down toward the river
seemed darker and more forbidding because of the tint of red on
their tops, while at the ground they melted in inky blackness
with the earth. Beyond them I visioned the muddy pond that
I had never waded because of the undetermined depth of its
mysterious ooze.

Mentally I was abnormally active. Picture after picture
rushed before my mind from years before down to the very
moment that was ticking away with ominous certainty. Not
only did I recognize the miserly allotment of time, but into
this superillumined awareness was crammed a consciousness of
the whole width, breadth and depth of the evening—the meaning to me of my parents and all the years we had lived together.
But the dominating note that with fatal sternness chilled every
tender impulse was a sense of strength. With an almost cruel
joy I seized the thought that at last I had become a man free
from all clowning with silly girls or vague dreaming of things
to be done in the future—yes, a man strong enough even to
resist the more subtle urge to remain and support my parents.

In my inner breast pocket I carried, carefully wrapped in
tissue paper, a woodcut of Michelangelo's Delphian Sibyl, by
Timothy Cole, which I had clipped from the *Century Magazine*. On the back of the picture I had written:

In my library.
I will leave tonight for Europe to study art. I have to
bum my way but I am going just the same. Good-by
home, good-by all. It's a big sacrifice but I must go.
Monday, July 29. DAVID EDSTROM.

Until two years ago I possessed this souvenir of my parting,
but at that time some cruel acquaintance stole my treasure from
me. In my heart, when I took this picture with me, was a
premonition that circumstances might arise in which I might
waver from my high resolve or even forget it, and the presence
of this mighty picture of Michelangelo would safeguard me
against such danger.

Out on the Wabash Railroad back of our house I heard Ed's
shrill whistle advising me he was there. Mother followed me
to the gate for a final good-by. For a moment she looked at
me in silence. But her voice was firm as she uttered her farewell.

"Don't come back until you've done what you've decided to
do," she said.

Down the long road Ed and I walked off at a brisk pace, and
although I felt my mother's eyes on my back and her strong
will demanding that I turn around and wave good-by, I did
not do so.

To Ed's utter disgust I insisted on going to the Armory in
the Opera House to say good-by to the boys of Company G and
secure a leave of absence from Capt. Laughlin. The captain
was surrounded by the company when I told him of my plans
and asked for a six-month leave of absence instead of a discharge. With a curse he commanded me to get into my uni-
form for drill, and the rest of the boys, when it dawned on
them that I intended to tramp to Europe to study art, commenced to push, strike and kid me unmercifully. At my
fierce resistance they let up shamefacedly. Grimly I left with-

out a leave of absence but with a very unpleasant threat from the captain of a dishonorable discharge.

With great care Ed piloted the way into the C. B. & Q. Railroad yards, where we looked around until a freight train headed east was found. Ed was an expert at this business, but the best accommodation we could find was a box car loaded with soft coal.

Ed in some way knew that it would be hours before the train would leave, so we climbed up on the roof and lay down, watching the stars. My comrade knew something of astronomy, and as he pointed out various stars he told me a number of legends about them. I was unable to listen well because there was a lump in my throat and I had to combat a nervous shivering. It seemed as if I were over on the other side of the river with Father and Mother, and that which lay here on the car was only the shell of a man, of little interest to me and with no real relationship to myself.

Not until three o'clock in the morning was the suspense of our waiting broken by a few rough bumps and then the smoother motion of the rolling train as it gathered speed. At dawn we arrived in Burlington. Here I experienced my first fear of the police, which Ed had inspired through instructing me how to evade being arrested. Without difficulty we got away from the train and down to the Mississippi River, where we shaved and washed ourselves. In getting out of Burlington I had my first experience in boarding a moving train. This is done on the outside of a curve, where the trainmen cannot see you from either the last car, the caboose or the engine. As soon as we got on the Illinois side of the river we were discovered by the brakeman, who saw some boys getting into our car. They had been out picking water lilies, of which they had great bunches. With some of these they bribed the brakeman to give them a ride, but as we two refused to give him anything, we were kicked off.

However, after a few hours we got on another train, which

carried us to Monmouth, Illinois. Here we made the acquaintance of a young Negro, a very nice boy with whom we decided
to dine. We found a grassy slope, a spring of water and a
couple of empty tin cans, and these two experienced wanderers
decided that I, being the most respectable looking, and therefore most likely to awaken sympathy, should go to a neighbor-
ing house and buy a loaf of home-made bread for five cents, but
not to forget to ask for a pinch of salt to go with it. I succeeded and came back with a mighty loaf of sweet-flavored
home-made bread which we divided and ate with great relish,
drinking deep draughts of water from the cool spring.

After our meal we lit up and the fragrant smoke of tobacco
added to our contentment. Flocks of heavy violet and gray
clouds stood like mountains of transparent splendor above the
horizon; above floated swiftly light white fleecy clouds so thin
that through them showed the blue sky. The sun blazed away
and in the heat I felt a distinct and active sense of pleasure as
I heard the cool ripple of the water running over the ledge of
the little basin the spring had formed.

Ed lay to my right, the Negro boy lay to the left stretched
out with closed eyes bathing in the sun, a straw of grass in his
mouth. I have seldom felt a warmer, fuller love of life than
on that hillside. The grass was full of chirping grasshoppers,
now and then a bumblebee buzzed by or hung dangling heavily
in the bosom of some frail flower. Then there was the twitter
of birds, flitting shadows, and the hot, heavy perfume of weeds.
I clung fondly to every detail of the surroundings because it
helped me to think clearly of the life behind—Father and
Mother—and the mystery ahead.

Toward evening, after having failed to get on several trains,
we found a car loaded with wheat that had been previously
broken into. In America this is a penitentiary offense that is
always relentlessly prosecuted when the culprit is discovered,
and although we knew that were we found in this car we had
every chance of being sent to prison, our disappointment in

being kicked off the other trains was so great that we took a chance.

The Negro boy had told us that Chicago had been for some days enclosed in a cordon of police and watchmen, to catch and arrest criminals who, like vultures, were stealing into Chicago because of the great railroad strike that was then going on. It was therefore imperative that we should get off the train before it entered Chicago to avoid being arrested.

We planned to stay awake, so that we would be sure to get off in time, but the wheat was so soft, and the rumbling of the train so pleasant, that we all went to sleep. After what seemed to me a few seconds I was awakened by Ed, who was shaking me and yelling in my ear.

"For God's sake, wake up!" he cried.

I stumbled to my feet, but in spite of violent cuffings and kicks, we could not get life into the Negro boy, and we were getting dangerously near to the outskirts of Chicago. Ed and I, therefore, had to leave him to his fate and crawled out on the bumpers, ready to jump as soon as the train slowed up. There was a drizzling rain and the night was black as pitch. All of a sudden, as the train was slowing down, a dark lantern was flashed on us.

"Here's two of them!" a harsh voice yelled.

Almost simultaneously Ed cried, "Jump!"

In a moment we were both running into the darkness, the police chasing after. Ed stumbled on something. There was a crackle and a flash. Whether we were shot at I don't know, but Ed gave out a terrific yell that halted me through terror. However, in a second we were both rushing on again in the dark—splashing into a swamp with long grass. After a short run through the morass, Ed stopped.

"Let's duck down in the grass," he whispered. "They'll never find us in the dark."

For a long time we heard them beating around, and then all

was quiet, but we sat there in the water, shaking and shivering with cold for a long time before we dared to move.

Finally, when it began to dawn, we crawled out and found a place where we could wash and make our toilet; but, strange to say, I have never been able to remember what kind of place it was.

X

ALONE

ED was sociable, good-natured and easy-going, and resented my unwillingness to fraternize with tramps. He was a tramp and wanted to be nothing else, but I refused to consider myself one. In spite of anything he may have felt about my snobbishness, he explained to me in detail much of the technique of hoboing and I absorbed all that I could, because I began to have the feeling that he wouldn't stay with me long, for I soon found that we had little in common.

Ed had a negative nature, ever seeking situations to interest and amuse him without costing him anything in energy. He was a natural vagabond and I was not. To me hoboing was a means to an end, whereas it was Ed's existence. I had already found that his glamorous story about going to Africa was only a dream, a springboard from which he could leap into a wandering stream that would take him any place at all.

A remnant of respectability persisted in him that made him invent an objective for each trip, and then as events were always impossible for a truly ambitious man, he created perfect alibis for his failures. Yet, although he didn't know it, he never really failed. He got just what he wanted—the adventures of the road—and happiness. Roaming over the world was to him an art in itself. Just as Schiewe loved art for its own sake, so Ed was a hobo by the grace of God, and found his delight in the practise of his calling. He needed no objective and never really sought one.

He had told me of crossing deserts and mountains—of having

been lost in sandstorms and snowstorms—but not until I had shared the road with him did I realize that his stories were true; and that in this business of pacing over the world without funds, he was great—a truly magnificent personality—I did not until years later appreciate. Just as an inspired musician is bored by the dull, fat, dowdy women to whom he must at times bow, Ed was bored by my bourgeois intensity of purpose. I was a person not able to understand the fine points of hoboing.

Just the matter of being awake—of knowing within minutes when we came to the outskirts of Chicago that night—was nothing short of genius. I marveled at the time and I marvel to this day over the fact that Ed—in the rainy black night, within a closed box car, after several hours' sleep—should be able to know when we arrived, not in the city itself, but at the first crossing, where the train slowed down before entering the city limits of Chicago.

Fearing to lose sight of him, I made Ed go with me to the Chicago Art Institute. My horror of being an outcast, a man chased by the police, sought a palliative in art. When we came to the Institute the sun was shining warmly. In front of the building was a large monument, and on the steps around it many hoboes were sleeping. At the sight of their relaxed positions, a great drowsiness came over me, and instead of going into the exhibition we lay down among the other outcasts and went to sleep. After a time, as the hot August sun came to mid-heaven, the heat woke us and made us both eager to get into the cool rooms of the Art Gallery. But I can remember only the gratifying coolness of the building's corridors, and not a single picture or piece of sculpture that I saw that day.

In the cool of the evening, near the yards where trains were made up for Buffalo, we went into a small grocery store, where we bought bread, smoked herrings and candy—to carry with us. The storekeeper was a talkative chap and gave us much valuable information. He told us in detail how to manage to find the cattle trains running between Chicago and Buffalo. The cars of these trains, especially constructed for the transportation of stock, had under the roofs hay cribs each of which was large enough to hold a bale of pressed hay. We were told that although the bottoms of these compartments were made of triangular wooden slats about two inches apart—not exactly the sort of thing you would choose for a mattress—if one had the guts to stick it out in one of these cribs, he could make Buffalo in forty hours without change of trains.

It was enough for Ed that he had never ridden in a car like this before. That fact made it automatically a desirable thing to do. As I think of it now it is amazing to me that we found, on that trip, one mode of travel he had never experienced. He was so avid for new experiences, so eager to go into anything that he had not known before, that it is almost inconceivable that he had never ridden in the hay rack of this kind of cattle car. As for me, I was delighted that we would be able to cover six hundred miles more of our journey in one jump like that, and we went gaily into the yards and, without difficulty, found two berths exactly as our friend in the grocery store had described them. We got two right next to each other, so that we could pass our salted herring and candy back and forth and talk.

But a few minutes' confinement in my cramped cage were enough for me, and I would have climbed out right then had I been given the chance. However, the train got under way almost as soon as we were settled into it and I could do nothing but suffer with my legs and arms and back twisted about in awkward positions, and the parts of me on which my weight rested tortured by the sharp edges of the corrugations.

Nor did I get any sympathy from Ed. Unable to stand the discipline of work and what physical effort went with it, he yet seemed utterly insensitive to any hardship of the road, and was so gay as we sped over the prairies of Indiana and Ohio that I was ashamed to grumble. Soon my senses were a blurred jumble of crucifying pain and weariness, accentuated by the stinging thirst which salt herring, candy, and butterless bread, without water, created.

After a nightmare of suffering we reached Buffalo at last and began the painful process of unwinding ourselves and trying to become men again. At first it was impossible. Out of the car and on the tracks neither of us was able to stand upright for a time; we crawled about on our hands and knees, limbering up. Ed thought it was funny, and laughed. And I laughed too, partly to keep Ed from seeing how I was suffering, and partly in sheer relief at being out of that hellish place.

A short way from the tracks we found a half-built house with some water barrels and from them we quenched our thirst. After shaving and washing, we hunted up a saloon and had some beer and free lunch. With the lunch they gave us each a huge bowl of rich soup—and all for five cents!

Afterwards we went to the post office, where I wrote to my parents, telling them that all had gone well and that now I would surely succeed, already being so near to New York, and asked them if possible to borrow fifteen dollars from a well-to-do man I knew and send it to me, General Delivery, New York. While I was in the post office writing, Ed disappeared. I waited around for many hours, but he did not come back. I decided then that I had expected this to happen, and that I must go on alone.

I took a street car to the east side, and then hid myself on a curve of the railroad track, behind some large packing cases, ready to board the first train that passed. I had not been there long before a freight train with several empty cars came along. As I ran, ready to jump into one of these, I saw another man leave cover from behind another box and dash for the train also. He was a bit ahead of me and didn't see me. But even in my breathless dash I noticed something familiar in his figure and gait, and, just as he swung up into a car, I saw that it was Ed. I had no time then to catch up with him, but I noted which car he got into and swung into another myself. The first time the train stopped after dark, I left my car and, finding his, climbed into it. After recovering from his surprise, he told me what had happened.

While I had been in the post office, he had been arrested and brought before a judge, who, after a short examination, had let him go. He had hurried back to the post office then, but when he did not find me there, he had decided that I had got tired of waiting and had gone.

We went on together without any adventures until we came to Bainbridge, New York, from where he was going to some place nearby to pick hops in order to earn money, he said, for his journey to the gold fields of Africa.

After separating from him there, my real difficulties began. I now realized what help his superior knowledge in the trade of beating one's way on the railroad had been. To get to New York City I had to pass through a corner of Pennsylvania. In Pennsylvania the laws against tramping were very severe, and, as a move in the war against it, railroad men were given immunity from responsibility for injury caused to any undesirable passengers who were bodily thrown from a moving train. I cannot remember everything that happened to me before I got safely out of the dreaded state. But I do remember that at one place, called Great Bend Halstead, I was thrown off seven trains without being able to get out of town.

Utterly desolate, wanting nothing so much as to weep, I gave up at last and sat down by the side of the track. If it hadn't been for my one disgraceful return home after having started on this same trip under better auspices, I think I might have given up the whole plan then and started back to Iowa from Great Bend Halstead, Pa. I knew that I would never have nerve enough to try to jump another freight in that town. I tried to remember what the date was, wondering, with a melting self-pity, how long it had been since I had slept in a decent bed, but I couldn't even remember what day of the week it was. My face sunk in my hands I sat there, without a plan, without an idea even on which a plan might be built, consumed by sympathy for myself.

Just as I was about to decide that my best bet would be to lay my head on the railroad track and wait for the next train to come along and end my suffering, I heard a gruff voice speaking just in front of me.

"What the devil are you so gloomy about?" it said.

I looked up slowly and saw a one-armed man in rough clothes regarding me quizzically. He seemed friendly enough, yet I couldn't answer his question. Nothing that I wanted to say could be said. I knew that if I opened my mouth to speak I would begin to blubber like a child. So I just stared at him tragically.

"Well, if you can't talk," he said, "come along with me."

With his one arm he helped me to my feet, then started off down the track and I followed. He asked me my name, but I couldn't answer him. He asked me where I was headed for, and still I remained mute. Every time I tried to open my mouth to speak I was seized with an almost uncontrollable upsurge of emotion and almost burst into tears.

Finally he quit trying to make me talk and we walked on in silence until at last we arrived at a neat little cottage set in the midst of fruit trees and flowerbeds, where he introduced me to his charming young wife.

She gave a shriek of laughter, as she looked at me, which started tears running down my cheeks. But when the man, seeing my grief, shoved me over to a mirror and I caught a glimpse of myself, I also commenced to laugh. I saw a big man, with half-grown, stubby beard, black as a Negro, with gray streaks where the tears had coursed down my cheeks, and the trembling lips and woful eyes of a child. Eventually I had finished my bath, and, well groomed, was seated at the dinner table, where I had eager ears to listen to the tale of how I was going to be a great artist.

Meanwhile I had learned that my benefactor's name was

John Tyler and that his arm had been lost in the service of the railroad from whose track he had taken me, like a stray cat, into the warmth and comfort of his home and his wife's generosity and kindliness. Before the meal was well started I felt as though I were in the company of bosom friends.

This was on a Saturday afternoon. I stayed with the Tylers that night and spent the whole of Sunday with them, most of the time in the garden, where I talked many hours of my past and my dreams of the future. They wanted me to stay with them for some days, but I insisted on going that night.

Mr. Tyler was employed in the railroad offices, and he arranged with one of the engineers, a Mr. Curby, and his fireman, to take me along on the engine of their train. They made a nice bed for me on the fireman's seat, and fed me on pie, after which I slept almost uninterruptedly until we arrived at Scranton, the end of their division.

In Scranton I went into a bar and took a glass of beer and a sandwich. And there the bartender unconsciously boosted my self-confidence tremendously by asking me a question which showed me he thought I was employed on the railroad. I had been afraid I was beginning to look like a tramp.

Tyler's kindness was the beginning of a series of kindnesses which were shown to me by railroad men. Most of the trains at this time of the year carried no empty cars east. I was therefore obliged to ride most of the distance through the State of New York either on the roof of the cars or on the bumpers. But one night I was invited, by the conductor himself, into a car half-filled with lumber, where he, the brakeman and I played cards all night by the light of their lanterns. Another night two brakemen found me standing asleep between two cars. They could not very well stop the train for a tramp, but to ensure themselves of my safety they took turn-about to keep me awake until we reached the next stopping place. Here they put me on the engine, where I rode to the end of their division.

New York was at this time a safe town for tramps. The

police paid little or no attention to unfortunates. I therefore rode boldly into the city in broad daylight on the bumpers of a New York Central freight train. I shall never forget the intense joy I felt as I left the train and realized that I was at last at a seaport, from which I could leave for Europe.

I left the railroad yards with little idea of where I was going to go. Chiefly I wanted food. Yet I had so little money that I was afraid I would not be able to satisfy my appetite in a restaurant. As I was wondering what to do about it I saw a little shanty nearby with its door invitingly open. Instinctively I turned toward it, and as I came nearer I smelled the enticing odor of frying meat. Without hesitance now, I walked up to the door and rapped gently as I looked in at the broad back of a large Irish woman who was standing over a stove. As she looked around I asked her a little timidly, with my eyes on her skillet, whether she would sell me something to eat. For a moment she appraised me from head to foot, her gaze dwelling on my face. Then, without a word, she turned back to the stove and, plunging a fork into a piece of the steak which was frying there, she put it between two slices of bread with a magnificent gesture and handed it to me.

"Now be off with you," she said gruffly, and I, with a hurriedly muttered "thank you" which I am sure did not sound half as fervent as I meant it to, went on down the street eating one of the most delicious meals I have ever tasted.

I soon found my way to the post office, but there was no letter for me. Somewhat discouraged, and feeling keenly my isolation, I went to the wharfs in Hoboken. Here, confronted by ocean liners fresh from the sea, the magnitude of my undertaking towered up before me. I felt very puny, and my voice seemed to be almost piping when I asked for work. The first day I had nothing but disappointment. Now and then the following refrain from an old song kept haunting my mind:

The Bowery, the Bowery,
They do such things and they say such things,
On the Bowery, the Bowery,
I'll never go back any more.

Somehow the song made the street seem familiar to my imagination, and toward evening I went to it. At first its noise
and blatant ugliness made me wonder why I had wanted to
come. I had only a very little money and didn't want to spend
any of it in any of the places of amusement. But I wanted to
get off the street. And so, when I heard the tune of a familiar
hymn, I followed the music into a stuffy little hall, where an
old man was conducting a prayer meeting. Almost the whole
congregation was asleep, and all seemed poor and forlorn. As
soon as I was seated, I also fell asleep, I was so tired. After
awhile I felt some one shaking my shoulder gently and woke to
see the old man who had been conducting the meeting standing
over me. He asked me if I had any money, and when I told
him I had, he gave me a card to a lodging house, where I was
given a small room for fifteen cents.

The next day I went on looking for work. I went aboard
the *S.S. Norge* of the Thingvalla Line and found the purser,
who was terribly drunk. He asked me if I was a fireman, and
when I answered "no" he sent me away having scarcely looked
at me. As I went out, I saw him pouring himself another drink
of whisky. I left the ship and walked about until I decided he
had had time for two or three more drinks. Then I went back.
As I suspected, he was barely able to talk when I faced him the
second time, and neither his face nor his voice evidenced any
recognition of me. This time, when he asked me if I was a
stoker, I told him that I was, and was promptly engaged.

After all it wasn't such a very black lie. I had done all kinds
of work since I had been a child, and I knew beyond all doubt
that I could do the work of a stoker. I think it is the only time
in my life when I ever told quite so flat a lie as that to gain a
personal advantage, and it hurt my conscience as I said it. But

the quick surge of triumph which I felt through all my being as I got the job, the realization that I was at last about to be actually under way, was a quick and potent salve.

Leaving the ship, I went to the post office again, where I found a letter from Father containing fifteen dollars. Secure and proud now in the knowledge of my job, I kept only four dollars and sent eleven back to him.

XI

HATE

THE engine room crew of the *Norge* was a shabby lot. The ship had a bad reputation along the waterfront. Her boilers were old and had long since passed the point at which they should have been retired. As a consequence she was difficult to stoke and few men made more than one trip on her. When she had docked at New York on that trip seven of the stokers and trimmers had deserted and been replaced, hit or miss, by a drunken purser who had picked them up much as he had hired me. But as I stood before the yawning fire pits about to begin work it all seemed beautiful to me. The fire boxes were more than fire boxes and the ship more than a ship, for she was taking me to the fulfilment of my ambition. I had no premonition of any real difficulties on the way—certainly no thought of personal conflict with any other members of the crew.

But on the very first day I received a warning that this was not to be a peaceful trip.

There was a young Dane in the crew, a man of about my own age, who was the most evil-natured man I have ever met. Why he seemed to take an instant dislike to me I cannot to this day guess. Perhaps it was something which went back far beyond my own existence, a hereditary conflict between the Danes and the Swedes. Perhaps it was fundamentally a hatred of himself which found expression in a hatred of me, so closely related to him racially. At any rate he began, the first time we did a job together, to show me that while he and I occupied the same ship there would be no peace.

I was working with him, placing some of the heavy steel plates which made the floor of the engine room, and which had been removed for repairs. It was a job which required considerable care and coordination between the two men doing it. As I was stooping over to place my end of the plate, he suddenly let go of his in such a way that, had it not been for my natural quickness and experience in handling heavy objects, I would undoubtedly have had my fingers crushed.

I looked up at him quickly, automatically expecting, I suppose, some word of explanation if not apology. But the thick bestial smile on his face quickly sent a flush of anger to my own. Obviously the man had dropped the plate intentionally, finding a twisted, ugly sense of satisfaction in the thought of injuring me. I think nothing which has ever happened to me has surprised or shocked me more than the realization I gained in that moment of the black ugliness which dwelt in the soul of this Dane who was my fellow workman. Had there been any grounds for hatred, any offense which I had committed against him, even though it had been trivial, I might have understood. But this empty, meaningless desire to hurt me I could not, and cannot now, understand.

But I quickly controlled my anger, and we went on with our job in silence. My one aim was to get to Europe. Already I had overcome hardship, hunger, and loneliness to get thus far. I would not be turned back by the ugly spirit of another man. And I did not want a quarrel.

Two or three days later I found that it was going to be more difficult to keep the peace than I had imagined. Since I was the last man engaged on the ship, I was given a number of nasty little jobs which no one else wanted to do. One of these was to clean away the soot which accumulated at the base of the smokestack. In order to do it, it was necessary to crawl in through the firing door (with the fires out, of course) along the grates of the fire box, and then up into the smokestack itself.

It was an unpleasant job at best. In spite of all precautions, chief of which was the careful closing of the drafts, the fine powdery soot crowded into the lungs, making breathing difficult. Yet, with the drafts and the fire door closed, it was safe enough. But once the soot was stirred up by a draft the place became untenable. More than one stoker, careless of safety precautions, had been smothered by the rush of soot.

I knew this and had been careful to see that all was as it should be before I began my work. But just as I had got a thick cloud of soot moving ahead of me, as I raked it clear, I felt a sudden rush of air past my face and up the stack. Before I could think clearly I was enveloped in a cloud of biting blackness which stung my nostrils and forced its way into my lungs. Choking and gasping, I tried to make my way back as I had come, but every breath I took was torture for me, and I suddenly found myself unable to move through the small opening through which I had to go to get back. Every way I turned and squirmed seemed to be the wrong way, and finally I fell, practically unconscious, all my effort spent on trying to breathe.

Fortunately another member of the crew happened to be passing the boilers and saw the Dane open the drafts. Being made of different stuff, he tied a handkerchief over his mouth and, crawling into the fire box, pulled me out, undoubtedly saving my life. Again the Dane's unreasoning, brutal, crazy, pointless hatred had found expression in trying to injure me.

Still I held my peace with him. The quarrel was of his own making, with no point or object, so far as I could see, save to hurt me, and, not understanding unreasoned hatred, I thought that if I refused to carry it on, it would die of its own weight. So I went on, staying away from him as much as I could, doing my dirty little jobs without complaint. And for a time I thought that there would be no more trouble. When the real fight came it was precipitated by a conflict with another member of the crew.

The Dane had a number of friends among the rough-and-ready members of the ship's company. Gradually some of them joined his campaign of persecution against me. My soap was stolen, and my body, lacking proper baths and irritated by coal dust and bilge water, became covered with sores. The food was abundant, but served in great pots from which every man snatched for himself, and the coterie headed by the Dane operated to keep me from getting my share.

At first I went hungry, but bit by bit my courage rose and my sensibilities declined, until I was reaching and snatching for the choicest bits of meat with the rest of the crew. But still they managed to keep me from having my two liters of Branvin (white mule) daily, and my share of butter and sugar.

By the time I had been a few days at sea, my body hardened and with it my sensibilities toughened up a bit too. It is a bit difficult to stick with the gentler habits of life in a boiler room. The bruises, the ache of muscles, the burns soon sweep away the thin veneer of civilization. Suddenly I began to enjoy the sense of brutal strength in me, and looked forward, almost with eagerness, to the day when the real fight would be inevitable.

The moment came at mess one day. Tired of going without sugar, I reached out my hand for a sugar bowl, whereat it was immediately seized by a stocky, broad-shouldered man on the other side of the table.

"Keep your hands off the sugar," he bellowed.

Suddenly all the torture of the days behind me rose to give me strength, and I answered by seizing a metal teapot full of hot tea and dashing it over his head. Just behind me stood the Dane, who had been waiting for some open violence. Without warning his huge hands encircled my throat and he began to choke me. With the conviction that I was fighting for my life, I wrenched myself loose. The narrow space gave me no room to use my legs, but I struck him several times as hard as I could in the face before he could close in on me. Then his weight took its advantage. In a moment he had me down on one of the bunks, pounding me in the face with his fists; after striking me perhaps a dozen blows, my head bobbing up and down on the pillow, he crawled off. As soon as I could get my breath, I crawled out and again struck him several blows in the face before he closed in on me, and then he beat me until I lost consciousness. When I came to, he was gone.

Wild with rage, I sought and found a large bread-knife and started down for the engine room, intent on killing him. However, one of his friends got down there before I did and gave warning, so I could not find him.

From that day until the ship docked, my anger never left me. I had learned at last the meaning of hate. All the restraint I had at first exercised with the Dane was gone, and whenever there was an opportunity I tried to attack him with whatever came to hand—a knife, a shovel, or the great iron rods used to stir the fire—but he always escaped me because of the protection of his friends.

Often my anger, which had become hard and fixed, turned toward the other men, and I did not miss an opportunity to take offense. One day—I don't remember now what trivial thing it was that stirred me—I knocked one of them into a pile of hot cinders. After that they took care never to aggravate me. I took my allotment of white mule, sugar and butter at mess in sullen silence and there was none to say me nay.

The mark of that trip was not obliterated from my soul for years. A hundred times after it was ended I dreamed that I was about to plunge a knife into the Dane—and awoke with a cold, bitter sense of frustration because he had escaped me again.

Even while I was still on the ocean in the stoke hole of the *Norge*, I realized that I had become a brute, and I liked it. But now and then I would sicken of it and, coming up from the fiery bowels of the ship into the salt, balmy ocean air with the August moon hanging like a great silver disk on the horizon, would feel the exquisite joy of detachment from it. The rippling waves made a shining path from the moon right up to the side of the ship. And the contrast between the stoke hole with its human bestiality and the clean magnificence of sky and sea, created in me a consciousness of the beauty of nature more intense than any I had ever felt before.

XII

I VISIT THE ROYAL ACADEMY

A RRIVED at Copenhagen, I collected my wages amounting
to fifty-two crowns—bought me some new socks, a sack,
some bread, cheese and sausages, and took passage across the
Bay to Malmö, with the intention of tramping to Stockholm.
But in picking my way from the ferry at Malmö with my sack
on my back, I caught sight of a smart-looking freight steamer,
the *S.S. Allegro*, from Stockholm, and going aboard, found that
I could get a job as a stoker, which seemed a much better way
of getting to Stockholm than tramping.

The stoking crew on the *Allegro* consisted of a young man I
remember only as Emil, three other men named Fallquist, Anderson and Carlson, and myself. And what a difference there
was between them and the crew on the *Norge!* The *Allegro*
crew was friendly, intelligent, and companionable. The boys in
the engine room were not only stokers but skilled mechanics
ambitious to become marine engineers. They would listen by
the hour to my tales of America, laugh at my funny American-
Swedish dialect, and now and then jump up and push me over
in friendliness and good humor when I told them something
that seemed too queer to be true.

But they drew the line at my story that I was going to the
Royal Academy. To them this seemed the beginning of madness and they set about to save me from it before I became completely insane. But I knew nothing of this at first. They were
so gay and friendly that I paid no attention when I saw them
with their heads together, or noticed that they would sometimes

stop talking and begin to giggle when I came upon a group of them unexpectedly. I reveled in their friendliness, in the seeming nearness of my goal, and in the beauty of my native land.

In the North during summer the atmosphere vibrates with a live, cold purple at times veiling and at times revealing land and sea through a mystic twilight, where transparent shadows in fantastic loveliness seem to fall and rise, sway and weave until it is all like a delightful dream or a mirage.

With eyes almost blinded from the glare of the fires and my clothes drenched with perspiration, I crawled up from the hot boiler room one morning about four o'clock. We were in the channel leading up to Stockholm and I wanted to be on deck when the city came in view. Excepting for the muffled throb of the engines, all was still both to the eye and to the ear. In the foreground the narrow channel twisted like a silver-scaled blue serpent between amethyst-colored granite islands and dark wooded shores.

It takes several hours from the Baltic to Stockholm. Sometimes you enter narrows in which you could toss a stone to shore from either side of the ship.

As the ship slowly felt its way the passage seemed to end suddenly in a lush green meadow—then the channel would take a sharp turn around some mighty crag, and as my eyes followed the turning of the boat a great lake opened up. My eyes could not detect an opening on the other side, but the ship sped on more rapidly straight across, and after awhile crept in again through another channel—or else between little islands that seemed to float in the blue twilight like fairy barks beside the granite-anchored mainland that had pushed up above the water level.

Far away a hazy blue curtain obliterated all contours, making heaven and earth one, and in it swayed grotesque shapes. Finally, breaking through the opaque horizon, a flicker of red and gold where the church spires caught rays from the unseen sun revealed the city toward which I had been traveling so far.

Bit by bit in the nebulous light emerged a vision of surpassing beauty. The church steeples, tremulous with subdued color, wraithlike and evanescent, seemed to be of some heavenly precious substance. The Royal Palace and the terraced hills, where building towered over building, all seemed to be made of translucent jasper and onyx. Here and there the rising sun caught bits of burnished copper in its flame and the blazing splotches, like yellow gold, suddenly imbued the blue and purple tones with vibrant life.

I saw the high and mighty granite bluffs which at first seemed to rise directly out of the water. Then my eyes found the majestic Royal Palace before which ran a terrific cold blue stream of water—the North Stream emptying the great Lake of Mälaren into the bay. The seafront of Stockholm is mighty and beautiful in a grand, austere manner unlike any other harbor in the world.

How my whole being expanded with pride and exultation! With all my harassing experiences behind me, my heart stretched out with profound devotion to the city of my dreams. She was like a beloved woman, won against tremendous obstacles, personified, warm and throbbing, waiting, now, to take me into her arms.

I had ten dollars more in my pocket than when I started my journey in a C. B. & Q. coal car in Ottumwa. Everybody on the *Allegro* from the cook's boy up to the captain liked me, and I was pleased and proud when the first engineer, with some embarrassment and hesitation, offered me a job as trimmer in place of Carlson, who was to leave the ship in Stockholm.

I knew why he was embarrassed. Every one on the boat was convinced that my plan was merely a tragic dream, and when he offered me a job his kindness made him afraid that I would think he doubted my chances of even getting an audience with the director of the Academy. I told the engineer that I could not give him an answer until I had seen the director of the Royal Academy, but asked him if he would please hold the place open for me a day or two. My comrades asked me several times:

"How are you going to get to see the director of the Academy?"

"Why, I'll just call on him," I replied. Since I hadn't a stitch of clothing other than what I had on, this seemed funny to them. They grinned—but as they looked into the eyes of each other there was a grave steadiness in their glances that I could not understand.

Before we tied up at the harbor they invited me to drink with them a glass of Swedish punch to celebrate my arrival. They started me with a tumblerful of the insidious sweet stuff, which I took happily. This was followed with another and another, until, when I came down in the engine room to work until noon I was so drunk I sank to my knees.

"My God!" exclaimed the second engineer, and immediately sent me up to the forecastle, to which I had to crawl on my hands and knees, not being able to stand. The deck was full of stevedores ready to unload the vessel, and when they discovered me, black as coal, crawling gravely and slowly and methodically bit by bit toward the head of the ship, they gathered around me with uproarious laughter, which set me off in a fit of drunken hysteria.

Finally two of the stevedores lifted me, one by the head, one by the feet, carried me thus like a sack, and tossed me into a bunk in the forecastle, where I passed out as soon as I struck the mattress.

It was twenty-four hours later when they finally wakened me by pouring cold water on me. When I realized that a whole day had gone by and I had not yet seen the director of the Royal Academy, I sprang to my feet furious. Now I realized what their many secret conferences had been about. Getting me drunk had been a planned performance. It was their way of trying to save me from the consequences of my mad dream. My American-Swedish was inadequate to express my emotions and my comrades knew no English, but so fluent and impassioned was my profanity that even in what to them was a foreign language they understood that I had risen to the occasion and that my cursing was hot and professional. During breathing spells I could hear their delighted remarks as they tried to guess what I was saying. As they were laughing themselves sick, out of simple humanity I had to compose myself for their sakes and quiet down.

But when they saw that they had only delayed, and not really stopped the execution of my mad plan, they began making up for the trick they had played on me. The wonderful jeans pants Father had given me were still serviceable, but from washing and rewashing had shrunk so that my hard muscles bulged out through them as if I had been wearing tights, and they did not quite reach my shoe tops. Fallquist was about my size, and he produced a pair of decent pants. Carlson gave me a shirt. Emil furnished a tie of great brightness and luminosity. From their united wardrobes they clad me in all the glory of a successful coal stoker. When their artistic labors with me were complete, Emil remarked:

"Say, fellows, do you see now I was right when down in Malmö I saw him asking the old man for a job and I told you guys that 'the finest-looking bozo I ever saw is trying to make the ship'?"

Sped at last on my way by their whole-hearted good wishes, I started out. I confess that, as I left the ship, I felt a warm sweep of nostalgic pleasure at the thought that I was to take this step, the most important in my life, in my native land. Here, if anywhere in the world, I would be at home. Here I would be understood and helped onward to the realization of my ambitions. But I had walked only a little way before I felt, with a vague unrest, that something was wrong. I was as little at home here as I would have been in China. The people looked stiff, blank-faced and forbidding. They wore dark clothes and there were no colors even in the ladies' hats. When they met

I noticed a mincing step, then both feet were brought together at the heels, then they made a mechanical bow from the hips; with faces fixed in a corpse-like gravity, with hands stretched rigidly at the sides, they finally spoke to each other, but without a smile disturbing the awful seriousness of just being alive. At first it seemed funny to me. Then suddenly it was frightening. I had felt out of place most of my life. Here I felt more out of place than I ever had before. I did not know these people. I did not understand them. I felt that I was completely shut out by them.

I gritted my teeth, tried to pay no attention, and hurried on. Surely at the Academy I would find a different atmosphere. An aspiring artist among artists, I would be made at home there.

The flunkies at the Academy tried to keep me out. They could scarcely believe their eyes when they saw one who was obviously of the lower order of workingmen, presenting himself with a demand to see the Herr Director. Had I really been a Swede instead of a Swedish-born American, I would have wilted before their freezing words and glances. But in this case their attempts to protect their sacred trust were futile. A man who had fought the crew of a freighter for his rightful rations of sugar and butter was not to be stopped by their dignity and wordy protests. I do not remember just what happened, but I do remember vividly standing at last face to face with Count George Otto Von Rosen, Director of the Royal Academy of Fine Arts, K.V.O., K.N.O., and a whole lot of other things like that.

I've never met a man who so much reminded me of a proud bantam rooster as Von Rosen. He wore a tightly fitting cutaway coat with the top unbuttoned to accommodate his protruding chest, which made him look like a pouter pigeon. He wore very high heels in his attempt to gain height, which made him seem almost to fall backward. His brow was perpetually set in a deep frown. But beneath the frown there were rather nice eyes trying to be piercing, but not quite able to conceal their warmth and alertness.

I should now have made the standardized bow, and stammered in a subdued manner to show profound respect, but I didn't. It wasn't arrogance, really, but ignorance which kept me from doing these things. I walked briskly forward, swaying a little on my sea legs, and reached out my hand, which he coldly ignored. Drawing back I flushed angrily at his slight, but he only appraised me for a moment, his face a mask. Finally he spoke.

"Well, what can I do for the Herr?" he asked coldly.

"I've come from America to study art," I replied, as calmly as I could.

Still he looked at me coldly. Finally he delivered judgment and it was in the tone of one who accepts his own words as the ultimate authority.

"Most seriously I advise the Herr to give up this foolish dream," he said pompously. "It is a very precarious profession and few ever succeed. Many years of study are required to arrive at any degree of skill for some one who has the means to support himself during his years of study. The Herr, by all appearances, is not possessed of earthly wealth. Most seriously I repeat again—give up this foolish dream."

I know now (for I came to know him later) that he was meaning to be kind, that he was telling me the thing which he believed thoroughly was the right thing to tell me, advising me in the only way that he thought made any sense for me. But I couldn't know that then. I was furious at his words, and when I spoke my voice was cold with rage.

"I have not come to ask you whether or not I shall become an artist. I've come to you to find out how I shall become one."

Immediately all his kindness froze up. He tried in vain to add to his height as I looked down on him with a sardonic smile. With quick clipped-off sentences he gave me the desired information without a change in facial expression.

"Before being eligible to take the examination for entry to the Academy, a three-year course in the Technical School is necessary. But," he added, "we take in only from three or four, up to ten, students every year, and sometimes there are as many as fifty applicants, all eligible, from whom we choose the best." As a parting shot he added: "I believe the Herr needs to cultivate humility."

Paying no attention to his last remark, I asked for the name and address of the director of the Technical School. Receiving it, I left.

The Technical School, I learned, would not begin before November, and we were now in the last days of August; so I decided to take the job as coal trimmer on the *Allegro* and add to my hoard of forty kroners, which I had over from the fifty-two kroners I had earned on the *S.S. Norge*.

In two months, I thought triumphantly, as I made my way back to the ship, I would actually have made a beginning!

XIII

I OUTRIDE THE STORM

DURING the two months and eighteen days that I worked as coal trimmer on the *Allegro* we made two trips to London and back. On each voyage we loaded the ship up north at Ljusne and Gnarp with pig iron and lumber. Here I first learned to know the peasant girls and boys of Sweden. While the ship took on cargo at night up north we went ashore, and sang and danced the polka, the schottische, and the Hambo polka. They were all vigorous, athletic dances, rhythmic and difficult far beyond any of the dances of today. A room full of these heavy boys and girls, whirling around to the tune of accordion and fiddle, was a room filled with the beauty of tremendous vigor and power.

My memory of these husky young people fills me with a sense of sorrow because I believe that never again will the earth produce such a clean, powerful race of people as the peasantry of the North in those days.

During the last voyage of the *Allegro* in November we encountered one of the worst storms known on the North Sea for many decades. A number of ships were lost in that storm and we had to fight hour after hour to surive the hellish onslaught of wind and wave. A more stout and seaworthy and friendly ship than the *Allegro* never pushed her staunch prow through the sea. She was a good ship and every one who ever became part of her company loved her. But the antics she could play in a storm were beyond description. She was like a bucking bronco, and no amount of seamanship could tame her. I was

seasick, and while the storm lasted I could not eat. The deck
was piled so high with lumber that it was like climbing down
a well to get to our forecastle quarters. Ropes were stretched
around to cling to when the great seas burst over us, and sometimes the battering and sucking power was so great that when
I was caught in one of these deluges I felt as if my arms would
be torn from their sockets by the terrible pull of the water. We
all had to work without rest to keep the steam up.

One day, for more than eight hours without let-up, I shov-
eled coal into the hungry maws of the boilers. You, who sometimes feel sorry for yourselves because you sit at desks without
leaving them for longer than this, can have no conception of
what eight hours in the stifling fire room of a plunging ship can
be like; how the breath comes in short and anguished gasps
from lungs clogged with coal dust; how the rhythmic motion
of arms and shoulders and back, swinging forward with the
shovel filled with coal, backward with it empty, can become torture; how the whole being can cry out for rest.

In addition to the normal strain of the work was that caused
by physical weakness, the result of seasickness and no food.
Finally, as I swung backward for a shovelful of coal, the miner's
lamp which I carried on my cap went out, leaving me in almost
total darkness, and, suddenly at the end of my endurance, I
threw myself with a cry of despair onto the pile of coal from
which I had been shoveling. Every mad contortion and twist
of the ship shifted the huge pieces of coal and filled the fetid
air with fine, choking dust. Now and then pieces of coal would
roll against me as if to cover me.

"Why am I here?" I cried to myself. "Why do I let these
things happen to me?"

And there, in the suffocating air of the coal bunkers, with
sweat rolling from my filthy body in the air heavy with the hot
breath of the furnaces, I saw a vision of a shining male figure
of surpassing beauty and power. It came as if in answer to my
question. In it I saw a reason for my miserable plight, some-

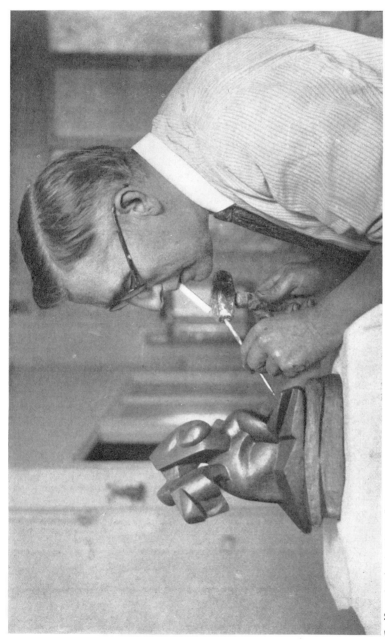

THE SCULPTOR AND "THE ETERNAL TRIANGLE"

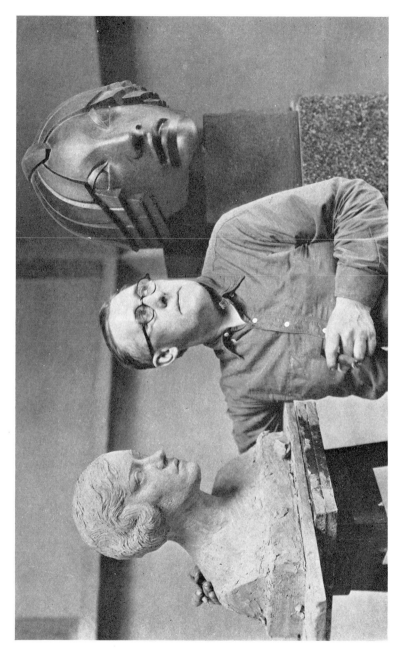

DAVID EDSTROM AT WORK ON A BUST OF GLORIA SWANSON

In background, Sphinx, black granite

thing which suddenly glorified my struggle and made even the filth and the physical agony of it beautiful.

It was as if, standing there before me, the figure said, "I have come to remind you what you already know but have forgotten. Acknowledgment of defeat means defeat. The greatest thing in life for you is the molding of yourself into a fine figure of a man. You have given up the struggle. Take it up again!"

In shame at my temporary weakness, and with new determination, I rose, lit my miner's lamp and went to work, never stopping again until I was relieved.

Finally the storm subsided and we anchored safely in the calm sheltered Thames. Every one on board ship was thoroughly exhausted, but we were all happy over having brought not only our stout *Allegro* into harbor, but with it all her cargo. Not one single plank of our deck-cargo of lumber had we cut loose for safety's sake. Other Swedish lumber boats had been forced to drop their whole deck-cargoes in that storm, and the crews of these ships we gibed and taunted for lack of seamanship when we met them in the sailors' taverns in the city.

I mustered off the *Allegro* on the twenty-seventh of November, 1894, when I was exactly twenty-one years and eight months old.

Through a policeman I secured a nice room with a family named Peterson, living at No. 13 Pretgardsgatan up on the high hills of South Stockholm.

About the twenty-ninth of the same month I entered the Technical School.

XIV

THE BAND BEGINS TO PLAY

I feel so light and gay,
I feel so light and gay,
I've got to take the dogs along
To keep the boys away.

MANY times during those early days at the Technical School I was reminded of Von Rosen's offensive advice to learn humility. And many times in the years that have followed I have tried to decide just what the word meant to him. Swedish custom at that time, and I believe even now, requires that whoever ranks above you must be allowed to walk on your right-hand side. In the army where everybody wears an insignia showing his rank, it is easy to practise this rule, but in civilian life, to know the intricacies of Swedish caste requires a lifetime study. The mouse bows to the rat, the rat to the cat, the cat to the dog, the little dog to the big dog. Everybody bows to somebody else in Sweden, and it is called humility.

From the first I blundered and violated many of the petty rules of Swedish usage, thus barring myself from a great deal of social contact. But I didn't care. I did not, in those days, allow myself to feel inferior to any one. The reproduction of Michelangelo's Sibyl that I had carried with me was evidence of the height at which I had set my goal. As if the picture had been a letter of introduction and recommendation from some mighty person, I would take out the packet in which I carried it, carefully remove the woodcut, and show what I had written on the back of it about leaving Ottumwa, Iowa, to bum my way to Europe to study art. Then I would finish my story with: "And as I left, Mother said, 'Don't come back until you have done what you set out to do.' And you bet I won't," I would add. How I must have bored my listeners!

A trunk from home had arrived by express before I came back from my last trip to London, and in it were my wardrobe and all kinds of papers establishing my identity; also all my juvenile drawings. In Ottumwa I had gone in for rather large-checked suits, smart according to the ideals of the times in Iowa. America used to be, at least in men's ready-to-wear clothing, original. My trunk also contained a brown derby hat unlike anything in Sweden. Eagerly I took these out and put them on in place of my coal stoker's clothing. Then, taking some of my drawings under my arm, I went again to call on the director of the Academy.

If Von Rosen had been surprised over the appearance of the coal trimmer, he was not less so at the apparition in the loud-checked suit and brown derby which called on him now. I am sure he realized, as he looked at me the second time, that he had met with an individual of at least dramatic possibilities. In the meantime I had gone to the National Museum, where a number of Von Rosen's works were exhibited, and had learned what a fine artist he really was. Although I had not "learned humility" in his sense of the word, I had gained an admiration for him as an artist which had made me choose him as my best friend in art.

He was still reserved, still completely on his dignity, but he looked carefully and with serious interest at my drawings and did not hesitate to say that he liked them very much indeed. But again he pictured to me the hardships of an artistic career and the small chances I had of succeeding, finishing his discourse with the same advice he had given me before: "The Herr must learn humility."

As time went on I saw him frequently, often taking him

examples of my work, and a strange and truculent relationship developed between us. His attitude toward me was made of a strange combination of personal dislike and interest in what he recognized as my talent and promise.

My hands were so stiff from the last few months of hard labor, so used to the feel of a shovel, that only with the greatest effort could I control so comparatively delicate an object as a lead pencil. And in those days no one could start at anything in Sweden without mastering first its ABC's. Accuracy was the first law of education. My art studies at the school, therefore, began with drawing straight lines. I was put into classes of boys only ten or eleven years old, who were apprenticed in different trades. Here I sat towering above them and scowling with my effort to do simple things which they, less concerned with the whole business than was I, did with ease. Fortunately Swedish boys are quite well behaved, and although I knew that they were amused at seeing a man of my age so awkward, they were not rude, and when I took my ineptitude with good grace and even asked their aid and advice, my position in the school became agreeably established.

When I called on Von Rosen I could not refrain from chewing tobacco. I could not have bowed and looked serious if my life had depended on it. I grinned, I walked erect with a swagger, I said what I had to say loudly and directly, without frills. According to all social rules I should have approached him with at least three formal bows between the door and the desk where he sat enthroned in his reception room. Then, after being spoken to, I should have coughed in an embarrassed way, murmured in an unintelligibly low voice a sentence of respect, then commenced in a cringing whine: "If the Herr Count would do me the great honor I would humbly like to show some drawings I made at the Technical School. I know they are indifferent and immature, but the Herr Count might in his kindness point out something that would help me to do better." Instead, I would swing in breezily with a broad smile and speak at once in a loud voice, saying: "Well, here I am again with a batch of my new efforts. It's hard work, Herr Count, but by Joe I am getting there. Just watch my smoke after I get the kinks out of my stiff hands."

At this point the Count would usually interrupt me.

"My dear fellow, why so dirty?" he would expostulate. "Your vest is a fright. Soap and water should not be beyond your means. I believe the Herr has talent, very much talent, but such pride, such arrogance will not help the Herr along to success. And such a filthy habit of chewing tobacco—the habit of a bum!"

My face would flush with anger, then, and I would prepare to depart. But the Count would break out in a humorous smile. He was human, after all, and a great artist. He would unbend and take my drawings, his face lighting up as he looked at them, and in a moment he would be immersed in discussions of what I was to do next.

But as sure as heaven above, before I could get away he would freeze into his lordly manner and I would leave in a huff and with a feeling that he was laughing at me behind my back.

It became a game. He was insistent on starting me on the way to being a gentleman, and I was just as determined to continue to be myself as I had been in Iowa. I worked, I starved, I became thinner and less vigorous in my movements, but never did I yield an inch from my brave, noisy, American front.

Before the end of the first school year I entered the drawing classes of a man named Sjostrom. Von Rosen knew him and his methods of teaching and advised me to be very attentive to Sjostrom and above all not to irritate him.

"He is the greatest teacher I have ever known anywhere," the Count said, "but he is a very ill man and unless you are careful he will not make an effort with you."

I tried to follow this advice and, as a result, learned from Sjostrom one of the most important things I ever learned in art—how to establish absolutely the angles and relations of lines and details in a drawing.

"If you can master a detail with absolute exactness," Sjostrom would say, "you can master any complexity of form correctly."

He advocated synthesis of details into a whole instead of, as most teachers do, the generalizing of an object and working into details gradually from a general form. The latter method is, of course, easier and brings quicker results; but it never gives the strength and beauty achieved through the former, which is tantamount to building the whole out of well-established parts instead of throwing the parts into a careless heap and trying to arrange them later.

My father and friends in Iowa sent me now and then small sums of money—sums ranging from a dollar and a half to twelve dollars. This unusually large sum of twelve dollars, which I once received, constituted the proceeds from a concert given by the Swedish church for my benefit. The reader may smile at the amount, but it was a great and honorable sum in the estimation of the poor folks who contributed it.

The pathetic loyalty of the old folks and friends in Ottumwa spurred me to an exacting devotion to my studies. I wish now that I had not taken things quite so seriously. I would have fared better in the long run, and perhaps have developed a calmer philosophy, had my student life been spiced with a little more play.

I had practically only one form of diversion, and even this I took as a seeming necessity and always paid for it with hours of depression afterwards. Feeling that I did not have time to have sweethearts, yet unable, as I have always been, to live without women, I would deliberately not eat for a day, now and then, in order to pay for a few hours' love. The type of women my poor finances could afford were a shock to my fastidious nature. And what a strange boy they must have thought me, as I tried to make a transient relation as romantic and as clean as that which I desired in life! I would never go to a *liaison* with one of them without an apple or a little bouquet for her, and, as I paid in advance the agreed-upon fee for her services, I would accompany it with kind words and compliments.

Then one day I met Greta, whose heart was even more hungry for refinement in love than was my own. I met her on a stairway one night—a petite, brown-eyed young thing. She had a small squalid room behind a tawdry pawnshop owned by a crass and feelingless pawnbroker, who rented it to her for twice its worth. I was poor, but to her I became not only a Prince Charming, but also a man of power and distinction. And she wanted her landlord to be impressed. So one day she gave me five kroners, which she had saved by I don't know what sacrifices, and asked me to buy grapes with it—a luxury in Stockholm in those days for only the rich.

"Send them around with a messenger from yourself so I can show him up," she told me.

She was the only person I've ever met who surpassed me in the art of make-believe, and that interlude with her is a bright spot in that first hard year in Stockholm. But it was not to last for long. The dear child was stricken with appendicitis and died after we had known each other only a few weeks.

Meanwhile I helped to support myself by giving lessons in English to workingmen. But I was such a poor business man that I charged only one crown (28 cents) for an entire class. I had only time to give one class of an evening.

As long as I lived with the Petersons, the family to which the policeman had sent me, I got along fairly comfortably on my earnings and the help I received from Ottumwa. The Petersons charged but six crowns for my room and two or three times a week would invite me to dinner. Quite often, too, in the morning, before I went to school, Mrs. Peterson would open the door of my room and stick in a tray with coffee and trimmings, saying that she had just baked some new cakes and wanted me to taste them.

But my ridiculous snobbishness—as bad as that of the Swedish caste system to which I objected so—soon put an end to my good fortune.

One day as I was going to school I heard a street organ being played in a court and a woman singing a popular song. Idly I stopped to listen. Suddenly I stiffened with shock, for I saw that it was my landlord Peterson who was grinding the organ and one of the daughters of the house singing. The great artist David Edstrom was living in the home of an organ-grinder. Preposterous!

All through life I've had to pay for this trait of snobbishness. Love, appreciation, duty, and fortune, I've cast away when my particular rules of caste became involved. A prostitute had honorable traditions: Aspasia, Rahab of the Bible, etc.; a certain type of tramp was all right—Ulysses himself was a wanderer—but an organ-grinder was something *déclassé*. I have always held the same attitude toward the imitative artist. The hanger-on, the plagiarist, however famous and wealthy, to me has always been as the organ-grinder, the vender of tunes ground out without creative instinct. Yet it is evident that ninety-nine per cent of all successful artists are men of imitative, unoriginal talent.

I moved away from the Petersons' at once and took quarters with one of my students of English. Here I had to share a room with three others and pay the same sum as I had at the Petersons'. The ventilation was bad and, being undernourished, I soon developed a cough and a fever. My hands were sweaty and I could not keep drawings clean. My intensity, my eagerness and will power kept me from realizing that I was gradually becoming a very sick man.

At last the school year was ended. I was given high marks in all studies except in plan drawing and perspective. Soderman, my teacher in sculpture, offered me a job at his country home, Sturehall, as a gardener for the summer, and I gladly accepted it and took up my work there. And then, in the surge of nostalgia which came to me on America's greatest national holiday, I almost sacrificed all I had gained.

On the Fourth of July I asked a day off and went into Stockholm. I was homesick for America, and somehow I hoped I might meet some Americans on the Fourth and get a whiff of something from home. The day brought me a treat beyond my wildest expectations. The American battleship *Marblehead* lay in the harbor, and I soon joined some gobs and we proceeded to paint the town red.

I was the guide, of course, knowing the city and the fine points of Swedish drinks, and could act as interpreter with the girls we gathered unto ourselves. It was a marvelous sort of homecoming abroad and before the night was over I had agreed to sign up on the *Marblehead*. My celebration continued to the next day when I was passed by one of the officers as fit material for stoking coal. The doctor was not on board ready to examine me, so we ambled on shore again for further celebration and then, suddenly, the reaction set in.

Sobered, I found myself aghast at what I had been about to do, and quietly returned to Sturehall, sicker than a half-drowned cat from my two-day debauch.

XV

I FINISH WITH THE TECHNICAL SCHOOL

BACK at Sturehall I plunged into my strenuous job as man of all work, but the experience with the sailors, through which I had almost sacrificed all hope of being an artist, had frightened me and driven me back to my ambitions with renewed fervor. I felt that I could not wait until fall to be at creative work. Consequently I began to model a bust of a little peasant girl named Esther, a sweet and lovely child of thirteen who was as shy and quiet as a mouse. In order to have an hour for modeling every day I used to get up before four o'clock in the morning.

Then, almost before daylight, my hour of modeling over, I would plunge into my heavy physical work. After that was finished it was time to go to bed, but I seldom did so until much later. Two lovely girls lived in a cottage on the Soderman estate, and Soderman's son Carl and I, with the girls, used to make up an almost nightly foursome, not infrequently spending the whole night in singing, dancing, talking, and having a friendly and congenial time generally, so that often I would go directly from them to my hour of modeling, without having had any sleep at all. As the result of such a summer, my health, when school opened in the fall, was worse than it had been at the beginning, in spite of the good food and out-of-door life which might have been my salvation had I let it be. I had only the bust of Esther (which I still have) to show as a positive gain for the summer.

Von Rosen had told me that it would take me three years

to do the required work at the Technical School, but I had
made up my mind to do it in two. And so, when I returned, I
continued living badly, eating little, getting too little sleep,
until physically and mentally I was close to the point of dis-
solution.

It was at this time—the worst time it could possibly have
happened—that I got a letter from home which told me that
there was a rumor in Ottumwa to the effect that I was not going
to school at all, but was spending my time and the money the
kind friends at home sent me, in pool rooms and gambling
places, wasting my life carelessly.

There have been plenty of other rumors about me since,
which I have not liked, but none that seemed so degrading and
unfair as that one. Its cruelty seemed infinite, the burden which
it placed on me unbearable. Once more, as I had done before,
and as I have done many times since, I pondered in futile agony
over the cruelty of mankind. I remembered suddenly a day
in Paxton, Illinois, during our first months in America, when,
as a child, I had come into striking and confusing contact with
empty, meaningless, destructive cruelty, which had completely
confused me then, and confuses me equally now.

Father had come home one day with a huge, gorgeous,
colored kite. Neither he nor I knew what it was, but he had
bought it in an impulse of affection for me, knowing only that
it was a beautiful plaything for a boy, and trusting the other
boys of the neighborhood to explain its uses to me.

I ran out into the street to find some boys to show me what
to do with it. Finding them, I asked simply and directly what
it was, and they, strangely delighted at the width and depth of
my ignorance, promptly told me it was a target. Putting it up
against a fence, they began to throw stones at it. After a few
holes had been made in the beautiful creation, they saw the confused look of pain in my face and, bewildered themselves by my
passivity, their mood changed. In a few minutes they had
secured paste and some newspapers and mended the kite. Only

when the patched-up beauty was tossing in the sky, did my ponderous Scandinavian mind begin to wonder what pleasure they had found in mutilating it, and I have wondered ever since. If I could have answered that I would have known why Christ was crucified.

But in those days I was a healthy child, and could throw off the depressing effects of such wonder as that. Now, with my health broken, my frayed nerves in constant turmoil, my body and mind at the point of exhaustion through illness and worry, I was incapable of taking it, and decided that I would commit suicide. Only by dying could I avenge myself on the person who had started such an abominable lie.

Steeped to the marrow in Victorian romanticism, I planned my exit to be beautiful. I thought of Castle Island, which had so delighted my eyes on the morning when I had first entered the harbor of Stockholm. Rising in a sheer cliff at one side, it overlooks the cold blue waters of the bay, resplendent in its loveliness. To jump from this cliff seemed to me to be the most desirable exit I could devise from a life which had become intolerable.

It was an angry, stormy, cold night early in winter, when I set out to raise the curtain on what was to be the last act in the tragedy of my life. The water was black as ink in the dim starlight. As I walked along I thought darkly of how noble was this final evidence of my creative genius. No one could have planned a more magnificent death than mine was to be. I pictured the faces of my false accusers in Ottumwa, when they would hear of my death. I saw the fear in their eyes, heard the awe in their voices as they spoke of it in lowered tones, felt their shame as they realized, too late, to what they had driven a man so much their superior in ability and courage. I thought myself very much a splendid martyr to their stupidity and baseness, as I slowly walked to the edge of the cliff.

And then, as I looked down toward the water which had seemed so beautiful to my imagination, I saw in the depths of night only a sullen blackness through which came the impersonal, meaningless muttering of the waves below; the beauty of the spot was shattered for me and only brutality and ugliness remained. A plunge into those impersonal, body-breaking depths could not be the magnificent thing I had pictured, but only something hideous and degrading.

I decided to go to the other side of the island, where the beach was low, sloping gently to its junction with the sea, and where I could lie down and let a great wave come in and carry me out, as though I were a creature of the gods. Turning, I made my way to the other side. And here, as I had planned, I lay down and a great wave of ice-cold water dashed over me.

And suddenly, as though I had been drunk, the cold water brought me back to my senses and, aghast at the danger of catching cold, I struggled to my feet, shaking off the icy grip of the sea and my morbidity, and hurried home and into a warm bed, where my kind-hearted landlady brought me a hot toddy.

The result of my discovery that I could not commit suicide was a renewed and more feverish intensity in my studies. I plunged into the task of making a half-life-sized copy of the famous Greek statue known as "The Gladiator from the Villa Borghese." Undernourished as I was, and in ill health, I finished it only by the most tremendous effort. Too late I realized how much better off I might have been if only my snobbishness had not driven me from the home of the Petersons, who had taken such good care of me. But I finished the statue. And then, at last, I collapsed.

The day after I had the gladiator in plaster, my condition was so bad that I had to go into a hospital. It was the end of the school year and I had just taken the examinations, the result of which would tell me whether I could enter the Academy in the fall. I had done my work at the Technical School in two years—but how? I did not know in what classes I had passed and in what I had failed until one day one of my fellow students visited me and brought me the news that I had received the highest honor in sculpture, with which went a small financial prize, and high markings in all studies but one. And then as I lay there, my face flushed partly from fever and partly from the sense of triumph which his words brought me, he spoiled it by saying, "They, of course, know of your great poverty and sickness."

For several days I lay there, trying to forget, in my sense of triumph, the sting which had come in the student's intimation that my award had been made out of charity rather than through recognition of merit. And then came the official report from the school, which, at first, seemed to dash all my hopes. For it bore the crushing news that I had failed in perspective and plan drawing, and thus would not be given the certificate which would enable me to enter the Royal Academy.

Wild with disappointment, I sprang from the bed and began dressing. I must go to Von Rosen at once. I must tell him what had happened before he left the city for the summer. Somehow, in spite of all the conflict in which we had engaged, I felt sure that he would be able to do something about it. A nurse rushed in when she saw me dressing, her face a picture of astonishment and terror. When she could not prevail on me to go back to bed, she dashed out again, returning at once with a doctor, who at first tried to reason with me, telling me that the gravest consequences might attend my leaving now. I must stay several weeks longer, he said, before I could be allowed to get out of bed if I wished to retain any hope of recovery. When this failed he tried bullying me, but I went right on dressing, and when I had finished I left the hospital at once, and, going to the school and my room, collected the work on which the Technical School had passed such harsh judgment. Then I went to see Von Rosen.

I went to him with my arms full of drawings and explained that Architect Anderson, the head of the department of architecture at the Technical School, had refused to pass me, not because of any faults in my drawings or in my ability to pass the oral or written examinations, but because the drawings were slovenly. I explained that my hands were constantly dripping with perspiration because of the trouble with my lungs, and it was this, not a lack of knowledge, that had made them messy.

It was then that the Count proved his sense of fairness and his integrity as an artist. Without any attempt to conceal from me his fury at Anderson, he told me to go back and demand a certificate to the effect that I had made the drawings, promising to have the Academy committee of entry pass upon them instead of accepting the Technical School report.

Hopeful again, I returned to Anderson only to have my hopes shattered once more by his flat refusal to give me the document for which I asked.

"You intend to become an artist," he said, in a voice which reproached me for such presumption. "You have not the means nor sufficient talent to warrant me to help you in such a foolish endeavor. It is for your own welfare I refuse. Some of the drawings have been so erased that the paper is almost worn through. It is preposterous that you should submit such drawings either to me or to the Academy. I will not do anything to help you and you may tell the Herr Count this from me."

In despair I rushed once more to the director of the Academy and reported our conversation word for word. If he had been angry before, he was furious now. I stood and listened with delight while he delivered himself of a stream of profanity which would have commanded some little respect even in the engine room of the *Allegro*. Finally he calmed down enough to give me instructions.

"If you have the imagination and ability to make an original composition showing real creative talent to submit with your drawings and models," he said, "I guarantee you that you shall not be turned down because of any petty technicality."

Delighted, I left him, my mind busy with ideas for the com-

position I would submit to win my entrance to the Academy.
One idea after another I rejected, settling at last on a group
representing Cain and Abel just after Cain has murdered his
brother.   It was not an accident which made me choose this
subject.   For a time I thought that I would do a statue of the
shining male figure which I had seen in the coal bunker of the
Allegro, the night when I had almost given up the struggle
with the storm; but that was a figure of triumph, and must wait,
I thought, until I had experienced triumph.   The cruelty of
the boys who, in my childhood, had almost ruined my beautiful
kite before they had patched it up to fly it, the realization that
their action was unfortunately characteristic of mankind in
general, and the more recent incident of the rumor which had
been started about me in Ottumwa, all contributed to my desire
to make the Cain and Abel composition—the first group I had
ever made in sculpture.

Meanwhile I had my livelihood to think of, and I turned
again to labor.   There was a great boom in the building industry that summer and, after joining the plasterers' union, I
secured a job making plaster moldings for buildings.   At this
work I made as much as ten dollars a day—a huge wage for
those days.   The unions had everything their own way in
Stockholm that year.

At nights and on Sundays I worked on "Cain and Abel."
The group showed the two brothers the moment after one has
passed from life into death.   Abel lies stretched on the ground,
while Cain bends over and forward in mute surprise at what
has happened, as if it were inconceivable that a man could die.

There was a closer connection between the composition and
the event which, such a little time before, had led me close
to the brink of suicide, than is at first apparent.   In the lie told
about me in Ottumwa I saw the path of the serpent, the father
of lies.   It was he that made Cain a murderer and a liar, and
ever since then we have all had in our veins some of Cain's
blood.   The liar is ever surprised over the power of his lie.

A blow will kill. How strange! Next time he will lie even better and more deliberately!

The fifteenth of August, with fourteen other applicants for entry to the Academy, I was locked up in a large studio to make drawings from plaster casts. Here, under strict supervision, we worked two weeks. Each one had beforehand submitted his works and certificates. On a certain Monday, we were informed, there would be posted on a billboard in the Academy the names of the successful candidates.

When I found my name with three others as one of the successful four to be accepted as students in the autumn of 1896, I looked long and hard before I could believe, could know, that at last I was a student at the Royal Academy.

XVI

THE BEAUTY OF BONES

I HAD become a sedate, somber-faced young man by this time. I entered the Academy with the greatest seriousness, determined to let no mistake of mine mar the opportunity it gave me. To earn my living I secured a job at the Royal Opera as a supernumerary, and, working there, I continued my education in human nature as well as earned a little money and heard glorious music every night.

A celebrated bass singer named Elmblad was director of production. He had been manager of the Berlin Opera previously and was considered one of the best artists and producers of the day. He was a tall, powerful man with a vitriolic and sarcastic tongue. His eagle eye kept track of every one from the lowest supers, members of the ballet and chorus to the world-renowned soloists in a performance. He gave them their orders and expressed his uncomplimentary opinions of them in such a way that there was never any uncertainty about the way he felt. Of the several hundred people employed at the Royal Opera there was only one man with whom he never quarreled, or to whom he never said anything unpleasant. This man was the darling of the whole nation, the tenor Odman. Yet Elmblad detested Odman, and refrained from openly venting his dislike of him only because of the tenor's immense popularity.

I was a beginner and did not know the ropes nor who was who, nor what I might be called upon to do, and Elmblad, knowing this, used me as a pawn to play a malicious practical joke.

One of the first operas produced after my entry was "The Crown Jewels." I was given a small part, and at the first rehearsal, as I was standing in the wings ready for my cue, Elmblad came up to coach me.

"Mr. Edstrom," he began, "you are now a villainous outlaw. You must stride into that gloomy forest where Mr. Odman, the lonely tenor, is singing so ardently. When he has finished his aria you are to seize him and take him and bring him out right here where you entered. Be fierce about it. Ready—now go!"

I did not know Elmblad's style of humor, nor that he sensed in me the one-time butcher and coal stoker, and so I did as I was directed. Stalking onto the stage in the most ferocious manner I could assume, I grasped one of Odman's mushy arms. To my horror the little man with a plaintive bleat sank to the floor, looking up at me in shocked terror. Aghast, I stood back, looking from him to the director in confusion, whereupon the tenor, seeing that I was not really dangerous, stood up quickly and, his face a picture of distaste and outraged dignity, fluttered to where Elmblad was standing and in a quivering voice, on the verge of tears, pointing at me, gasped out:

"He—he touched me!"

The director turned on me with a fierce scowl and clenched fists as if he were going to beat me and his voice rumbled at me.

"Oh, I say, Mr. Edstrom," he cried, "how dared you—how dared you touch Mr. Odman? You must never touch Mr. Odman—you must bow—you must always bow when you approach Mr. Odman and you must never, never come close to him."

I glowered at him in silence and never mentioned the matter again. After that I did as I had been instructed to do, but as long as I was at the Opera, Mr. Odman revenged himself on me in so many painful and comical ways for my one great mistake that I was cured for all time of my admiration for lyrical artists as persons. To me was revealed, as it was to the Greeks, that singing as a profession makes men soft and unmanly.

I made my work at the Opera a school in self-control and allowed nothing to mar my keen enjoyment of the gorgeous ballet, the glitter and glow of costumes and scenery, the surge and pulse of the mighty orchestra and chorus, or the rapturous content of the impassioned soloists.

Gold is where you find it, and I've enjoyed few singers as I did the divine Odman. He may have had the heart of a rat, the general intelligence of a moron, and the manhood of a flea, but his voice was beautiful and his musical soul that of an angel. He employed only three movements to dramatize his emotions —right arm out—left arm out—both arms out. These three movements were made with such uniformity in whatever character he played that he seemed like a stuffed doll whose limbs were pulled with a string. But what mattered his sausage-shaped body, his ridiculous character, when through his throat burst forth such a flow of golden song?

Meanwhile my studies at the Academy were so absorbing that I was ready to call black white or white black, smile if I was sad, seem sad if I was happy, in order to avoid a minute's contention with any one that might take me away even in thought from my problems at school.

I loved all my studies at the Academy, but the one which fascinated me was anatomy. For this I have my teacher, Dr. Karl Curman, to thank. With such firmness and such infinite wisdom and beauty did he ground us in this most important of all subjects for a sculptor, that for a time I considered seriously abandoning art to become an anatomist.

Curman was, in every sense of the word, a great man. Yet he had little conception of his own greatness, nor had the other members of the Academy faculty, nor most of his students. He was nearly seventy years old when I was his pupil, but his carriage was erect, his movements as easy and dignified as those of an athletic Greek philosopher. His nature was such that the destruction of a continent or the tragedy of a human life, even though it be his own, would be only a small incident to him in the great evolution of life as a whole. He was like a god to whom the crash of a solar system might sound as the rustle of autumn leaves in a breeze sounds to us.

Around Von Rosen there were always arguments, petty impassioned words. Around Curman there was no commotion, only a calm pursuit of wisdom with a sweet and humble gratitude for every fact, every bit of information gleaned from life. His voice was deep, vibrant and resonant—yet capable of exquisite nuances in his lectures. In personal conversation he was gentle and humorous and became incisive and rasping only when positive facts of science were challenged.

I can see him now, standing before his class, holding up a piece of bone and demonstrating its structure with the delicacy of a woman showing a friend a priceless pearl. Yet there was nothing dreamy, vague, impulsive, romantic or haphazard about Karl Curman. He was a true scientist and his whole outlook on life was determined through the findings of exact research. Yet he saw the human body as a thing of beauty, from its general construction and mechanical function down to the infinitesimal integration of cellular structure. An ardent lover could not regard the miraculous charm of his beloved with more awe and tenderness than Curman did a piece of bone from the body of some unknown person. The manner in which nature fastened a tendon, the law of mechanics worked out by nature in the application of energy to propel the body, the action of nerves, arteries and veins, the flow of the blood, the tension and relaxation of muscles, the application of the physical forces that give the face the power to convey emotions such as love, hatred, fear, determination, laughter, scorn, indifference—were to him the most overpoweringly fascinating matters in the world, and he conveyed as much of his love and wonder to us as we were capable of taking.

His tremendous grasp of the united complexity of the human

body, and a mastery of the Greek ideals of beauty, placed Curman above all other anatomists of all times. Indeed he had gained a thorough knowledge of medical anatomy, normal and pathological, and a medical degree, before entering the field of plastic anatomy. After having been graduated from the Academy, he spent years in Italy and Greece, studying Greek sculpture at first hand. He thus not only mastered a knowledge of man's evolution as an animal from lower to higher functions, but he also learned to know the forms that expressed the noble inner life of the great Greeks of ancient days.

The pure mechanics of anatomy from a plastic angle have been intelligently and exhaustively worked out by Richet, the great French anatomist, and by distinguished Germans in still greater detail, but Curman is the only anatomist who has united the immortal concepts of Greeks with modern science. Leonardo and Michelangelo both studied anatomy and were far ahead of their time in the knowledge of the body from an anatomical point of view, but their Christianity limited their outlook on life. Though Greek calm and dignity were somewhat evident in the art and personality of Leonardo, he was tainted and poisoned by the restlessness of the Christian era.

Restlessness is always manifest when the instincts of nature are condemned as evil. The control of the instincts by the ancient Greeks was inspired by the same attitude that they showed in the training of muscles in their athletic games. No one calls a muscle a bad name because it is weak or overdeveloped. Sensible points of view are applied to the task of correcting a muscle, without any soul-anguish or flagellations, fastings or brutality to oneself. Curman, though a modern scientist, had the Greek attitude toward life. There were no bad names for natural things in his vocabulary, no littleness in his mind.

He was a very wealthy man and was therefore able to spend a fortune and thirty years of his life in concentrated work on a treatise on plastic anatomy. It was his ambition to give to the world an exhaustive, conclusive and final work on the sub-

ject. But, to the world's great loss, the several hundred thousands of words of text, and hundreds of colored drawings from
his own hand, which made the book, were burned up in a few
hours with the publishing house in which they were to go to
press the next day. Thus through the mysterious agencies of
Fate was destroyed the life work of a great man.

As I think of some of the difficulties of decision which I faced
in the closing weeks of my first year at the Academy, I am reminded of a poem called "Frogs" which was written by a little
Norwegian boy in Chicago.

What a wonderful bird the frogs are!
When he hop, he fly—almost;
When he stand, he sit—almost;
He ain't got no tail either;
When he sit, he sit on what he ain't got—almost.

Are we some frog, what?
I guess, maybe;
When we ask ourselves whether in the frog-pond of this wild and
        weary world
Is it better swim, hop, or fly?

"Is it better swim, hop, or fly?" This was indeed a question
for me to decide as a new and unlooked-for problem obtruded
itself upon me at the close of the school year. Not only had
I passed my examinations, but the rating of my work at the
Academy was so high that in the fall, when the great carved
doors would be opened again after vacation, I was to be given a
large free government studio for my private use. In it I was
to make an original statue.

And then, just as I was feeling triumphant about that, my
mind was harassed by the intrusion of a basic conflict which,
for a time, threatened to make me leave the Academy.

Just as we are all slaves to fashion in clothes, so are the
denizens of the art world slaves to the changing taste in paint-

ing, sculpture, music and architecture. In the arts, longer or shorter seasons of style come and go, and a picture that ten years ago won a gold medal may tomorrow be laughed down from a palace wall as readily as a woman is laughed out of society for wearing last year's clothes. While I was feeling proud of my association with the Academy, the style, the fashion, the essential value of what my professors were teaching, was being challenged by the fashionable intellectuals of Sweden, and the seriousness and nature of this challenge was revealed to me by my friend Karl Milles, a student of sculpture at the Technical School. He stood out above all my comrades as being both a young man of talent and a man of good sense. Therefore when he told me he was going to Paris to continue his art studies and explained his reasons for so doing instead of following his sister into the Academy, I was much impressed by his determination and at the same time deeply shaken in my loyalty to the Academy. Milles was so obviously of great talent that there was no question of his being accepted at the Academy had he chosen to seek admittance, wherefore his attitude carried convincing weight with me.

Both my time and energy had been so engaged merely in getting on at all from month to month that I never looked at a newspaper or attended any art exhibitions, so that I was most ignorant of anything outside of my immediate school work. I therefore did not know that the French Impressionistic School of painting and sculpture had become established in Sweden through an aggressive and powerful group of artists calling themselves "The Artists' Society" (Konstnarsforbundet). This vigorous young club was, unknown to me, even undermining my beloved Royal Academy.

After having had my attention aroused to the situation, I started an investigation and an analysis of the whole problem so as to know what my own position should be. I soon discovered that Rodin was considered by the adherents of the new school as the greatest sculptor since Michelangelo, and I also learned that my own teachers considered him an incompetent, if not a faker.

Milles was level-headed, practical, a master of himself, and at the same time he possessed an artistic fervor and ability that I dare say has already placed him among the immortals. At this time I liked him intensely, and even after my liking had curdled, my esteem for his ability grew year by year.

I almost followed his lead to Paris, but I had sense enough even then to know that what I must do was not merely to decide whether I wanted to continue at the Academy or go to Paris, or whether this school of thought or that held the true secret of art, but to mature and ripen my own basic idea of what constituted art itself. And this was a matter for thought and solitude, of living with myself and searching my mind and heart.

Fortunately I found a way to do this and at the same time live in a situation in which I could find plenty of fresh air for my harassed lungs. The celebrated Emilie Rathou, a pioneer leader in Socialism in Sweden, had an apartment in a building which included a huge tower, constructed for the personal enjoyment of the baker who had built the building and who was now dead. In return for two English lessons a week she rented me the tower room, and in this magnificent eyrie I settled down to spend the summer of 1897 and establish a point of view.

Around me up there thousands of telephone wires hummed and played night and day like a gigantic Eolian harp. Because Stockholm that year had a great international exposition, the bay below me was cluttered with men-of-war from all nations. Night after night, through the blue resonant air I heard their bands playing at the large fêtes given on the ships, and now and then, if the wind was favorable, there came to my ears the sparkling laughter of men and women at play woven with the mighty symphony of the city. Across the water lay the great exposition buildings crammed with the products of modern art and industry.

My landlady, Emilie Rathou, was a fairly well-educated woman, but a fanatic in her faith in the salvation of the world through Socialism. Her heated efforts to convert me to Socialism made me aware of an effort to start a new fashion in politics.

I was, however, on the alert here, as well as toward the new art movement to the investigation of which Milles had stimulated me. I was not easy to convert. I had never forgotten how my father had been kicked out of his church in beautiful Burlington, Iowa, because of a new fashion in theology. It was very vivid in my memory how the whole congregation had become holy and absolutely without sin through a new apostle, and how poor Father had been treated with cruelty because he could not become perfect even as the angels. I had become afraid of people who were so serious that their eyes became fixed and shiny when they talked of God, art or women. I had become afraid of all assurance that the truth, the one and only truth, had been neatly pinned down and labeled.

At the exposition Rodin was showing plaster casts of his monument to Victor Hugo. Through the generosity of his great heart he offered as a present to the Swedish National Museum the whole collection of his works on exhibition, but the gift was refused by the Royal Academy and Museum authorities. King Oscar, to avoid a nasty political mess over this discourtesy, wrote a personal letter to Rodin and asked if he would change his gift and make it to him for the Royal Palace instead. The radicals all over the world shouted with delight and Miss Rathou indulged in an unholy glee, ridiculing to my face the stupidity of my Royal Academy.

But I was becoming impervious to the assaults of opinion. With my decision made to return to the Academy in the fall, and my loyalty to it firmly fixed, I had settled down with an open mind, free from dogma, to decide what beauty really was and what art should be.

First of all I proved to myself that the true artist must be original. Originality was a thing from within, something which grew from a simplicity of spirit that found the facts in nature for itself and did not follow any fashion in art. I began to see clearly that it did not matter much where I was located. Passing styles, passionate radicals with the latest fads, composed the swift current of life, and an artist must resist it and become rooted in the eternal facts of his own faith.

In the previous two years, whenever I had touched the bitter depths of loneliness, poverty and sickness, I had found relief and peace in looking at a picture by Rembrandt in the museum. In it a very old bearded man is reading. He is just ready to turn a page. The light comes in through a small open window, and outside you see a bit of blue calm summer sky. The shadows in the corners of the room are cool, dark and mysterious. The old man is interested in his reading, but also restful and full of repose. The light plays softly on his high forehead and the pages of the book.

The picture might have been called "Peace." I cannot remember a time when a half hour in front of this picture did not give me peace and courage, no matter how harassed I had been when I approached it. Here was the whole solution in a nutshell. Art should create peace and happiness.

XVII

ELIZABETH

AS the fall term opened I had the good fortune to receive financial help from a man namel Aspelin, one of Sweden's wealthiest men and a most liberal patron of the arts. With sufficient funds now, with the dignity conferred by an appointment as keeper of the stiffs used for dissection in the anatomy classes, and as one of the privileged few to possess a private studio, I began my second year with grave dignity and supreme pride. During the summer I had allowed my beard to grow. It was fine-textured, reddish brown in color, shiny and luxurious. I twirled my mustaches to a pinpoint and made them stick out like a pair of horns. Day after day I made my trip to the Royal Academy with the aloof and haughty bearing of a Leonardo.

The approach to the Academy was magnificent and palatial. At the head of the innumerable steps of the great outside stairway was the bulletin board where, only a year before, I had read my sacred name as one of the elected few. Then came the immense carved doors, then another grand stairway, and then the large T-shaped hall containing reproductions from the masterpieces of Greek sculpture. On this floor was the anatomy room.

Now that I was to create an original statue of my own, the study of anatomy took on an even greater significance to me because now I must use my knowledge in a practical way in this work. On the second floor was my private studio. Not only was this magnificent room, with its wide high northern window, all my own, but I had an Academy credit for materials and models.

The statue upon which I was working I called "February," and in it I endeavored to portray the earth's restlessness, the painful dreaming before the sun has completed its liberation from the winter's cold and bondage. It was the tinkle, tinkle, of a hidden spring under the deep snow that had given me the idea during a walk in the country the previous February. That night I had been very homesick for Ottumwa. I had felt myself to be snowbound—unalive—without any one to love. Home was so far away and I was very lonely, when my ears caught the faint tinkle, tinkle far down below the snow. "Spring is approaching," I mused, and just as an acid is neutralized by an alkali, so this thought changed my mood. Winter would soon pass away, I realized, and all the woods and meadows be full of flowers and singing birds.

As my exultation rose over this thought I saw in the spirit, tossing restlessly under the earth, the figure of a young girl more beautiful than any girl I had ever seen in real life. "This is the February of my own life," I reasoned, "not only the February of the year 1897. Soon the Spring of my life will break loose and the fulness of joy and freedom be mine."

More intense than love in real life is the artist's dream-love. I felt a deep love for my "February." If I had lived in old Greece instead of in Sweden, perhaps the gods would have granted me the same blessing as they did Pygmalion when they gave life to his statue Galatea. If my chaste February could have smiled back at me, talked and exchanged thoughts, told me she loved me as I did her, she might have turned the tide of my life into a different channel. Then I could have continued to abide in that rare and perfect abode built through the alchemy of the soul's dreams.

But another fate awaited me in the shape of a young woman surging with ardor and eagerness for earthly experiences. I look back at the experience now with unpleasantness, as to an affair into which I went unwillingly and at the cost of loss to myself. I had known women intimately, of course, but had avoided any lasting attachment to any one of them as something which I did not yet want to face, something which I feared as well as desired.

How much of my attitude toward this is the result of the fact that I am an artist, and how much the effect of my childhood teachings about religion and sex, I do not know. When my father in Smaland had turned aside from his holiness at the insistence of the sexual urge, it had been Skam. When I, in my childish ignorance and wonder had thought of Loke, and set out to find him, it had been with that throbbing, choking mixture of keen anticipation and dark fear with which the wrongly instructed adolescent mind turns to the thought of sex. When I finally encountered sex experiences, I went into them as something which constituted a necessary evil, and after each I was depressed for days. Now I found myself plunging headlong into an attachment which was not what I would logically have wanted at all. What I really wanted to do was to put all this passion for the beautiful into my "February." But instead I gave way to a more fleshly passion.

Years later I met a priest who gave me the only practical formula by which the temptation of love may be resisted. Had I had such wisdom at this time perhaps I would have been better off.

"Son," he said to me, "the love of women is one of the sins you cannot overcome through will power. The more you will not to love them the more intensely you yearn for the sweetness you try to resist. There is only one way to escape this temptation and that is to flee from every thought of women. Here the better part of valor is to run as fast as you can."

Even though I sigh with regret over my downfall, I cannot even to this day keep out the memory of Elizabeth's warm softness, her exquisite sparkle, her ensnaring perfume, her throaty murmurs, her liquid chatter, and the awful fact of her resolute will to make me a creature of her ambitions. A male in love is a creature insane, whether he be cat, fish, dog, fowl or dromedary. And human males are as mad as any. They may pluck the stars from the sky in their madness, squeal like pigs or roar like lions while the convulsions last.

Elizabeth was a blonde with thick hair so alive that it crackled when she combed it. Her eyes were bright blue, set in a smooth, beautifully shaped, rosy face. Her mouth was ever half open and the glistening white teeth seemed a defense to a luscious interior. I met her at the age when the malignant power of a girl of her type over men is at its height.

She was a student of painting in the women's school of the Academy, a part of the school of which I saw very little, for I felt then, as I do now, that a woman hasn't the remotest chance of ever achieving greatness in art. This deep conviction made me evade the acquaintanceship of the girl students. There were no mixed classes, so this was not difficult to do. And I had heard so much discussion of Elizabeth by the other boys of the school that she seemed especially poisonous to me.

The dissecting room of the anatomy department was available for the male and female students at strictly different hours. However, most of the students hated the smell of the corpses and few of them spent more time in the dissecting room than was necessary. I, however, was so ardent in this study that even the stench of putrefied flesh and carbolic acid seemed sweet to me because of the association of this odor with a revelation of the intricate beauty and wisdom of nature's integration.

One day, as I sat perched on a high stool, delicately unraveling a bit of material, the door opened silently and Elizabeth poked her head through the aperture. Her parted lips and baby stare seemed to say: "It's only me." Clamping the thumb and forefinger over her nostrils with one hand, with the same fingers of the other hand she lifted her skirts and tiptoed across the room to fetch some article she had left. Obviously she wanted me to see the revulsion she felt toward the corpse

I was dissecting. But, seeing this, I saw too her dainty ankles, her lovely hips, small waist, budding breasts, velvety neck, red curved lips, and beautiful blue eyes.

Instinctively I tried to combat their power with sarcasm.

"If the smell is so intolerable to the young lady, why does she pursue such a serious calling as that of an artist?" I asked, irritably, as she passed me.

With a stricken look she fled from the room, leaving me with trembling hands and complete loss of concentration in my work. I cursed all girls, especially girls who are art students, and most fervently that fool Elizabeth, who did not have sense enough to stay away from the anatomy rooms at an hour when she had no right to be there; but still my hands shook.

Just as I was about to throw down my work and quit, she came back. Turning her glorious blue eyes full on me, she let them fill with tears that ran down her cheeks and dropped on her working smock. Then she began, with racking little sobs, to tell me how very unhappy she was because I considered her nothing more than a doll and not a serious person. She was really very, very deep and serious, she told me.

"It is hard," she said, "to be a girl and not be able to make any one understand your true nature."

And I, being merely a male creature, did what other males have done under similar circumstances. That day, for the first time in my life, I kissed a girl of culture and good birth to comfort her, and, as my lips touched hers, I said good-by, without knowing it, to that detachment from women which an artist needs.

I should have died at the end of the winter of 1898. During that most glorious year of my youth I was tense and vibrant, and a constant light fever gave me the appearance of a genius burning his candle at both ends—a spectacle that the world loves. It was a mean trick Nature played on me and my surroundings when she gave me such fine thick bones, a digestive system nothing could upset, good nerves and a lot of horse sense, and at the same time made me an artist, a poet, a dreamer of dreams that, coupled with a slight tubercular ailment, made me seem as one of the beloved of the gods, destined to die beautifully, heroically, and young.

The secret of a fortunate life is to know astrology before you are born and make your entry when the heavenly bodies are in a benign state of relationship to one another. But when I chose my parents and the date of my birth I must have been ignorant. My whole life has been a succession of contrary events. I have failed when I have been expected to rise to sublime heights of fame, survived when I should have perished. What is most difficult for me to bear is that because I am determined and strong-willed, the world blames me, makes me responsible for everything I have done, when it would automatically take responsibility for a weaker person. I suspect that even when I die it will happen at a time and under circumstances of which no one will approve.

In those days of my youth I had a very affectionate nature and wanted to make friends and share the lives of others, but something within me always seemed to get in my way and kept me from letting friend or enemy fit me into his scheme of things. Yet I felt that I deserved, and knew that I needed, friendship. My dreams and aspirations were so magnificent that only a soul ready for heaven, a very darling of the gods, had any right to shoot so high. Except in moments of artistic frenzy I was sober and cleanly, careful with my funds, studious. Yet I stood alone, wanting to share my life, my aspirations, my dreams with my kind, yet feeling constantly lonely. And it was in this fertile field that Elizabeth sowed the seeds of love.

I fought valiantly to keep my love life with Elizabeth within bounds. I do not think I spent two hours with her indoors all that winter. Every morning between half-past six in the morning until school began at eight we took long walks in the forests of Haga, and my most vivid memory of her is of her young vibrant body breasting keen cold winds of morning as she strode along at my side. My love of her reached its greatest height during moments when we stopped to rest and turned our backs against the swirling wind and snow. Out of breath, her laughter came in thrilling little gasps, her cheeks were red and white, and her long eyelashes were beautiful with clinging frost. Our love was an out-of-doors, winter's love, and we joined each other in fighting the primordial urge of our young bodies. We became intellectual about it, read Nietzsche and, in our desire to be "supermen," declared that we did not love each other. Love was Christian and degenerating. Sentimentality had no place in the life of a "superman."

Day by day I worked dutifully and lovingly on my statue "February," attended meticulously my classes and lectures. At odd hours I made sketches of great schemes for the future. There was one in particular that exalted and excited me so much that, when I had made a rough sketch of it, I called out to myself, just as Archimedes had done upon his momentous discovery: "Eureka!" ("I have found it.") I have given this idea many names, none of which is quite satisfactory, but as a name is necessary I choose in my narrative to call the composition "Cain's Dream."

Meanwhile I was finishing my "February." Because of the insistent requests of Von Rosen, I reluctantly changed its name to "Spring." "Every one thinks of February as cold winter," he said. "No one would understand what you meant by calling your statue 'February.'" In a letter to my mother in which I told her about the statue, I wrote as follows:

"Both hands and one foot are not finished, and they must be completed by Tuesday. I am going to name her Spring. She symbolizes awakening. It is a young girl trying to get up. One leg is numb—the other is moving slightly. The head makes an effort upward and one arm presses against the earth to aid the arising. The eyes are closed, the lips slightly opened, giving her a childlike expression—yet I've tried to show a promise of voluptuousness and sensuousness. The statue expresses a degree of pain from the blinding snow, and intense longing. She has received tremendous praise, but perhaps I'll never get her finished. Sometimes I hate her, she seems so cold and dead—and then sometimes when I come into my studio I feel as if she were full of life; I can hear her sigh, as her heart beats and sends blood and warmth through the numbed limbs—and then I am so happy I caress the budding, immature form and I love her more than anything in the world."

And then, just as the year was ending, two things happened which changed many of my plans. I had finished my "February," and received, in recognition of it, a scholarship for the succeeding year.

But as I was feeling happy over this Von Rosen walked into my studio one day and, finding Elizabeth there, became purple with rage. Unknown to me he had fallen in love with her, and, finding her with me, regarded me as an interloper. The situation had its comical aspects, to be sure, but I could not see them that day. I suppose that I was still smarting over his initial admonition to me, "The Herr should learn humility," and this final demand that I practise humility to him was a sharper sting than even my male jealousy or my anger at Elizabeth for having allowed this situation to develop. At any rate there was a very unpleasant row, the details of which are better left untold.

And then, close on the heels of this, came the decision of my doctor that my lungs needed serious care, and I was told to go to the North where I could breathe the cold clean air of the country. I left Stockholm determined upon the attitude of a misogynist, telling myself darkly that Elizabeth's flirtations meant nothing at all to me.

XVIII

ROARING WATERS

THE Fallforsen is a roaring, boisterous waterfall of the Umea River in northern Sweden. Only a few rods below the falls, in a peasant's cottage perched on top of the steep brink, some three hundred feet above the rapids in which the falls dropped, I found shelter during my vacation. The Umea River is a deep, mighty stream and at this place hurtles through three or four tortuous granite passages, where at the same time it tumbles down successive chasms with a terrible churning and rocking that seem to make the granite fastnesses tremble in the overtones of a symphony of reckless fury and violence no orchestra, however large, could produce. The grand finale of the enormous volume of water and foam striking the bottom of the abyss is like the beat of a giant's drum. The dark recess receiving the falling water was a deep basin in which the water sped with incredible swiftness, in great, smooth, oil-like eddies going round and round before rolling into the furious rapids below.

I became expert in maneuvering the odd-shaped skiffs used in these waters, whirling round and round in the dizzy eddies, and at the same time catching "harr," a tender, delicious game fish with which the waters abound. I never caught one above a pound in weight, and ten or twelve during a whole day's work were a good catch. It was the extreme difficulty of getting them at all that made this fishing so fascinating. The deafening roar of the waters, the capriciousness of the eddies, the constant need of alertness and dexterity in order to escape disaster, gave me such a thrilling occupation that the days melted into weeks and the weeks into months before I was aware of the passing of time.

For a period the river became gorged with great logs that spoiled my fishing. Then came a gang of loggers cleaning up the jams and stray logs stuck here and there on the shores. One day, in watching a gang of these men breaking a great jam of tens of thousands of logs above the rapids, I was seized with a mad urge to have a pike-pole in my hands and be working with them. I looked up the gang foreman and asked for a job without pay.

"All right," he replied casually. "One of our men was drowned yesterday. Go find Forsman—he needs a man in his boat."

In the slaughter-house in Ottumwa I had worked for periods in the gang that rolled five-hundred-pound pork barrels. These were handled with pike-poles, so I had some familiarity with the wonderful tool I would have to use on the logs.

Forsman took me into his little skiff and we tied it to one of the logs. The jam was in the very middle of the river. Climbing through the slippery, crazy jumble of logs while the whole mass was shaking and trembling from the battering waters was a breath-taking maneuver in itself.

With Forsman and three or four others I tackled log after log. It is practically impossible to find the source of a jam, and the method we used was to strike our pike-poles into the most promising log at hand and then, to the rhythm of a sing-song, give a heave and loosen it, strike again and sing-song and then another heave, until it went spinning into the water. Thus we liberated log after log until a cry warned us the mass was moving. Like monkeys we scrambled each into his boat and then rowed like demons to escape the advancing mass that was threatening to pull us into the rapids.

I stayed with the logging gang until we reached the sea and then reluctantly went back to Stockholm. Too soon the summer had passed. Too soon, I felt, I was forced to leave the active, violent life which I loved. Much as I loved the Academy and my work there, I went back to it sadly.

But I was not to stay long. Though I seemed the picture of health, a few weeks after my return I collapsed again from the tubercular ailment which had not been cured by my short stay in the North, and this time the doctor told me emphatically that I must make my choice between spending at least a year or more out-of-doors, and facing an early death.

Again my incomprehensible friend Von Rosen, he with whom I had fought over so many different sorts of matters, came to my aid. Through his offices a patron, who asked to remain unknown, came forward with funds for whatever period was necessary for me to regain my health. Other wealthy friends presented me with several cases of fine wines, cognac, and whisky. Members of the Nobel family gave me about a dozen suits of the most wonderful silk-and-wool underwear I have ever seen. Mr. Petrus Cantor of the Catholic Church, besides a case of Barzac wine from the church vineyards in France, presented me with a beautiful crucifix of silver and ebony. There was magic in this gift, not only because of its beauty and religious significance, but because this dear man showed such a profound Christian love in his gift. The crucifix gave me great comfort, though I had no Catholic leanings.

During the previous summer I had heard so much about a beautiful lake called Tavelsjo (meaning literally "Picture Lake") located about eighteen miles from Umea, that I decided to go there. It was said to be teeming with big fish, and the surrounding forests were described as being full of ptarmigan, foxes, and wood grouse.

I arrived in Umea in November and a peasant named Karl Holmgren from Tavelsjo met me and drove me to my destination. Before we had driven many miles I came to a fearful realization of what a dreary country I had chosen in which to seek health. A more desolate and lonely landscape I had never seen than that which unfolded before me, mile after mile.

It was the anguished period between the bright green summer of the North and the white winter. The sun began to sink long before we reached the end of our trip. Mile after mile we passed through ragged forests darkening in the deep twilight, black marshes and moors. A flurry of snow beat against my face, enough to heighten the dreariness of the day. At one place a lone fox stood on the road. With that strange stillness peculiar to wild things in repose, he looked more like a master-piece by a taxidermist than a living creature. As we came nearer, with soft, light, indifferent leaps he disappeared in the brush.

Holmgren drove me directly to a little inn at Tavelsjo Village, kept by an old couple named Koenigsons. At once, as was the custom in this part of Sweden, they served me hot milk, coffee, and Branvin (white mule). When dinner was ready I broke boorishly into fretful criticisms of the food. This beastly habit had come over me during the preceding few weeks. If no one stopped me, I might continue in a peevish mood for hours until like a child I wore myself out. I was in such a state of irritability that I was not fit to live with any one. But after a few days I managed to rent a vacant farmhouse on the shores of the lake, where I could be alone.

Holmgren secured a female pup for me which he said was half fox, half Irish setter. I moved into my cabin with my belongings and my dog, a most forlorn and lonely young man. As I awoke to my penurious surroundings and isolation from the world, I quaked with apprehension as to what would become of me. It seemed as if I had, through lack of judgment, buried myself alive instead of finding a place where I would recuper-ate and gain health. I thought to myself: "This is the end of David Edstrom."

I had so much of the primitive in me, however, that here in the North I did what I had done before when I became very unhappy. I went to sleep. Many a time I have slept twenty-four hours or more when deeply disturbed or gloomy. Disappointment in love, pain, hunger, anything and everything that has upset me too much I have slept away. The following quotation from a story by Irvin Cobb which I read in the *Saturday Evening Post* describing a Negro characteristic, fits my own case completely, though I have not a drop of Negro blood in me.

"Jeff, why is it that white people are forever committing suicide on account of their private worries, but you never hear of a darky killing himself for the same reason?"

I studied for a minute and then says:

"Well, Mr. Dallas, I reckon it's dis yere way: A white man gits hisse'f in trouble an' he can't seem to see no way to get shet of it. An' so he sets down an' he thinks an' after a w'ile he shoots hisse'f. A nigger man gets in trouble an' he sets down an' he thinks an' he thinks an' after a w'ile he goes to sleep!"

Presently the great lake froze up and was covered a couple of yards thick with snow. Into this wide spread the undulating white meadows and fields merged so gently that no shore line was discernible. Dark evergreens covered the hills, and on the edges of the forests were groves of birch trees that at a distance looked like an irregular bright purple border painted around the somber green of the firs.

From the hilltops the red farmhouses looked like cranberries strewn carelessly on a sheet. Every house was painted the same shade of red.

Trees, bushes, flowers or hedges were not planted by the peasants around their homes. No frills or decorations either indoors or outdoors or even in the thoughts and habits of the inhabitants seemed to be permitted by Mother Nature up there.

My red log house, nestled in the vast crystalline white bed of snow, came to mean home to me. I bought several cords of birchwood logs, and however low the mercury sank, or however hard the wind blew, the crackling open fire kept the place comfortable and warm.

With my goodly supply of liquor, a young beef's carcass frozen in my storeroom, a collection of fine pipes and pounds of the best tobacco money could buy, I did not lack visitors as soon as I had slept off my sense of misery and damnation. Many of the old men of the neighborhood who came to see me were wonderful story tellers, and this remote corner of Sweden was rich with tales about supernatural beings living both in the lake and in the forest.

Even my house had a ghost. Per Olsa, the poor man who had built it, was known far and wide as an authentic "revenant" from the other world. And he was real enough! I saw Per Olsa with my own eyes and described him in minute detail to a group of old-timers before they told me about him. Native tact had kept them from telling me of my ghostly tenant until he had shown himself to me.

But ghosts you may see any old place; of greater interest was the fact that up here lived and flourished witchcraft, and the lake and forests were inhabited with "Vitra," a supernatural race much more interesting than the fairies of Old England and Ireland.

Few cultured people have had any authentic experiences with these beings or are even able to reason intelligently about them. Holmgren was my nearest neighbor, and, being an adept in magic, he more than any one else helped to paint for my mind a series of new pictures that became, as Alice says, "curiouser and curiouser" the longer I stayed up there.

Gradually there grew, between the Holmgrens and myself, an undemonstrative but deep friendship, the memory of which I cherish to this day. I came to love them and to feel an infinite gratitude for their presence.

One night, which I remember especially, after having been lost for hours on the lake in a snowstorm and finally reaching Holmgren's house, I ached with joy at being with them. But

the natives were as stoical as Indians, and you could talk of anything under the sun except personal hardships or personal emotions.   At the time I wanted to weep and babble about how
happy I was to be alive and with them, and instead I sat silent
while Mother Holmgren fed me hot milk.   But though I said
not a word about the hours of hellish struggle, moving on and
on, not knowing where I was, in an impenetrable blanket of
snow, I felt they knew all about my state of mind as definitely
as if I had told them.

The peasants at Tavelsjo made their own wagons, sleds, skis,
yarn, cloth, knives, shoes, in fact almost everything they used.
Even Holmgren's rifle was home-made, and it was accurate to
a degree I have never known a factory-made rifle to be.   It was
about twenty-two gage and he had killed bears with it.   A
miss with this little muzzle-loader would cause him a day's
gloom.   A twentieth of a cent would more than cover the cost
of a charge in the gun, yet this petty amount was a large sum for
him, did it not bring down a bird, a rabbit or some animal of
value.

One day some one called out to me: "The Lapps are coming."
I hurried on my skis over a hill indicated, and in the distance
on a great white plain I saw a black blur of little moving spots
and here and there a swiftly agitated spot moving back and
forth.   I sped on, and after a time I came to the moving body,
consisting of some four or five thousand reindeer and a score
of Lapps.

As winter moves on, the Lapps move southward with their
herds and toward spring they move north, finally to spend the
summers either within the polar circle or on the high mountains where the snow does not melt.

I became very friendly with the young men of the village at
Tavelsjo and was taken into their comradeship.

A curious method of wooing was practised in this part of
Sweden.   Secretly on Saturday night we all met at a place previously agreed upon.   Then the whole crowd went to the

nearest house where there was a marriageable girl—or several of them. One of the boys then made a funny drumming noise on a windowpane, and after a short wait the entire crowd would be invited to enter the sleeping quarters of the girl—or girls, as the case might be. Here we would all sit down while the girls cuddled up under their sheepskin blankets. Then would begin a special sort of conversation which I was never able to master. Through ingenious double meanings, mixed with haphazard words without any meanings at all, in a code spontaneously improvised for the occasion, one or more of the boys would gain permission to return later in the night. The object in the conversations was to make the appointment in such a way that none of the boys not concerned could guess what was happening. After a few minutes of this confusing badinage and chatter, we would all troop away to the next house where the same thing was repeated.

As the visits progressed from house to house, one boy after another would disappear. Each young man spent the rest of the night with his chosen inamorata, but, contrary to what you might expect with a more sophisticated mind, nothing but the most innocent kind of caressing happened. The process was very like that of "bundling" in the early days of New England.

The interesting thing was that so secretive were the relations between the young people that when a couple married it was generally a surprise to the rest of the village. There would be plenty of guessing, plenty of rumors of engagements, but when marriages were announced they were usually in contradiction, rather than affirmation, of the rumors.

The daily diet in the Holmgren home consisted mostly of sour milk and barley prepared in many different ways, and a great deal of coffee. Thirty to forty cups of coffee a day was the average consumption for each member of the family. The coffee was cooked indefinitely until all the virtues had been extracted from the bean. Salt was used with sugar as seasoning.

Rye and wheat do not grow in this district. The bread was

baked in thin sheets about the thickness of wrapping paper. A great deal of skill was required to throw into the brick oven the thin sheet of dough about thirty inches in diameter, let it bake a few seconds, get it out, and, before it stiffened, fold it into a napkin. One of these bread napkins had about sixteen folds. As soon as the bread was cooled it was as crumbly and dry as a soda cracker.

Even barley raised in this district has not the time to mature before the frost and therefore has the slightly bitter taste of green grain. The method of baking, however, makes a bread of great delicacy without a taint of bitterness.

The milk is soured in wooden vessels about twenty inches long which look like small flatboats or dugouts. When it is ready to use it has the toughness of thin dough. You crumble fistfuls of the bread into the sour milk, stir it about, and eat the mixture with a wooden spoon. It is delicious, and you never tire of it.

On weekdays barley mush with the milk instead of bread furnished variety. On Sundays and holidays the head, feet or other unsalable parts of pork, mutton or beef were boiled for hours until the meat left the bones. Soup meat and perhaps potatoes would then be served. All the milk was skimmed and no butter used. Everything that could be sold and converted into cash was a luxury not indulged in except on unusual occasions such as funerals or weddings.

Although the peasants lived largely from their cattle, cheese-making was not practised in this district. It was a surprise how well-fed, happy, healthy and contented these people were on their monotonous and limited diet.

There was no evidence of any sense of poverty, but rather an atmosphere of opulence, dignity and pride. The respectability of the congregation at church on Sunday was even oppressive. The wealthiest man in the village was quoted as being worth twelve thousand kroner (about forty-five hundred dollars).

Huge iron boilers were used in the stable to warm the water

for the cattle in winter. On Saturday nights the pots were used to heat water for bathing. Once a week every one took a hot bath.

Holmgren was under a bit of a cloud because of his hunting and trapping, since hunting and fishing were looked upon with disapproval by the older and more conservative natives. It was argued that these activities made a farmer neglect his work. Also the hunter came into too close contact with the "Vitra." To wrest a living from that meager soil during short summers for long winters required all of a man's energy and thought. Hunting and fishing were dangerous to the character. They not only brought a hankering for delicious meats, but relaxed a man from the austere hardness necessary to see him through the years successfully.

As evidence of this view there was always held up the example of a very ill man in the village. I believe he suffered from cancer. He and his family were supported by charity, and it had all come about because he had neglected his farm for the rod and gun. But I, in spite of the bad influence he might have on me, spent many happy hours listening to his extraordinary tales about wild life.

He told me that in the lake lived a pike weighing several hundred pounds. He said this fish was so old that moss had grown over its body making it look like the log of a huge dead tree. He told me many anecdotes of futile efforts to catch this pike with hooks he had forged especially for the purpose. He did not worry as much over his illness as over the fact that he had never been able to catch this magic pike. His greatest achievement, the one in which he felt the most pride, was outwitting and shooting a famous elusive fox after several years of effort.

In trapping foxes, witchcraft was an important feature. The magic formula to vanquish the fox was a deep secret and neither Holmgren nor the man with cancer would reveal even to me the recipe for brewing fox magic.

But Holmgren taught me some minor charms for keeping cattle from running away, snaring rabbits and woodcocks. To concoct a really serious magic (Troll skott) to get revenge on or safety from an enemy, distant magicians (Troll Karlar) farther away north were engaged. However, I was not told of an authentic case of the exercise of this higher form of witchcraft, and more than ordinary detective work would have been required to get evidence of such a case.

The church and authorities in Sweden were fighting vigorously against all superstitions. On Sundays, my friend Holmgren became all Christian. After church services in the village he would read aloud from the Bible and the Psalm Book by the hour. If on a Sunday I referred to some plan for the coming week concerning hunting or trapping, a fearful look came over his face, and instead of answering me he would read louder, or say the Lord's Prayer. However, Monday morning his hearing regained its habitual devil-may-care air, his cap a cocky tilt, and his language became again picturesque and human.

At Tavelsjo each home had stored away enough barley grain for a whole year above what was needed until the next harvest. Banks and modern means of communication had not been able to make them give up their old and proved methods of insurance against famine (no-dar). There were vivid records handed down from father to son of the time when whole districts had starved to death and of how the eating of the tender inner bark of fir trees had ruined the health of those who survived. In the North, famine has been a scourge of which people in the South have no conception. The long-headedness and foresight of northern races have been gained through cold and hunger.

After a few weeks I acquired the most extraordinary vitality and strength. A run to Umea and back on my skis for supplies in a day seemed an easy jaunt. In trapping and hunting I must often have covered over fifty miles in a day through the roughest kind of territory.

I became quite an expert on skis, but now and then on a steep wooded slope I'd lose control and shoot downward at such breakneck speed that every rock and tree in the way threatened broken bones.

The Lapp style of skis was universally used. They are broad, short and light. A strap traversing the ski under which the toe of the shoe was pushed held the ski very insecurely to the foot, but you could kick it loose in a second in a moment of danger, whereas with a laced ski this is impossible. On several dangerous occasions I saved myself by kicking free and diving headlong into the snow. This meant, however, perhaps an hour's floundering around in a sea of snow before I could recover my skis.

To see a Lapp careening down a precipitous rocky and wooded mountainside on skis is the most thrilling sight I have ever seen. His sidestepping and dodging are too quick for the eye to follow.

Day by day Holmgren described the great Winter Fair at Lycksele and always referred to this place as the "Lapp Capital."

Here, at midwinter, trappers, Lapps and traders meet to buy and sell. It is quite near the Arctic Circle, and the desire to experience still greater cold and see the business machinery when the time came made me engage Holmgren's eldest son Edward, a husky sixteen-year-old youth, to drive me to the Fair. In a one-horse sled it took us several days to get there. The moods of that journey I treasure in my memory as precious possessions. Driving hour after hour, the mystery of the arctic winter filled me with a great peace.

Up there only for a few hours the sun is seen like a flat bright disk of gold—soaring low over the southern heavens. But long, long after the stars and the moon are hung out from below the edge of the world an emerald green glow is reflected in the sky. Then suddenly, like a Titan's searchlight, Aurora Borealis may throw a blinding flash from out the great depths beyond the horizon; or again she may take a notion to give a long performance and in weird splendor from nowhere set off one burst of silent ghostly fireworks after another.

You simply cannot arrive at a rational notion about Aurora Borealis. In a clear sky the air burns; bright rays and flares glow, run, flutter, shiver and dance in fantastic formations coming from nowhere; coming out of nothing between you and the stars, which themselves seem near enough to be targets for a high-powered rifle; yet the Aurora Borealis, though dazzlingly evident, is remote and intangible, and even the imagination is unable to speculate or theorize about it.

To add to the sense of being in a place beyond the beyond, one evening I saw a dull red meteor as big as a balloon float leisurely below the silvery moon for a minute or so, seemingly only a few hundred feet above the earth.

During our journey the mercury hovered around forty degrees below zero Celsius.

At one of the inns where we stopped were two mute dwarfs. These two deformed little beings were considered by the natives to be "Vitra." I listened to serious discussions as to whether they belonged to the "mountain Vitra" or to the "under-water Vitra." Their hands, arms and bodies were examined minutely to determine this momentous question. Each dwarf had a large iron savings bank into which visitors put coins. The little fellows grunted with satisfaction every time a coin clinked into the iron boxes. They seemed very happy, contented, and well taken care of, as became denizens from another world.

The Fair was held out of doors, and as I recall it, there must have been several thousand people buying and selling. Huge piles of furs and all manner of merchandise were displayed in open booths. Even with thick underwear, a heavy homespun suit, fur boots and a long fur coat, I found it difficult to keep warm. I saw many faces terribly disfigured from frostbite.

Since the only evidence of frostbite was a white spot on the frozen part, which could be seen by others but not felt by the person on whom it occurred until thawing set in, one was expected, upon seeing such a spot, to tell the victim, whether stranger or friend, at once. The cure was to rub snow on the afflicted place until the circulation returned.

The United States Government was at this time inspecting reindeer for the Eskimos in Alaska. The decrease of fish and game in Alaska was threatening large numbers of Eskimos with extinction, and to aid them the government took steps to teach them to live by the reindeer as the Lapps do. The reindeer is a domesticated caribou and lives on the moss growing under the snow. Having heard rumors of this, and learning that I was an American, some one spread the news that I had come—with a great deal of money—to buy live reindeer.

One drunken Lapp followed me all over the place, determined to make a sale. He thought my trying to evade him was my way of beating down his price. When he made a new reduction in his demands he would accentuate his concession by striking his hand against the ground. He was so limber that this was quite as easy for him to do as for any one else to strike a table with his fist.

The Lapps marry at these fairs with ancient heathen ceremonials. I tried to get entry to one of the marriage services, but the natives, unwilling to have profane outsiders, refused to admit me.

It was forbidden by law to sell liquor to the Lapps, but they got around the ruling by eating shoe blacking prepared in alcohol, drinking patent medicines and perfumery, and getting quite satisfactorily drunk.

One of the things which struck me on this trip and which I have never seen mentioned anywhere is the delicacy of certain parts of the tallow from the reindeer. It was so delicious that even to eat it raw was a delightful experience. It had a bouquet resembling violets. Not even American terrapin or fresh salmon from northern streams is as delicate as this tallow is.

The Lapps use a peculiar method of castrating the reindeer

bulls. The young bull calf is tied and then the man operating destroys the glands by chewing them to a pulp without lacerating the scrotum. It would be interesting to learn whether this method of mutilation has any merits over that used by farmers in more civilized districts. Primitive people have often very profound reasons for their traditional customs.

Upon my return to Tavelsjo there was awaiting me a letter from the world-famous feminist leader, Ellen Key. Elizabeth, with whom I had been in constant correspondence, had told her that I was living alone in the North for my health. She wrote, among other things: "Take the care of yourself that you would of a frail chalice containing a lifegiving elixir that it was your duty to bring to the lips of humanity." Thus, through a poetic and thrilling letter, which did much for my self-confidence, did I come into intimate contact with the great spirit of a woman who was later to have a marked influence on my life.

One day spring burst loose. The thick layer of snow over hill and dale had not begun to melt when a million birds filled every nook and corner with whistling, warbling, cooing, squawking, chattering, stuttering, wheezing, babbling and many other sounds for which words have never been invented.

I lost interest in hunting. For hours at a time I would lie bundled up in furs at a point over the lake where the forest grew up on the banks. Here I could watch and listen to thousands of sea fowl and birds of the woods carry on. I was city bred, and it was the most exciting experience I'd ever had, to hear, see, and feel the terrific agitation of a natural world gone mad in lovemaking.

Below, above, everywhere, water was running, murmuring and splashing. Soon a million wild flowers added with their perfume to the ecstasy of a new epoch in the history of the world. When spring comes in the North, a new era, a new life is born.

When the ice in the lake broke up I began to fish and caught pike weighing from two or three up to and over twenty-five pounds, and in such numbers that to this day I can't stand the odor of a pike, much less eat one.

Sport has always been to me more of an excuse for being out of doors than an occupation thrilling in and of itself. In fact, I've never enjoyed killing any creature, not even a snake or a beast of prey. It is, therefore, natural that I remember and treasure the memory of my dreams in the North most of all.

The queer things I heard from Holmgren about the "Vitra" caused me to have long, logical and dramatic dreams. I remember most of them in minute detail—and to illustrate the influence the country had on my thoughts during this period I will tell one of these dreams.

In it I saw a strange girl, unlike any human being I had ever seen or even conceived of in my imagination, soar into my room. Silently she beckoned me to follow. I became light as a feather and with her flew through the thick log walls. Over mountains, streams and valleys we flew for an indeterminate time until we stopped at a far-away place in a deep ravine impossible for any human being to reach by ordinary means.

Here the mystery lady showed me a rock and asked me to remove it. When I had done so I found a small cave and in it a stack of smooth stone tablets on which were scratched strange hieroglyphics. The girl taught me with surprising rapidity to understand the language and read the story inscribed on the tablets. She made me promise that I would write down the alphabet of the language and the history written on the tablets the next morning before I had anything to eat.

There were, she told me as an introduction to what was written there, two distinct races of beings on the earth millions of years ago, the human family to which I belonged and the race to which she belonged. These two races were elementally separated—that is, the difference was greater than between men and any of the animals we know. The very elements out of which the two races had their existence differed. As the meteorological life on the planet changed, her race vanished from our knowledge—because the very elements in which this race lived became too refined for our vision. But they were still aware of us.

After I had studied the remarkable narrative on the tablets and thoroughly memorized it and the language, she asked me to replace the tablets and seal the cave with the stone. She then led the way over another route to a high mountain. Here she led me through the solid rock into a great hall where hundreds of her own kind were congregated. I met and fraternized with them.

Then we all went out of doors, and they began a strange chant, a rhythm—seemingly lively—yet winding and long. The time was kept by clapping the hands, and soon we were all dancing to the chant. But what a dance! Each step was a leap into the air fifteen or twenty feet, and we only touched the top of grass, flowers, bushes. The most slender flower stem or grass blade gave sufficient resistance to enable us to make these astounding leaps.

Suddenly the singing and dancing ceased and we trooped into the vast hall in the mountain again. Admonished not to forget my instructions, I was given a slight blow with a hazelwood stick—and woke up in my bed.

The language and story on the tablets were very vivid, and I started to write them down, when it occurred to me that never so long as I lived could I forget them. To prove to myself this fact, I had my breakfast before writing the story— and the alphabet and analysis of the language. When I had finished I sat down contentedly to write—and found to my dismay that I'd forgotten everything but the first letter in the alphabet.

Years later I described this letter to a friend who is a famous psychoanalyst, and he told me that the letter meant dreadful things—such dreadful things that I refrain from revealing them. I don't know a thing about psychoanalysis and don't take much stock in it, but for the sake of discretion I withhold the mysterious letter which he said was the key to the whole dream.

All too soon the summer was over—and after a sad leave-taking from my many friends in Tavelsjo, I returned to Stockholm.

XIX

NEGLINGE

MY long stay in the North had brought back all my old audacity, and I was hard, bronzed, and good to look at when I met Elizabeth immediately upon my return to Stockholm. There was a crisp tang in the autumn air when we made our first rendezvous out at Haga Forest, where we had known so many winter walks together. Her cheeks and lips were cool when I kissed her—cool with that smooth delightful freshness of young flesh that hates warm clothes because it is secure in its own pulsating vitality—and with the coolness of our lost passion for each other.

I was very happy to meet her, but not thrilled. She felt my lack of response, and a note of dissonance crept into our conversation. We tried desperately to seem excited and exuberant, each feeling that it was the thing to do for the other, but there was a subtle poison in our very demonstrativeness. And she, suddenly angry because she could not move me deeply any more, suddenly finding it necessary to her pride to rouse me by some act—any act at all so long as it got a response—took a burning cigar out of my mouth and pressed it against the top of my hand, burning a sizzling wound in the skin. Though the pain was keen, I did not flinch, but looked into her eyes, smiling as well as I could, and said nothing.

It was the worst thing I could have done, of course. If I had been angry—even if I had struck her in a rage—she would have liked it better. But now she was defenseless. Jerking the cigar away, she flung her arms around my neck and burst into tears. Between sobs, her head close to my shoulder, she told me everything that had happened while I had been away. It is her story and I have no right to tell it, nor has it any place here. Enough to say that the things which had happened to her since we had been together had left her feeling shaken and lost.

Her warmth, her youth, her beauty, and the vehemence of her despair overwhelmed me. It was a tragic story she told and I wanted to help her. I tried to apply my mind to her problem in an orderly way, but to every suggestion I made came more floods of tears, and at last, after my many helpful suggestions, she told me calmly, and in a practical manner, what she wanted.

To her there was only one solution and that was that I marry her. There had never been any deep, mature love between us, just a sweet, natural attraction and an inability to resist each other. I have recently read over her letters, which I still have, and found them all sparklingly humorous, natural and unsentimental. But now, as at the very first day I talked with her in the anatomy room, I gave in to her power over me.

"All right, Elizabeth," I said. "But we shall need more money. I'll see what I can do to get it, so that we can be married."

I did not want to marry, but if I had wanted to, I would rather have married Elizabeth than any other woman in the world. I felt both mentally and physically unfit for marriage, and I became very unhappy. But I was too weak to resist her and accordingly I set about trying to find a way to grant her wish.

I decided at once that I must get Ellen Key's moral support. I knew that she was a friend of Ernest Thiel's, an immensely wealthy man and the most generous patron of the arts in Sweden at that time, and I decided that I would try to reach him through her. The letter I had received from her while up North gave me a good excuse to call on her, and so I went.

She received me most fervently, and if her letter had been flattering, her attitude on meeting me was even more so. She pleased and flattered me at once by showing that she was familiar with my past, my work, and what my teachers thought of me. Thus when I asked her for a letter of introduction to Thiel, she sat down and wrote me one immediately. As she gave it to me she told me how to approach him and what I might expect from him.

She told me of a home for young artists that Thiel had established in Neglinge, a small suburban town near Stockholm. In this home, she said, was staying a famous young artist and poet named Hogstedt, as well as the poet Jansen and others. She told me that Thiel would probably invite me to live out there.

"As to your plan to marry Elizabeth," she said, "at this time it is foolish, but I will help to get Thiel interested in you and I am sure you and Elizabeth will act sensibly."

When I met Thiel I found a man about thirty-five years of age, an erect, proud, dark man with the air of an Arab warrior chief more than that of a bourgeois banker. He had been knighted at twenty-two for negotiating a great foreign loan for Sweden, was an eminent chess-player, had made an excellent Swedish translation of the works of Friedrich Nietzsche—and had now under way an art collection that was later on to be rated one of the finest in the world. But just as had been the case with Von Rosen—as has so often been the case with men in a position to help me—I took an immediate dislike to him, and felt that he, also, disliked me. There was a boldness, a decisive finality about his treatment of every subject we discussed that I resented.

As Miss Key had predicted, he asked me if I would like to move out to Neglinge, and I accepted his invitation and was moved into a fine large bedroom and an ample studio of my own. Here I met for the first time young men who were considered geniuses. To me they seemed crazy—yet perhaps unknowingly I was the craziest of the whole outfit.

ERNEST THIEL, PATRON OF ART
Bronze bust by Edstrom, now in the Thiel Gallery, Stockholm, Sweden

"CHRIST AND MEDUSA"
Bronze in the collection of the Swedish Club, Paris, France; also in that of
Marchesa Montagliari, Florence, Italy

There was one young chap named "J" who had a notion that ghosts were pursuing him. To keep them from getting into the house, he climbed upon the roof, put a board over the chimney, and sat down on it. As long as there was no fire in the building, we didn't mind how many hours he sat straddling the chimney, but as soon as it got cold we had to climb up and pull him down. However, in spite of our watchfulness, suddenly the whole place would be filled with smoke and we would know "J" had gotten on the roof again.

Although none of the others were quite as difficult as "J," the place was like a madhouse, and it is a source of constant wonder to me that those of us who were not mad when we went there did not become so from being there. Indeed, poor Hogstedt did.

He was a most amenable and sweet-tempered youth, and no one would have suspected him of having a disordered mind until he began to make bouquets from bits of weeds, straws and colored rags, and then stand outside the house of a certain fashionable lady by the hour until he could present her with his strange flowers. Finally he had a complete breakdown and before I left Neglinge he was taken to an asylum where he spent the rest of his life.

One day, after I had been at Neglinge for a few weeks, Thiel called on me. We talked in my studio where, in the best place I could arrange for it, stood my statue "February." As soon as he saw it he asked for it in his usual sarcastic, superior manner.

"I want that statue," he said, "and I want it in marble. How much will it cost?"

My dislike for him flared up immediately and my lips parted as I was about to make some arrogant reply, but he stopped me.

"No, don't tell me now," he said. "You are one of these chaps that if you do not ask enough you will regret it. Come and have lunch with me tomorrow and tell me then."

His manner was so arrogant and bold that it made me furious and I decided to ask him the highest price that had ever been paid for a small statue of that size in Sweden. I learned that Hazzelberg, at that time the most famous of Swedish sculptors, had received four thousand kroners for a half-life marble of his girl figure, "The Frog," and I decided to ask Thiel the same amount and let him take it or leave it.

But it seemed such outrageous effrontery to me that, when I came to his house the next day my courage failed me and as I rang the bell my price had come down to fifteen hundred crowns. However, as soon as I met him his cold superiority angered me again and when he asked me what I was going to charge, I blurted out:

"Four thousand crowns!"

I expected him to look shocked and angry, but he only grinned and put his hand on my shoulder.

"My dear young man," he said, "that is too little. Let us make it five thousand. But," he added, "there is a condition. I have been making inquiries about you and I have come to the conclusion that those asses in the Academy don't know how to take care of a man like you, nor the doctors who have handled your case taken the pains they should have. I know a specialist—Professor Edgren—and if you want to get this order for your 'February' you must go to him and then do as he advises."

Something within me rebelled violently against accepting the help of this man, but I felt powerless. My cough had returned, and I knew that I must do something for it. Yet everything in him stimulated the wrong things in me. The luncheon which followed our talk was disagreeable. I don't remember what we quarreled about, and I suspect now that I did most of the quarreling. I do remember that Mrs. Thiel tried to keep the discussion within polite bounds, but the air was thick with dissension.

Elizabeth was very excited and happy over the way things were moving along, but I was in the depths of depression and felt as if the bottom had again dropped out of everything. Poor

Elizabeth! She had not hitched her wagon to a star when she had decided that I was the way out of her difficulties.

Dr. Edgren, and other doctors whose names I did not try to remember, gave me a series of examinations, using methods of finding out what they wanted to know which none of the other doctors had used. They were most charming and tactful and seemed to enjoy my descriptions of the North and my views on art.

In a few days I received a letter from Thiel, asking me to call at his home. When I arrived he chuckled in his diabolically irritating manner. His chuckle and superior air seemed to say: "Now, don't talk. I know all about you. Anything you say is worthless. You know nothing about yourself at all."

Not until he had looked me over wordlessly for awhile did he say anything.

"The doctors verified my own diagnosis of your case," he said at last. "Please don't be offended at my frankness. The doctors say that your organs, save for a slight affection of the tip of one lung, are perfectly sound, but that you are sick mentally—through depression. You are discouraged with life and very unhappy. You need to have a lot of money, dress in elegant clothes, be free, easy and happy. Edgren says Davos, Switzerland, is the only resort that suits your case. It is a fashionable, expensive place that specializes in treating consumptives. Now to go to Davos you must first of all be outfitted by a first-class tailor and have everything in keeping to feel at home at this place. Don't worry over the cost; that will not come out of your precious five thousand for 'February' when you get that finished. I will take care of everything for as long a time as you need to be in Switzerland. Then I suggest you go to Italy and get thawed out physically and mentally before you come North again. Your minimum expenditures must be seven hundred kroners a month. If some special kind of expensive wine should happen to seem necessary you might spend more. Don't hesitate—it's my party. How about it?"

Of course I accepted, yet not then nor for years to come was there ever to be exchanged a genial word between me and my benefactor. If he had been my worst enemy I could not have disliked him more thoroughly, and though he was self-controlled I felt that his feelings for me were the same. He intimated this to Ellen Key when he said to her: "Edstrom has great talent, but is the most uncivilized young man I've ever met."

My chief quarrels with Thiel centered around Nietzsche and his own contempt for the common people. I was proud of being of peasant stock and of having been a workingman. I knew then as well as if I had already lived through all the long years ahead that I would never change on this point. In a letter lying before me now, written by Thiel to me some years later— in continuation of the quarrel begun on the day we first met— he says, among other things:

"A people is to you a wonderful material, to a poet a glorious objective, to a ruler a necessary condition for his popularity; for me a people is only something that smells bad, smells of filth, dirt, sweat and mob. I can have nothing to do with that which is common. You realize that my words refer also to spiritual values as well as physical. Democracy includes for me all the strivings of modern life, all such things as peace congresses, woman suffrage, universal suffrage, altruism, charity, the same right for all, etc., and all these things are to me equally obnoxious."

I was as great a fanatic in my admiration for Nietzsche as he was, but we differed as to what "superman" signified. To him it meant an aristocratic class with material power. To me Nietzsche's "superman" meant an aristocracy in all places and conditions. To me neither wealth nor education seemed to make an aristocrat. Nobility meant a noble life wherever and under whatever conditions that life was lived. If wealth and power were to be made the criterions of moral values, it seemed to me that existence would become intolerable and without hope.

In this connection I often thought of Molly Anderson in Ottumwa, who, although she had never been my sweetheart, had always called forth my deep admiration. No woman I had ever met or seen in my new life equaled her in character and nobility. She was a servant, and years later in mature life I met her in the same modest conditions as I had known her in youth, the mother of grown children, and the same queen of women as she had been as a young girl.

I did not at this time really know Thiel. The time was to come when we were to be the warmest of friends, but many years lay ahead before that day was to dawn.

Mrs. Thiel had an even more remarkable personality than her husband, and for many years I admired her in the same degree that I disliked her husband.

Elizabeth and I met as often as it was feasible and discussed our plans. Our situation, however, was very complicated. Von Rosen was still madly in love with her and had thrown all dignity to the winds by discussing her with me and frankly showing a bitter jealousy. I would have desired nothing in the world more than to have seen him marry her, but he could not do so because of his secret marriage to a Grecian woman.

At last I decided to ask Mrs. Thiel what she thought about the advisability of my marrying Elizabeth before going to Switzerland and taking her with me.

One evening after dinner with Mr. and Mrs. Thiel, during the period of my preparation for departure, the opportunity came. After finishing our coffee and liqueur that evening she said to her husband:

"Ernest, you read while I show Mr. Edstrom my jewels."

He laughed and threw her a smile of such warmth and kindliness that it surprised me. I had not known that he could feel such warmth. I felt that I had never seen real devotion in a man before I saw the flash of lovelight in his eyes.

From a wall safe Mrs. Thiel took out handfuls of the most beautiful gems I had ever seen—pearls, diamonds, sapphires, rubies and emeralds, great opals, jades, and a bewildering quantity of deep-tinted semi-precious stones. Throwing handful after handful of necklaces, bracelets, rings, tiaras, brooches and pins in a heap on the carpeted floor, she squatted down like a child beside the piled-up treasures.

"Now sit down right here close to me," she commanded.

Awkwardly I complied, flushing and thrilled. She seemed like a fairy to me, so beautiful and ethereal. She soon had me at my ease and we talked, laughed, fondled and admired one jewel after the other. So interested was she in her jewels and so excited about showing them to a sympathetic onlooker that she seemed to become more lovely as the moments passed and I almost forgot what it was that I had intended to talk to her about.

Finally, however, the moment came when there seemed a break in the flow of our talk about precious stones and their settings, and I began to tell her about Elizabeth. As I talked I kept watching my hostess. As I described Elizabeth's eyes, I saw how bright Mrs. Thiel's were. As I talked of the glorious hair which my fiancée had, her fine figure, her talent, I was as much aware of Mrs. Thiel's. But I could not have had a more sympathetic listener. She seemed to bubble with excitement at my descriptions and insisted that I must invite Elizabeth to see her.

When I subsequently saw Elizabeth I described Mrs. Thiel and told her of my talk about ourselves, and that she wanted to see her. Instead of being happy, Elizabeth wept and said: "The cat has hooked you."

She did not understand that my obvious enthusiasm about Mrs. Thiel was not an infatuation, or that Mrs. Thiel's interest in the problems of a struggling young man was something more general than an interest in the young man's person. The truth was that the woman who had concerned herself with Elizabeth's

problem and mine had been a sort of fairy godmother to many
of Sweden's leading men of letters, art and music. Levertin,
Thor Hedberg, Heidenstam, Liljefore, Carl Larson, and many
others had had occasion to be grateful for the warm friendliness
of this remarkable, many-sided woman, long before I had ever
met her. Ernest Thiel had, before this, written a book of
poems to her—poems that have stood the test of time. Alven,
Sweden's leading composer, has set them to music, and they are
sung wherever Swedish songs are sung. She was a woman who
belonged to art, and my interest in her and admiration of her
were nothing to cause jealousy. But Elizabeth was jealous.

Nevertheless I persuaded her to call, and she did so. At the
first meeting Mrs. Thiel commissioned Elizabeth to do her portrait, plainly in order to add to our marriage fund, and sittings
began almost at once. During the time the portrait was being
made I did not see either of the women because I was so busy
completing pieces of unfinished work, having fittings with my
tailor, plaster casting and packing my sculptures.

And then abruptly, without any word from Elizabeth, her
family announced her engagement to a famous French poet
visiting Sweden at the time. Following this, one night Elizabeth gave me a surprise visit out at Neglinge, and started such
a violent quarrel with me about nothing at all that I had to
carry her out of the house to get rid of her.

What Mrs. Thiel and Elizabeth had discussed together, or
what had caused the latter to drop our plans so suddenly, or
what had created her violent anger at me I could not, and cannot now, understand. Nor would Mrs. Thiel tell me anything
about it. But I was willing not to question any one too closely,
and, with a sense of freedom which transcended whatever hurt
pride I felt, I turned my thoughts toward the future.

At last all the loose ends in Stockholm were taken care of,
my many sketches and models packed away, clothes finished,
and fine new leather trunks and suit-cases packed. As I looked
at them, and smelt the delicious odor of the new leather, I felt

a sense of well-being that I loved. Count Von Rosen and Baron Gustav Cederstrom, another professor of the Academy, were going to Germany to be present at the opening of a memorial art exhibition of a famous German painter to be given in Berlin, and they invited me to travel in company with them as far as Berlin.

It would have been a most happy journey had not Von Rosen insisted on talking about Elizabeth at every opportunity. He was taking his loss so much harder than I did mine. I was so tired of the subject that the very mention of her name made me want to swear.

There was one other thing which Von Rosen talked about, however. He disliked Ellen Key intensely, and had frowned at the growing friendliness between us and at most of the things it had led to.

"They are turning your head," he said fiercely. "It is very unfortunate that Thiel has bought your statue. You know nothing yet about art. You must come back and spend two years more at the Academy before they have completely spoiled you."

He was still telling me, I suppose, with greater elaboration, "The Herr must learn humility." But I was taking it with a better grace now than I had when he had first said it.

And so I left Sweden for the first time since coming there as a coal stoker. But how different was my situation now! Beside me sat two men who were not only among Sweden's most famous artists, but were representatives of two of the country's most heroic and historic families as well.

I stayed over in Berlin two days and with my two teachers visited the art galleries where I met many men of distinction.

It was fine and exciting, but when it was over and I settled down on a train for Switzerland, the reaction set in, and I faced the future with a weary heart and a discouraged mind.

XX

THROUGH THE CITY OF LIFE AND DEATH TO THE CITY OF FLOWERS

E VERY day the puffing engines, climbing painfully the long steep grade to Davos, twelve thousand feet above sea level, pull trains loaded with cough-racked invalids, hopeful of the miracles which mountain air, correct diet, and scientific supervision may work. Every day trains pass down the mountain, with grinding brakes holding them against the pull of the steep grade, filled with sunburned, happy men and women who have been cured of a dread malady, and by their sides silent, hopeless creatures who are going home to die. And some, who did not leave soon enough for this last privilege, who hoped on to the end, leave silently at night, borne in coffins on the shoulders of hospital attendants, to the baggage car, with as little as possible said about the matter.

Davos is a silent city, dazzlingly white, bathed in almost perpetual sunshine, and so sheltered that there is seldom a breath of wind. Here at the time I arrived, in the winter of 1899, were five thousand feverish, cough-racked souls battling for their lives.

I had expected to find silence and depression among the patients, an atmosphere of death, a consistent somberness in which the pleasant aspects of life, laughter and playfulness and love, were forgotten in the grim fight for life itself.

But what I saw instead was bubbling gaiety and an accelerated, rather than diminished, sex interest among the patients. For days I was bewildered by the phenomenon. And then one of the doctors explained to me that this exuberance was one of the sinister symptoms of well-developed tuberculosis and that it made the physicians anything but happy. I also learned that in consumptives there seemed to be an intense glandular activity which stimulated all the senses—smell, feeling, sight, hearing, taste, and sex desire.

The problem of the physicians was most difficult. Music, dancing and gaiety were most essential in the treatment, yet they must be kept within bounds, for disastrous results would follow too much physical exertion or excitement. The physicians had to be not only doctors but detectives as well, to watch over and prevent patients from leaving secretly at night for amorous rendezvous in the cold. When a patient showed a sudden turn for the worse it was always something like this for which the doctors looked. The escapades of patients who made ropes out of their sheets to get out of second- and third-story windows, and slip into each other's rooms, were the wine and meat of never-ending gossip.

When I arrived at Davos I had a slight fever hardly noticeable unless I took my temperature. The cough, though continuous, was seldom painful. During the daytime I was made to lie down on an open veranda in a long wicker chair, clad in furs, with my head and neck covered in a cap and a long muffler. At night, although the temperature was from five to twenty or thirty degrees below zero, I slept with all windows wide open.

My diet was rich and varied, and included a quantity of milk every day. After about a week's absolute rest I was told to walk for five minutes, and every day after that another five minutes was added to the length of my walks.

My improvement was rapid, and though the doctors spared no effort to keep many patients in more serious condition than I was away from excitements and sports, they encouraged me day by day to take ever more severe exercises and to indulge in the entertainments available at the resort.

When, in January or February, I received an invitation to

visit the Thiels at St. Moritz, the doctor advised me by all means to accept the invitation. They were staying at the Engadiner Kulm Hotel, and to this day the two weeks I spent there remain as the gayest and most sparkling of my whole life. It seemed a winter paradise where all the gay, beautiful and wealthy young people in the world had come to be happy. There was a continuous round of bob-sleighing, skiing, skating and dancing. Never before had I seen so many beautiful gowns and lovely women, or so much sparkling jewelry, as in the ballroom of that hotel. I was so happy that I even forgot to quarrel with Thiel.

After my return to Davos the doctors advised me to leave the resort, forget my symptoms, and get to work again at my art. And so I began to carry out the second part of my bargain with Thiel: to go to Italy to "thaw out."

I wrote to Sweden and ordered the plaster model of my "February" to be sent to Firenze in care of the American Express Company, so that, while "thawing out," I could also complete my commission for Thiel. At Firenze there was a marble cutter who had been recommended to me to rough out my statue. I bought a Cook round-trip ticket south as far as Rome, then north by way of Paris and Berlin to Stockholm. From Davos I went to Thusis on the Rhine, where I spent a few days.

Here I made the acquaintance of a Baroness Helen von Goldberg, from Munich, and her two charming young daughters. Traveling with them was a young banker from Berne named Oppenheim. We four young people constituted an inseparable foursome with the charming Baroness as a guiding fifth. From Thusis we traveled by stage through the Splügen Pass down to Chiavenna. Here spring had already arrived, and into this town countless little streams cascaded. Little canals disappeared under houses and sidewalks, came out of the ground in yards and disappeared around corners. As I remember it, it seems to me that I laughed gaily from morning to night. I was well, and happy and free!

From Chiavenna we went to Lake Como, and on that tiny
lake steamers meandered from one little resort to the other,
staying at each as long as it pleased us. At Milan we stopped
several days, taking in several operas at The Scala. Each day
was like a pearl matched perfectly with every other day.

Finally we reached the dream city of Venice. The Hotel
Danielli seemed to me a corner of Paradise itself, so luxuriously
was it appointed. The food and wine were superb. San Marco
Cathedral, with its porphyry pillars, bright mosaics and carv-
ings, floated like a castle from the Arabian Nights in the sun-
drenched air.

Venice has all the glory the Orient has dreamed of but never
achieved. Nights, rocking in a gondola, listening to the lapping
waters and the thrum of guitars and male quartettes floating out
of the indistinct blur of shadows and moon glitter, by the very
intensity of their charm awakened me to the passing of time,
and I suddenly remembered the commission I had left behind
me, forgotten in the timelessness of my pleasure.

I realized that I must move on to Firenze at once and get
the work on my "February" started. I wanted also to study the
masterpieces of ancient sculpture in Firenze and Rome in the
meantime. Just as I was becoming drunk with happiness in the
company of some of the most genial and lovable people I have
ever known, I left them in Venice and entrained for Firenze.

I had been in love with women, and with art, but these, for
awhile, seemed minor loves to that which I felt for Firenze
after I had seen the city, felt it, and become a part of it. Day
after day I became more deeply lost in its beauty, more deeply
in love, and before I had been there a week the thought of
going back to Stockholm and the Academy, as I had agreed to
do, became intolerable to me. Secretly I began to lay plans not
to return. At once I set about to establish myself before any
one could change my plans. Time enough, I reasoned, to write

to Ellen Key, Thiel and the Academy authorities when I was so well entrenched that I could not leave.

I applied to the Academy in Firenze for admission, and after I had shown proof that I was a student of the Royal Academy in Sweden they accepted me. To make my step as irrevocable as possible I took a lease on the smaller Villa Rondinelli at Fiesole on the western slope of Fiesole Mountain, overlooking the city. "Cook's" gave me a refund on my ticket, and only then did I write a series of explanatory letters to everybody I could think of who might criticize my revolt.

It was typical of my character that, instead of thinking up any practical reasons to justify myself, I wrote ecstatically in prose and verse about the beauty of Firenze. To Ellen Key I felt the greatest responsibility. She was at this time gaining world repute and power in the feminist movement and was attacked right and left for anything she did. If I did not make good I knew she would be blamed. I felt extremely guilty and the only thing I could think of to defend my irrational ways was a repetition of: "She is the most wonderful lady in the world, my City of Flowers."

Meanwhile, like a disobedient child, I had avoided making any logical explanation to Ernest Thiel. To Ellen Key I could write as I felt. To him I could not. And then Ellen brought me up short to a realization of my responsibility.

> I have seen Thiel [she wrote], and he is not annoyed because you have remained in Italy, but he was very exasperated over the fact that he cannot get a single sensible word from you. "Has he," Thiel asked me, "gone out of his head or is he in love? I can't find out when I can expect to have my statue finished, how much money he needs, and although I've had several letters he has forgotten to give me his address. He writes about the red petals of the rose mixing with the white blooms of the almond trees and of nightingales singing in the rain, but not a word of sense."
>
> Promise me, David, that you will sit down now before you

forget it and write Thiel the practical facts he wants to know. He is a banker, a business man, and does not fancy so much gush, my dear. We all understand how you feel after all your unhappy years in Sweden and that you are hungry for sunshine and happiness, but for goodness' sake don't melt away in slush.

XXI

CALIBAN

THERE is something in the sun of Italy which brings to life in a man (and especially in an artist who takes his moods and emotions as seriously as a beautiful woman does her complexion) the keenest realization of his needs and his desires. In the North, under the cold mystical light of the Aurora Borealis, I had experienced an exquisite sadness and a strange sense of projection from the present back into the dim ages of the past. My consciousness seemed detached from my personality, unconcerned with my body, unimpressed by the possibilities of the present. But in Firenze I became newly alive, keenly aware of the stimulation of the senses, concerned with what lay about me and the tangible delights which I could make mine simply by reaching out and taking them.

My villa on the slopes of Fiesole Mountain was a delightful spot and I determined to make myself fit my setting. My first move was to order a dozen white suits of clothing. My notion to be clad every day in spotless white fascinated me. Then I stocked up with delicious wines, cognacs and liqueurs and the finest blends of coffee and tea I could buy. I engaged a married woman named Emilia to cook and to take care of the place, and gave her the most detailed and careful instructions as to her duties, even to the specific items of food with which she was to serve me. I would tell her each day exactly what I wanted, and I would expect, I told her, to get exactly that—no less and no added items on the menu. The Vieusseux Library was well stocked with all recent literature and I carried home armfuls of books. Then I settled into the business of living as I thought a great artist should live.

I arranged with the marble cutter to rough out my statue "February" which I was making for Thiel, and then set about enjoying myself. All there is in a body is stimulated to intense aliveness in Italy in the summertime. Every day was a round of pleasure with the gayest and most congenial of companions, loafing, singing, telling stories, and walking.

I soon made friends with a group of young intellectuals. Of my new friends Giovanni Papini has since become the most famous. He was delightful, but I found his books unreadable.

I made a bust of him and felt that he was the ugliest man I had ever modeled. His face seemed that of a death's head covered with youthful, healthy skin. The teeth were so large the lips could not stretch over them. His eyes were too big and constantly as bright as two stars. Yet his smile was exquisite. I loved Papini. I never in all my life knew a man so witty, so charming, and who wrote what was to me such unreadable nonsense.

Years later, when I modeled Ellen Key, I felt the same way toward her. She seemed the ugliest and the most charming woman in the world. And her books, like Papini's, were things which seemed worthless to me. But the world has not judged them according to my measure.

At the Academy I began to study Phidias and Michelangelo again. I attended life classes with growing excitement, for, although I had spent two years in Stockholm studying classic art, when I came to Italy I found what seemed to me the beginning of understanding.

Suddenly a disturbing element entered the well-ordered contentment of my existence. At first it made itself known by something which to most men would have been a minor irritation at worst, a definite cause for pleasure at best. Almost every day strange items of food appeared on my table, little delicacies, beautifully arranged to tempt the eye as well as the palate.

Although this was in direct violation of my order that nothing was to be brought to my table which I had not ordered, I remained silent at first. Emilia was a good housekeeper and I did not want to lose her. However, when the phenomenon persisted, and the additions became large and more elaborate, I finally became furious and voluble about it.

At first Emilia was silent, her gaze on the floor, her face flushed with embarrassment over my violent reproaches. Then, her eyes still downcast, she spoke, wringing her hands with grief over the depth of her dilemma.

"What can I do?" she moaned. "It is the signorina who sends the food for the signore. I cannot throw it back at her."

Then I realized what had happened. Over my garden wall was a garden which belonged to the house of a retired colonel who lived there with his two sons, one a lieutenant in the army, the other a lieutenant in the customs service, and his daughter, Antoinetta. Often, as I strode pridefully into my villa, dressed in my immaculate white clothes, I had seen the girl watching me, only to turn her head away modestly as my gaze met hers; but I had not known that she had conceived a romantic infatuation for my white-clad figure.

Encouraged by the strange declarations which came to me by the medium of food, I made my way over the wall and our lips found ways to say things more eloquently than her offerings of food could do. An Italian garden, a young man, and a beautiful Italian girl with warm red lips and dancing eyes—could there have been any other result? But her brothers were less interested in this perfect setting and personnel for romance than they were in Italian conventions, which did not permit young men and women to meet without a chaperon. One day one of them found us kissing each other and I made a hasty and very undignified exit over the wall.

After that I was constantly on the watch for days. Antoinetta had warned me of this brother's violent, murderous temper, and I had decided that it would be better to stay out of his way for

awhile. One night, as I was starting to walk in the bright light
of a clear moon, I suddenly saw, coming at me from the high
wall by the side of the garden gate, the shadow of an upraised
hand clutching a knife. I leaped backward out of the way and
started racing madly down the steep hill toward Firenze, but
not before, in one quick look, I had made out the figure of Antoinetta's brother. All the way down the hill I kept thinking
that I saw his shadow, flowing beside mine on the ground,
striking at me again and again with his knife. To this day I
do not know whether that was what I actually saw or whether
it was a hallucination.

However, Antoinetta and I did not stop seeing each other.
We were more careful about it after that, and to quiet her fears
I let her understand that we would be married.

Elmquist, the famous Swedish sculptor, lived only a few rods
away from me in another villa. He was at the time perfecting
a new method of casting in bronze. I remember him most
vividly because of the constant arguments we had over my positive assertions that within ten years I would be world-famous.
We made a bet of ten crowns about it, but I have never collected, even though I actually won the bet long before the ten
years had passed.

Gustav Steffen, later known as a political economist, became
one of my most intimate friends. Steffen also at a later date
became the first Socialist member of the upper house in the
Swedish Senate. He had been a very intimate friend of Strindberg and told me many amusing stories of this half-crazed
genius, of which I will relate one. Strindberg and Steffen were
both living in Paris and planned a summer's vacation together
in Switzerland. They had spent many enjoyable hours discussing their itinerary and the things they would do in the Alps.
At last they were packed, had their round-trip tickets purchased,
and arrived at the railway station in Paris ahead of time for
their train. While they were waiting for their train to pull up,

Strindberg excused himself, saying that he would be back in a minute. Steffen waited for hours, but Strindberg did not return. The train pulled out without either of them, and Steffen set about to find his friend, fully convinced that something serious had happened to him. For several days he stayed in Paris searching, but Strindberg had apparently disappeared from the face of the earth. Finally he went on to Switzerland alone. He never saw Strindberg again, but a year or so later, when Strindberg's next book was published, he found what he believed to be himself, under a suggestive name, one of the chief characters in the book, a man characterized as a terrible person who had tried to get control of Strindberg's brain for some diabolical purpose.

One day Ellen Key came to visit me at my villa. With her was a Swedish girl, Anna Levertin, sister of the famous Swedish-Jewish poet, Oscar Levertin, now dead. Ellen told me that together they had leased an apartment in Firenze facing the Arno, and that I would be expected as a frequent guest. She was quickly surrounded by a group of artists and intellectuals, some of them international figures, and I became a daily member of the group.

After a few days I found myself neglecting Antoinetta for Anna Levertin, and Anna was at least as much interested in me as I was in her. When Ellen saw what was happening she became as upset as a hen who sees one of her chicks straying. So far as I was concerned the affair was only a mild flirtation, but when Ellen told me frankly to my face that she would rather see Anna marry the devil than marry me, she threw a fine dramatic element into our relationship. Of course I immediately began to argue the matter with her, whereupon she cut short her stay in Firenze in order to get Anna away from me.

They had been in Rome only a few days when I received a sorrowful letter from Anna, telling me where they were, but

adding that I must not follow them. Of course after such a
letter and with Ellen against me I took the first train available
to the Eternal City. Here occurred the most devilish thing that
ever happened to me. I developed some kind of nervous itch
that drove me nearly wild. Nothing but chloroform would
ease the irritation. I felt as if lice were creeping all over me.
I consulted a specialist and he said it was not an infection but
a nervous disorder. Often when I was out with Anna in some
romantic situation I would have to excuse myself suddenly and
find a place where I could douse myself with chloroform. I
smelled like an operating room.

It was a terrible handicap for a lover, but somehow I managed. Darling Ellen was in a stew. Never have I seen any
woman so like a hen cackling over two ducklings.

"Oh, what shall I tell Oscar and your mother?" she wailed
to Anna. "They put you in my care and here you are mixed
up with—him!"

"But you like David!" Anna would reply.

"Of course, I like him; that's the trouble. He is so likable
but so utterly impossible."

Ellen was the frankest woman in the world and I adored her.
Years later when many of her gloomy prophecies had come
true, one of her letters to me began: "Boy child whom I received for my many and grievous sins." Poor Ellen Key! She
took to heart, as if she had been a mother, the faults and mis-
takes of all of whom she was fond.

I never read her books during all the years we were intimate friends, and I do not know to what degree the conservative world in the early days of the century was justified in blam-
ing her for the wildness of youth. Some of her severest critics
seemed to think the giddy flapperish young things of those days
were immoral because of Ellen Key's books. What grounds
there were for thinking this, I do not know, but I know that
her personal life was as pure as a lily.

Sweet Ellen Key passed on to her fathers without knowing anything concerning the things she wrote about: love, marriage, and children. She told me once in great confidence that when she was very young she had loved a man who died.

"I am of the kind, David, who can never forget. I've always been true to his memory."

I know she told the truth. Every other woman I've known excepting Ellen has been unable to tell the truth. Ellen was incapable of telling a lie even when it might have been a moral duty to do so.

Thiel and Mrs. Thiel visited me in Fiesole, and brought with them Richard Bergh, the famous Swedish painter who, years later, was to reorganize the Swedish National Museum. At the time they came I had just made a group of father, mother and child, and of course I showed it to them. At first I was pleased at their enthusiasm. But when Berg, who was a marked sentimentalist, read into my composition what seemed to me to be mawkish sentimentality, I became angry at once, and when a little later he said that my "February" was as good as a work of Rodin's, I felt a dislike for him which has not left me to this day. Thiel ordered the group in bronze, but as they all left I found myself still so furious at Berg's misinterpretation of my meaning that I could not bear the sight of it, and before they had been out of the house fifteen minutes I had turned on it in a rage and smashed it into unrecognizable pieces.

Thiel was furious when I told him the next day what I had done to the father-mother-and-child group. We had a new topic to quarrel over now: my artistic temperament.

"If the law would allow it I'd have you put in the care of a guardian!" he said angrily.

But I only laughed at him and went on setting my teeth eagerly into life. With Anna out of town I found Antoinetta— and others—charming again.

There were no heating facilities in my villa. The only way

to produce any heat at all was by lighting a scaldino, a small earthen pot in which you heated up small pieces of charcoal. At best one of these contraptions warmed your hands. To keep myself warm I was gradually increasing my consumption of liquor. I discovered that a constant mild intoxication was delightful. I developed the habit of sitting in my window in a fur coat, looking over the beautiful valley, with a fiasco of wine, a bottle of Spetagliara cognac, a sputtering coffee pot and a box of cigars within reach from morning to night. First I would drink a little of this, then a little of that, and write a poem now and then.

I must have kept up a constant mild drunk for several weeks when I developed an acute attack of neuralgia from drinking such quantities of red wine. I had a very good English physician named Tidey. He forbade me to touch liquor of any kind until I was well. To relieve my agony he gave me some suppositories containing morphine, belladonna and atropin to use if the pain became unbearable. The prescription was for three of these things, but the druggist suggested that I have a dozen made at one time, and I followed his advice. I did not have an idea that they contained three deadly poisons.

On the night after I first got them, being seized with one of my agonizing attacks, I took several of them before I got relief. Suddenly I realized that I was getting drowsy and had lost all feeling in the lower part of my body. When it dawned on me that I was poisoned, I was already so far gone that it required a great effort of will to get out and tell a neighbor what had happened and have him call a doctor. I had hardly touched my bed before I became unconscious.

For hours and hours my life was as complete a blank as though I had been dead, and then gradually, as if through tremendous effort I were struggling back from some far place, I began to be dimly conscious. At first it was only in snatches alternating with recurring unconsciousness. And then gradu-

ally, before I could even move an eyelid to open my eyes and
see what was happening, I heard a man talking directly over
my face. There was a pompousness and an expository quality
in his voice as though he had an interested audience.

"The heart is a muscle," he said.

I tried valiantly to open my eyes but felt myself slipping
away again, hearing only vaguely the rumble of his voice, which
my distorted senses kept translating into the statement he had
just made—"The heart is a muscle, the heart is a muscle, the
heart is a muscle," reiterating it over and over in my frantic
attempt to retain such consciousness as I had and increase it to
the point at which I could grasp my surroundings.

Finally I won the battle enough to get my eyes partly open
and see the hand of a man opening and closing, opening and
closing, in demonstration of the heart's muscular action. Then,
seeing the stir of my eyelids, the man standing above me bent
over, his hand on my chest, and I heard a little murmur of
satisfaction.

"He has a strong heart," he said. "He will not die," and a
little answering murmur of pleasure went about the room.

I tried desperately to move, in my effort to throw him off
of me, but the effort ended in a sudden fading away of everything as I began to sink into unconsciousness again. But suddenly the ebbing flow of my senses was checked by the quick
jab of a hypodermic needle and again I heard the monotonous,
unctuous voice speaking.

"Remember, my friends," he said, "that caffeine is the anti-
dote for all derivatives of the poppy."

And suddenly, as the strong stimulant coursed through my
blood, I was fully conscious again. My eyes wide open now, I
looked about the room and found it filled from wall to wall
with a curious crowd of neighbors. Furious, I sprang off the
bed, and though I swayed a bit on my feet, my weakness did
not diminish my wrath.

"Get out!" I cried. "Get out, every damned one of you!"

In shocked surprise they looked from one to the other and slowly filed out of the room, muttering to each other their low opinions of the uncivilized ways of foreigners.

"How could any one who is *sympatico* allow a neighbor to die alone?" I heard one of them remark. In Italy not to be *sympatico* is worse than committing murder, mayhem or arson. *Sympatico* is the great general designation of those who are good.

There must have been at least forty persons in the room, all of whom, in conformance with the absurd Italian custom of making any one's death a public show, had come to watch me die.

At last I managed to get in touch with Dr. Tidey and he told me the Italian physician had handled my case most excellently.

"Had he not cared for you so well, young man, you would have been dead by this time. You had enough poison in your system to kill five men."

Recovering, I went to work again on a bust of a sweet little American girl from Texas named Daisy Hardy. While working on this, I turned for variety to the task of making a bust of myself in which I tried to reflect all the things I hated in myself.

In a sense, I suppose, I was seeking absolution through confession. There were so many things I did in Italy that made me feel I had wandered far from the austere line of action I had set out to live up to in America and later on had enlarged and perfected in Stockholm and the far North. Yes, I'd tell all about myself in a bust.

One day Steffen came to my studio while I was working on my worse self and burst into enthusiastic admiration.

"I say, Edstrom, what a wonderful Caliban!" he cried.

I remember clearly to this day how thrilled I was and proud

over the distinction I found in the name. Yes, of course, that was what it was, that was what I was—Caliban.

When I had said good-by to Anna I had intended it to be final. I found that, when I was not with her I did not love her, and it seemed madness to think of marrying her. And, consoling myself for the mess I had made in following her to Rome, I had become involved in so many other relationships that when Anna suddenly returned to Firenze I was at my wits' end. Anna, with complete justification, considered us engaged to be married. So did Antoinetta, and they kept me in constant turmoil with their bitter jealousies of each other. In an attempt to escape them I had let myself fall in love with a married woman, which complicated things beautifully. In addition there were Leonia, a beautiful model, and other lesser ones to make life hideous for me.

One day in desperation I took a train for Rome to get help and advice from Ellen Key. I told her every detail of the situation with distressing emphasis on its hopelessness, while she listened patiently and with obvious disapproval. My narrative ended with what I intended to be a dramatic climax.

"I cannot see any way out of it except to kill myself," I said tragically.

But if I had expected violent protest and sympathy I was disappointed. Looking at me unwaveringly and without smiling, she nodded her head.

"I agree with you, David—you can't possibly escape in any other way," replied Ellen.

Her words were like a pin which pricked the somber balloon of my egocentric despair. I had always been sure that she had no sense of humor, and I do not to this day know that she was not actually advising me to commit suicide. But my suicidal mood was gone and I suddenly, unexplainably, felt gay and reborn, as though I had just come back to life from death. Laughing, I jumped to my feet.

"To hell with them!" I cried. "I'm through with all of them!"

Then I threw my arms around her and hugged her gaily. And suddenly her head was on my shoulder and she was crying like a baby. I could not understand her tears, but I wanted to comfort her.

"Don't cry, Ellen," I said. "Let's, you and I, get married. In your care I would be safe."

Of course, I didn't mean it. Ellen was nearly thirty years older than I and our marriage would have been absurd. But she only smiled wanly and said nothing. Later, when I left for Firenze she came to see me off on the train, and, as I told her good-by, suddenly she began to weep again, so that my one vivid memory of that parting is of the tears rolling down her cheeks and my ponderous and futile attempts to understand her emotion.

XXII

BRIEF FREEDOM

RETURNING to Fiesole, I tried to forget the complications of my love life in work. It did not occur to me that instead of having simplified the matter by calling on Ellen I had perhaps only complicated it further. I was determined that I would stop thinking about the women with whom I was involved and do better work than I had ever done.

One day, while walking through the Uffizi Gallery, I stopped and looked at the Roman marble copy of Laocoon and his two sons, which was restored during the Renaissance by Bandinelli, Michelangelo's bitter enemy. I had at the Academy drawn the group from a plaster cast and knew it intimately, but on this day I suddenly saw it in a new light. In the old Priest of Apollo, who with his two sons was being crushed by the two serpents, I found a great exposition of pessimism. The father and the two sons were dying with eyes helplessly turned upward in hopeless supplication to the gods.

Returning home, my mind full of my conception, I went to work rapidly, almost automatically, making a sketch of the father and the two sons. But instead of turning their heads heavenward in futile supplication to heaven, as in the conventional group, they were bending over in concentrated combat against the serpents. Unconsciously I had taken my first step in giving form to an idea depicting man as the conqueror rather than the plaything of Fate. The birth of that little sketch enslaved me to an ever-growing idea that was to be my blessing and my curse during many years.

Following my idea of portraying man the conqueror in the form of a reversed Laocoon group, I conceived a Perseus statue in which I tried to express the same general thesis in another form.

The third composition of this period, which later on in life brought me such fame, was "The Sphinx." In the head of this figure I did not so much try to portray the animal and the human as to portray two distinct functions or activities in existence as a whole.

Another composition of this period that for a time was the subject of much discussion was my "Hermaphrodite." In this statue I tried very much to express the same general conception as in the Sphinx, that is, the duality of Nature. I would have been horrified if any one had suggested that I had portrayed an abnormal creature. It was a symbol pure and simple of the whole of life—male and female—the eternal cycle of existence.

The large Perseus group I destroyed and kept only the hand with the two heads of Christ and Medusa. At a later date this fragment was sold to the Marchesa Montagliari at the International Art Exhibition in Venice.

The general conception of these three compositions entered, years later, into my "Man Triumphant."

But, as my conception for "Man Triumphant" was actually (unknown to me) in the throes of birth, I was far from being triumphant myself. With the coming of spring Ellen Key came to Firenze. I saw her the first day, of course, and we had not been together long when she reminded me of the suggestion I had made in Rome that we get married. What had been to me a gay and playful remark had been to her a serious proposal.

"I have been thinking about it ever since," she said, "and have come here to ask whether you still want me."

"But there is Anna," I cried, defensively, and to myself I

added, "and Antoinetta and Leonia. My God! I am expected to marry four women!"

As a matter of fact I had picked out Anna's name because I thought that that would be the most effective excuse I could find for telling Ellen that I couldn't marry her, not because I really expected to marry Anna. I had written Anna firmly and definitely telling her that I felt we were incompatible, that I had my career as an artist to think of, and that I probably wouldn't be able for years to support a wife; I thought I had disposed of her for good and all. But I had assured myself too easily.

For while Ellen was still in Firenze I received a wire from Anna, sent from Stockholm, which called me back to a frightening realization of reality.

> Meet me in Venice. You shall to my face tell me that you no longer love me. Will stay at Hotel Metropole.

I had scarcely recovered from the shock when a second arrived.

> I am now in Copenhagen on way to Venice where you will meet me and to my face tell me you no longer love me. Will stay at Hotel Metropole.

Some hours later a third wire came from Berlin.

> In Berlin now on my way to Venice where you shall meet me and tell me face to face that you no longer love me. Will stay at Hotel Metropole.

Thus from one city after another came wire after wire as she progressed southward toward Venice. They were like an inexhaustible flock of gnats against which there is no protection. Finally, in a panic, I rushed off to Ellen Key and flung the whole batch of wires into her lap.

"What am I to do, Ellen?" I cried. "I can't see her."

For a moment she was silent. Then she looked at me sadly and, as she had always done, offered to help.

"I am going to Venice," she said. "Would you like to have me see her for you?"

Like a drowning man seizing a rope, I grasped her offer.

"Tell her, Ellen, that I absolutely do not want to see her again," I said.

Ellen left that day for Venice and I breathed a sigh of relief. The next evening, free, for the moment at least, of two women who wanted to marry me, I told Antoinetta about the wires I was getting from Anna and she immediately became furious.

"She is coming to get you," she screamed. "She will take you away from me."

I comforted her with assurances that I would not see Anna. Antoinetta laughed hysterically.

"You don't know," she wailed. "You don't know anything!"

Furious now myself, I dashed out and caught the night train for Venice to be there the morning Anna arrived.

Hotel Metropole used to be popular with Swedish tourists, and Ellen Key was also stopping at the Metropole, but I was not thinking of her when I arrived about nine in the morning. As I registered, the clerk handed me a wire. It was from Anna and had been sent from Firenze. She had arrived in Venice sooner than I had expected she would, had seen Ellen, and left immediately to find me.

> Ellen told me you would not come [I read], so came here to see you. Please wait in Venice. Will arrive this evening.

As I read the wire I burst out laughing, and while I was still writhing in mirth I looked up and saw Ellen Key sitting nearby, her face filled with disgust and anger. I did not have a chance to say hello before she commenced to upbraid me.

"What a devil! What a devil you are! I am through with you for life," she said.

I tried to pacify her, but in vain. She was for once angered beyond my power to assuage her. She was so angry that she cut her stay in Venice and left for Sweden.

Night had fallen when I met Anna at the station. We did not say a word, but clasped hands and walked down to the canal and took a gondola. For hours we did not speak, but lay in each other's arms and kissed as the gondola moved on and on in the magic moonlight of Venice.

We spent two weeks in Venice and then parted in Padua. Anna's train left before my train for Firenze. I saw her wave to me as long as the train was in sight, and then as it faded away in the distance a sudden flood of disgust and nausea swept over me. I knew now that I couldn't resist her when she was near me but also that I would not marry her for anything in the world. I did not love her mind, her character or spirit, although my body could not resist her.

As soon as I got back to Firenze I wrote her a letter saying this bluntly and brutally, and I felt absolutely certain that because of my cold brutality I was forever free from her.

Now I set about to consolidate my life, to put to use the freedom I had acquired with such difficulty. Ellen and Anna now both understood that I would not marry them, and Antoinetta, her jealousy appeased by my unqualified dismissal of Anna, accepted my ultimatum that there was to be no talk of marriage. My life seemed suddenly simplified. Only one thing bothered me.

The street cars from Firenze to Fiesole quit running about eleven o'clock at night, but I was seldom home at eleven. Four or five nights a week I would leave Firenze after midnight up a steep old Roman road between high dark walls—the road down which Antoinetta's brother had chased me with a knife. These old Roman roads are so narrow that two small donkey carts would have difficulty in passing each other. I had always been somewhat nervous going along it at night, and since the one attack which had been made on me my nervousness had increased. There was one dark turn which I especially feared.

Gradually my fear grew almost to the proportions of a phobia. I felt sure that some night I would find an enemy waiting there to kill me. I pictured the attack in all its details. I imagined that he would stand barefooted in the dark and creep up from behind and hit me on the head with something or slip a knife between my ribs. Whenever I came to that corner I would hurry by with a cold chill running down my back.

One night, about three in the morning, in a drizzling rain and so dark I could hardly see my own hand, when I came near this place I felt "Tonight he is there." What should I do? I was too proud to yield to my fear and go back and take an hour or two to go the long road around the mountain. I had an umbrella and the absurd notion came to me that I would charge into the corner and spear the man I suspected to be there on the point of it. Then it occurred to me to run by as fast as I could. My dignity rebelled against both of these suggestions and so I finally decided to do the manly thing and walk calmly into the dark and grab him by the collar. When I stretched out my arm it actually encountered a man and, shuddering, I grasped his rain-drenched coat only to have him crumple together like a sack of meal with a grunt of fear. Who it was I did not stop to investigate—probably some poor devil who had no place to go for the night.

As a result of my feeling about the road and my two somewhat violent experiences on it, I decided not to renew my lease. I moved over to Viale Petrarca near Porta Romana, a place as far from Fiesole as I could find. My new studio was very practical but infested with hundreds of scorpions and not fit to live in, so I rented separate living quarters with the postmistress of the neighborhood.

After ridding my studio of scorpions I entered upon the most wonderful work period of my whole life. Antoinetta, the little Italian girl, managed to slip off once or twice a week to come to see me without any one suspecting it. All other affairs were done with. My life was perfect. Anna was completely for-

gotten—I had a pleasant playmate without any resulting obliga-
tions. It would have meant death for both of us had our meetings been discovered, so I knew she would never try to cause
me any trouble. In addition, I had been invited to send a collection of my works to an exhibition in Gothenburg and life was
very sweet.

During that summer I made my "Hunchback," the "Lone
Cliff in the Sea," and many other things. Ever since I had
been a sailor I had dreamt of modeling a cliff on which was suggested a titanic male figure. Seeing, years previously, a cliff in
the North Sea, it had suggested itself to me as great will determined to rise above the level of common things—a remnant
in the middle of the sea of a fierce force that had flung itself
toward the stars when the world was young.

I decided one day to make this figure in heroic size. Hurrying to a dealer in art materials, I asked for two thousand kilos
of clay (four thousand pounds). The dealer looked at me in
astonishment and said that he did not have so much on hand
and must write to Lucca for it. It might take a week or ten
days before he could deliver such a large quantity, he told me.

"Telegraph, telegraph!" I ordered. "I must have it at
once." And then I rushed away without leaving my name.

I turned down a street leading to a hardware dealer to buy
the iron for the skeleton of the statue, but just as I was about to
turn into his store it suddenly occurred to me that I had better
make a sketch of the statue before proceeding any further. I
returned to my studio and started a very interesting composition. When it was well on the way, however, I realized that
it would not do for a large composition. As a small thing,
which would stimulate the imagination to visualize the cliff's
grand proportions, it was fine, but to make an imitation ten or
twelve feet high would be an absurdity.

With consternation I suddenly remembered that I had
ordered two thousand kilos of clay! Now what was I to do with

all that dirt? The easiest way out was the way I chose. I solved my dilemma by deciding not to take the clay.

Firenze was a small town and if the dealer found me I felt I would be in a mess. I still had my beard and was very proud of it, but for the sake of disguise I did what so many crooks before me have done; I shaved off my whiskers. Later the matter of the huge order for clay became a subject of current gossip in the town. One day an artist friend told me about it.

"Say, Edstrom," he said, "was it you that ordered that lot of clay from that artists' supply dealer on Blank Street? He said a crazy foreigner came in one day pulling his mustaches and ordered two thousand kilos of clay, and that he never returned. He is up in the air—doesn't know what to do with it."

"Why, no, that is impossible," I replied. "I have no beard or mustaches."

This summer was the best, the calmest and most normal time of my whole life, and there is very little to relate about it. Caley Robinson, the famous English painter, was my most intimate friend of this period. Later in life he became a Royal Academician and gained great fame for his paintings of the scenery for Maeterlinck's "Blue Bird." He has produced scores of other inspired pictures.

I met many celebrities off and on, but I was so absorbed in my work that summer that they left no impression. Antoinetta flitted in and out, a slender wisp of a girl with dark hair, luminous eyes and warm red lips. She made me feel absolutely free. She was the perfect sweetheart.

XXIII

BONDAGE

I HAVE been criticized by many of my friends for my attitude toward women, for my general lack of chivalry, and my treatment of certain specific women. I do not see any virtue in being chivalrous, but quite the contrary. When I describe the troubles and losses which I experienced through marriage, I do so feeling not only that I am right, but also that I am adding to useful and essential knowledge. The female is the master mind, the captain, the one who holds control in all sex affairs. She is not the weak and needy one which chivalrous tradition makes of her.

Beautiful plumage, combs, manes, strange pouches, designs and decorations of all kinds are characteristic of the male among all species in nature. The voice of the male also is louder, and among the birds even takes rhythmic form. The female, on the other hand, is modest in color and plumage, often humbly soft and with a whining voice.

In the early days of history men followed the example set by males in other species and dressed in gay garments. Among savages even of our day the fine feathers are worn by the men, not the women.

But as civilization progressed, a thing called chivalry was created and men began to allow the women to wear all the decorations and devised for themselves conventional, modest raiment. Yet male superiority and social preferment were not given up until very recent times, when women began to gain political and economic equality. Now women have equal rights with men and still wear all the fine plumes, yet hold grimly to all the advantages of male chivalry. If the balance of power in early human history was on the side of the male, in our day the pendulum has swung far to the other side in favor of the female.

While I was staying in the North to regain my health, I spent long hours watching the mating frenzies of birds. The ptarmigan was the most interesting, for in him sex madness was so great that it overcame his fear of man to such an extent that I could bring the male to me in the mating season by imitating the female call—but not the female by imitating the male call.

Not until all the other birds in the forest had become quiet did Mr. Ptarmigan deign to seek adventure. On toward midnight the birds, one family after the other, would stop their racket. The last were the magpies. At last, however, a few minutes before midnight, they also were still. Then, as silence reigned, I would make the female call in a very low, petulant tone, a noise like this: "Nja! Nja!" with a few seconds' interval after each utterance of it. After a time I would hear far off a harsh baritone voice, sounding as if it were not made by a bird at all: "Tooba! Tooba! Ha! Ha!" interspersed with other noises impossible to imitate in words. I would then repeat the low, petulant, nasal noise, "Nja! Nja!" The male would again sound and then, always before I was expecting it, he would be careening all around me, scraping his wings on the snow, sputtering and ruffling, jumping and stuttering. Often I had him running over my head, his claws scratching my face in his wild response to my "Nja! Nja!"

Just so do women, with a whispered "Nja! Nja!" bend men to their wills. When a little girl follows age-old instincts and shows what a helpless, weak, lonely, unhappy little thing she is, small boys stand on their heads, jump, run, yell and in a hundred different ways show how strong, brave and able they are.

Yes, it is the female who always has the whip hand. She is not in need of the male's weak chivalry.

My monumental conceit, the sense of being a kind of none-such in everything, was my undoing. Until the autumn of 1901 I had escaped beautiful girls, gentle girls, passionate girls, educated girls, but when the time came I found that all my struggles to escape were futile against the desire of a strong-willed, clever woman. If I had studied Schopenhauer instead of Kant, the cynics instead of Nietzsche's Superman, I might have been aware of the fact that Dame Nature is an ogress who cares nothing for the safety of a grand genius, a ptarmigan, a lion or a worm, who has no mercy for the sweetest of singers, the most powerful of sculptors, the noblest of architects, the most learned of scientists, the gentlest of prophets, the wisest of magicians. When their time arrives she throws them callously into the arms of whatever stupid, giggling, shimmying, babbling, cooing, silly wench suits her purpose.

I had no warning of my impending catastrophe. I thought everything was perfect. My spiritual life at this time was fed by two particularly unique kinds of devotion. I had found in the Vieusseux Library a book called *Have You a Strong Will?* which I read every day as no priest ever read his exercises. I also practised the exercises with wonderful results. Then I had a large photograph of Basaitis' "Christ in Gethsemane." Christ is praying gently and seriously in this picture. The disciples are asleep and there is a loneliness over the landscape more infinite than I had ever experienced in Lapland. In this book and this picture were concentrated all my devotional exercises. I felt superb beyond what I can describe.

I, David Edstrom, the greatest sculptor in the world, had triumphed over the world, the flesh and the devil. Every evening I went through with my will exercises. Leland's *Have You a Strong Will?* had shown the way. The system is to relax completely before going to sleep at night and formulate what you want to achieve the next day. When morning comes your subconscious mind tells you what to do and you accomplish it without difficulty. It had worked like a miracle. It was so easy. I smiled contentedly as I pitched into work that bright autumn day of 1901 at No. 77 Viale Petrarca.

My mood was exalted and firm. There was something rocklike and absolute in my mind. I was so grateful to the book for this mood that I dreamed of having a million copies printed when I became rich. The book should be given away instead of the Bible to the heathen and unfortunate. Why, the system could save the world!

The summer's achievement had been superb. I was thin from hard work and sparse eating. Everything had gone into the work. The days were too short for all I had to do, for I was determined that I would get everything done in time for the big exhibition in Gothenburg—my subconscious mind would see to that.

The sweat was dripping from my nose and I was all spattered over with plaster of Paris. I was working fast and furiously to get a mixture used up before it hardened. This was one of the big days when all was rosy. I had not quite finished what was in the bucket when the doorbell rang. I couldn't go to the door at once and the bell rang again more vigorously. I swore in Italian, telling the visitor to be patient. At last I was through and opened the door.

There stood Anna. In my ignorance I had thought that she was thousands of miles away in Sweden. I was seldom surprised at what any woman did and I was not surprised when I saw my visitor was Anna. I only realized she was more, much more of everything I had feared in her. The moment before I was all energy and hope, and the moment I saw her I wilted with a sudden sense of exhaustion and helplessness.

"Anna, I am too tired," I said. "I can't."

She looked so small, pathetic and sweet. In a low whisper she answered:

"I'll go back then." ("Nja! Nja!")

The rock of my determination melted. I fell on my knees and begged her to stay.

"No, no," she wailed. "I will drag you from your work. You said you couldn't when you saw me. That was your real, true thought."

But of course she stayed and we were soon dining together. Under the influence of wine and food I recuperated. I felt a warming glow, sitting there so close to her, looking at the smooth olive of her cheeks, which took away all my desire to have her go. But a warning whisper of caution, away down somewhere, was strong enough for me to insist on an understanding. She saw the seriousness of my face and tried to forestall me.

"Let's just play and not be serious," she said. "Let the future take care of itself."

But I would not have it so and plunged directly into that which she had really come to discuss.

"If we are to marry," I said abruptly, "we must have a definite agreement."

First of all, I told her, she must fully acknowledge and not only acknowledge but understand that I was the greatest sculptor in the world. I had in mind a letter from her friend, Jane Claine, in which I was compared to Rodin. There must be no comparisons. I was the one and only David Edstrom. This was the only basis on which I could think of marrying. Her realization must be so strong that even should any member of her family be ill or dying it must not interfere with my work. I might at just such a moment be in the middle of some grand conception and a diversion of my thoughts by her departure might jeopardize the realization of a divine dream. Unfortunately she agreed to everything.

After this thorough understanding I was somewhat reconciled to marrying her. Somehow, "Lucifer" was neglected. The little restaurants on the hills and down the river gave excuses for walks. Then there were sunsets to observe.

She told me that she supported herself by translations and managed to make ends meet by hard work. She had recently translated *Leone Leoni* by George Sand. We read her translation together. The central character is the very epitome of what a woman conceives as heroic. He is a fighter, a musician, a gardener; he is proud, he is gentle, he is cruel and hard, he is soft as mush, he is everything under the sun any man could be, ever has been or ever will be. George Sand must have put into this stew everything her many lovers had been and everything she had imagined each of them could have been, in heaven or hell. Anna reading *Leone Leoni* to me made me feel as if I were all the things *Leone Leoni* had been and in addition possessed mysterious qualities even more rare and superb than anything described by George Sand.

Then one day Mrs. Levertin, Anna's mother, came unexpectedly to Firenze and with her her sister, Mrs. Heyman, the millionaire oatmeal queen from Vargarda, and Anna's cousin, Hilda Heyman, a beautiful Jewish girl. I had been booked to be married right away and didn't know a thing about it. I had been relieved of the worry of deciding anything in this matter for myself altogether.

The plans to marry right away seemed to develop of themselves, and it was decided that the wedding should be in Rome. We moved into a fashionable boarding house. They paid for everything. The greatest sculptor in the world became an appendix. My clothes were threadbare, because I had spent everything on my work. I was soon tailored and groomed, and they started my education with a vengeance. In secret I read and reread my worn copy of *Have You a Strong Will?* and tried to stand against the tide. I gazed upon my lonely Jesus and resolved, come what may, I would keep my soul free always—be alone "in eternity."

Anna's mother gained tremendous power over me through her feminine sweetness. When I rebelled at something, she would turn her head sideways like a hen, flash her white teeth

in a smile, and whisper: "For my sake." For years this was all
that was necessary for her to get her will. There was a terrible
finality in this sweet phrase, "For my sake."

"How is the artist child?" mother-in-law-to-be would greet
me, and I was helpless before the honey of her tyranny. But
a book had made the weak strong before, and I hoped I would
in some way escape.

My sculptures were dispatched to Gothenburg, but without
"Lucifer." He stood unfinished in my studio when we were
ready to leave for Rome to be married. He was made of wax
and I constructed a fine box for him so I could take him as
passenger goods and finish him in Rome.

The next day we started. What a lot of trunks! I had
never seen anything like it. I was worked to the limit keeping
track of it all. I had become the head of a multitude. There
was talk and excitement. One couldn't think of anything but
hat boxes, trunks, coats and bags. I almost forgot my box containing "Lucifer." When I checked the baggage at the station
they refused to let "Lucifer" go by. I became furious. I
reached in and tried to get hold of the agent, but he jumped
away. Eating with beggars and laborers I had learned the
Italian lingo of the alley, and it rushed forth with fluency. After
having expended my fury, I told the American Express agent
who was waiting by my side to take the box with the "Lucifer"
to the express company's storehouse until I returned. With a
parting fling at the railroad agent, enlarging upon the fact
that the cow was more akin to what he really was than anything else, I dashed off after the ladies.

But before we could get into the train a silk-hatted man
tapped me on the shoulder and asked me to follow him. His
request was emphasized by two gold-gallooned, glittering
gendarmes, taking me one by each arm. My romantic mind
at once decided that I was being arrested as an anarchist or for
some sinister crime.

But suddenly a faint hope of escaping the trunks and the

four women changed my distress to a sense of triumph. My arrest seemed an act of Providence! I was willingly marched into a small room. The man proceeded to read some reason for my arrest, but I was too excited to understand it. Anna fluttered around in her bright green dress looking for all the world like an excited parrot. How intensely I hoped they would lock me up in jail and save me from these women! However, Anna out-thought me, and as the man read on she took charge of the situation.

"He begs a thousand pardons!" she cried, and, as I furiously disclaimed the honor of begging any one's pardon, she shouted more loudly, drowning out my voice, "He begs a thousand pardons!"

The man behind the wicket now caught my eye and a light dawned upon me. It seemed to be a grave offense to call an official of the railway a cow. Meanwhile Anna kept tugging at my sleeve and urging me in Swedish, French and English:

"Beg his pardon, beg his pardon."

I refused, but her frantic pleadings pacified them and I did not have the presence of mind to think of a new insult. Soon all was over and in a daze I found myself on the train surrounded by the laughter of our fellow passengers.

After arriving at Rome mother-in-law-to-be asked me to sign a paper. As I read it through I realized that it was an agreement in which I would renounce all rights to any property Anna possessed or might inherit. I refused angrily.

"Why, she told me she owned nothing," I said. "No, I will not sign this paper. Whatever she may own now or ever will own I must control. I will not be dependent and poor while she has a competency."

There was a big row and a flood of tears and again I had reason to hope that the whole marriage would blow up. But a number of wires were exchanged with Oscar Levertin and Anna's other brother, Judge Levertin, and unhappily for me they consented to my demand. Women at that time did not have suffrage in Sweden; thus through marriage I became the guardian of Anna, with arbitrary control of her property.

As I read other papers in which Anna's age was given, I found she was four years older than myself, not three years younger as she had made me believe. Just a little matter of seven years. What an innocent little lamb Ellen Key had tried to shield from the wolf!

On the fourth of January, 1902, Prince Doria of the Syndaco performed the marriage rite. Leaving the other three women in Rome, we started for Taormina, Sicily, to spend our honeymoon there. Taormina had been chosen because I had acquired a bad cough with fever after coming to Rome. An old Norwegian doctor I consulted told me I was in danger of having a relapse of my old ailment if I did not take care of myself.

The town of Taormina is located in one of the most gorgeous settings in the world. It nestles on the side of a mountain, where to the left, looking up from the sea, the volcano Ætna towers into the clouds. In the winter it is snow-capped, while on the slopes great groves of orange trees, heavy with fruit, feast the eye with their color and the nostrils with their aromatic fragrance.

Rising behind the town is a crag-like mountain on the outjutting part of which, like an eagle's eyrie, perches the town of Mola. All this, with the old Greek theater, the undulating slopes covered with millions of fragrant flowers, makes an ensemble of the titanic and awe-inspiring, the prehistoric and romantic, plus a fragrant Elysian loveliness, with the whole framed in that indescribable indigo blue of sky and sea peculiar to the Mediterranean.

The little town of Mola was the central beauty spot in the landscape. Its picturesque splendor fascinates every traveler from the moment he begins his drive from the station down by the sea up toward the resort. But Mola was not only the scenic wonder of the Taormina view, it was also a permanent joke and object of constant mysterious persiflage and discreet whispered banter. The jokes about Mola were whispered in the ear to wife or intimate friend—never mentioned aloud in company. Its secret caused only a humorous watering of the eye or a subdued snicker by those who had a sense of humor, or a chalky, angry stare by Mrs. Grundy. No large parties ever stayed long enough in Mola to see the real sights.

The town clings to a crag that seems unapproachable from below. For mystery and beauty it is incomparable. Every day parties were made up for a climb up there. But when you asked anybody how he had liked it, no one would tell you. Everybody upon his return acted mysteriously and looked knowingly at others who had been there, but would not reveal the mystery. This made visitors anxious to undertake the trip. The secret was that the place was filthy beyond description. From below it looked like a fairy town from The Arabian Nights. But once there, all the romance disappeared in filth. A visitor's book was kept at a little inn, and in it were a number of quips about the place. Hallstrom, the Swedish poet, had written: "See Mola, then take a bath."

Separated from my work, I was so bitterly unhappy that I would have left my wife then and there had not Anna had the inspiration to ask my collaboration in translating—from the French—Flaubert's *Salammbô* and *The Confessions of Alfred de Musset,* for which she had a contract with a Swedish publisher.

One day there came a long letter from my brother-in-law telling me of my mother's death. He described how South Ottumwa had been inundated; a terrible flood had covered our whole part of the town. Mother had been moved, with other refugees, into a tent during the flood and had become very ill. Then, as soon as the flood had receded, they were obliged to move back home, where it was still worse. Bedding, clothing, furniture—yes, the very walls and chimneys were sodden with water, and Mother, after an illness of some weeks, had died.

I would have expected to be prostrated by this news after the close relationship which had existed between us, but to my astonishment I found that I could not feel any great grief over Mother's death. Whether my unhappiness with Anna was so great that it crowded out all other emotions, or whether the struggles of the years had made me insensible, I don't know.

All that I know is that the days and nights were filled with my unhappiness and my quarreling with Anna.

"How could you write me such beautiful letters when you seem so stupid?" I asked her in one of our quarrels.

In anger she yelled in my face:

"I copied them from books to catch you—you poor fish!"

Soon the incomparable Italian spring came to Sicily and we began leisurely to follow the season north. We spent a few days in Naples and Amalfi, then went up to Rome for a couple of weeks, then spent a few days in Siena and Lucca, and finally came back to Firenze. I had kept my old studio on the Viale Petrarca and started at once to work on my "Lucifer." As model I used a young German-Italian athlete.

This "Lucifer" I meant to be a young god, the spirit of defiance and freedom. With clenched hands and head thrown proudly back, and mouth open, he stood hurling forth a challenge to the powers of heaven—to me exemplified in the conventions of the past. At last I cast him in plaster. Some days later I thought he looked too much like Phrimmet, the model, and in a moment of disgust I took a large hammer and smashed him into small bits. Over a year's work was sent to glory in less than five minutes. It was a pity, because I know now it was a fine piece of work. The mask of the "Lucifer" I saved and today it is a reminder that I, in a supercritical mood, destroyed one of the finest pieces of work I've ever made. Poor Anna! This was her first (but not her last) experience with my destructive moods.

Before I had left for Rome to get married, Antoinetta had

sent me a ghoulish souvenir. It was an étui covered with black velvet. Inside was mounted a silver crown of thorns, a heart pierced with a dagger, a death's head and cross-bones. The memento had given me the shivers because I did not know what it meant. When we returned to Firenze the girl sent us a magnificent wedding cake, with a very courteous note. I did not dare to eat of the cake because I was afraid it might be poisoned. I had not told Anna about the sinister present I had received, and I found it hard to explain to her why I would not eat the cake. In spite of my warnings, Anna ate some of it, and when I found the next day that she was not poisoned I also shared the delicious masterpiece of an Italian chef.

XXIV

DESPAIR

WHILE looking around for a permanent home, we rented a furnished room near my studio and here had one of the strangest experiences I have ever encountered. We rented the room from an Italian family of seeming respectability. The next room to ours was always locked and did not seem to be used for anything, yet at night we heard stealthy muffled noises in there. We became, both of us, puzzled and suspicious of what was done there late at night after we had gone to bed. One night, in holding my ear to the door, trying to discover what was being done, I caught a faint, nasty, but familiar smell that in a tantalizing way escaped classification.

The next day when we were alone in the house we decided to investigate. With a hairpin I picked the lock and we entered. Anna gave a scream as she saw what the room contained. Lying around were detached human heads, arms and legs, while in a great oblong vat floated other parts. To me the mystery was solved at once and I burst out laughing at Anna's fright. We had come upon the workshop of a skeleton maker.

"He is no doubt employed at a medical school or a hospital and as a part of his compensation he gets the stiffs not needed for study and makes skeletons of them," I said.

The next day we moved away from the skeleton maker and for a time rented the Villa Dolgorouki and then established ourselves permanently in a studio apartment on Via Manelli.

My revolt against the bondage of marriage was terrible. That Anna could stand my violence and tantrums has always surprised me. When I married her and found that she was seven years older than she had told me she was, and that she had a considerable fortune in her own name and had definite prospects of being very wealthy in the future, I began to suspect that she had deceived me in other things also; that perhaps there was a still more sinister secret in her past that I could not quite fathom. An elusive shadow of something I ought to know seemed to be just beyond the grasp of my mind. Some remark, some forgotten conversation had given me a glimpse, a revelation of evil that had bobbed out again and that I could neither explain completely nor abandon. My tempers, though caused by a deep intuition, uttered themselves over the most trivial matters.

One day, in one of these fiercely devastating moods, I took a china closet in our dining room and carried it out on the balcony overlooking the studio. This balcony was about fifteen feet above the floor of the *atelier*. With a mighty heave I threw the cupboard full of glass and porcelain down to the concrete floor below. The crash was magnificent and stimulating. It awoke in me such a passion for further noise and devastation that I rushed down into the studio and, seizing a large marble hammer, proceeded to break up into bits the works of my own hands that I had made over a period of several months.

In the midst of the orgy of noise and destruction I happened to notice Anna, who had come down into the studio. Her face seemed to be petrified in an expression of awe and despair. The expression was so unusual that I was fascinated by it. Although a moment before I had been completely destructive, now I wanted to create.

"For God's sake hold that expression!" I cried. "Get up on the model stand and sit down."

In a moment I had a mass of clay on a stand and in a fever of inspiration I made in a few minutes a head in clay which I called "Despair."

A few days later, during a terrible thunderstorm, the door

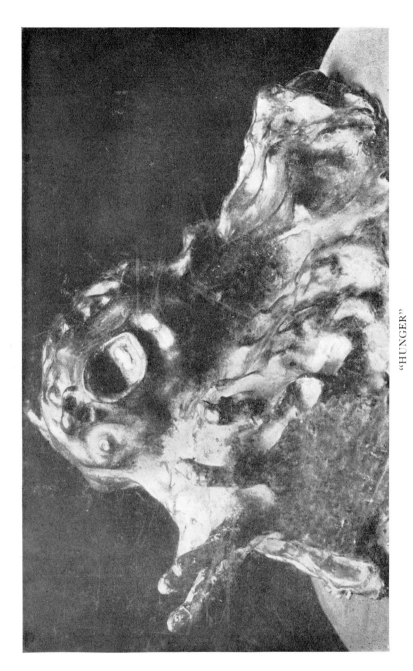

"HUNGER"

Bronze by Edstrom in the Gothenburg Museum, Gothenburg, Sweden

"PROTECTING THE FLAME OF LIFE"
Memorial to Florence Nightingale, modeled
in clay by the author in 1937

bell rang and I went myself to see who could be out in such
a drenching rain.   What was my surprise when His Royal
Highness Prince Eugene, brother to the King of Sweden,
pushed by me to escape the torrents cascading over the door
stoop.   Shaking himself like a wet dog and grinning, he
stretched out his hand.

"Well, I am glad to find you home, Edstrom," he said.

I pulled him into the studio and called up to Anna to get tea
ready.   She cast one hurried glance down over the banister
and then bobbed out of sight, and presently I heard the slam
and clatter of pans and dishes as she hurried to prepare a warming drink for our royal guest.   In the meantime I showed him
my works and among other things the study, "Despair," I had
made from my wife's head.   He thought it so remarkable that
he ordered it in bronze for his collection.

He stayed for a couple of hours or so, drinking tea, gossiping
about mutual friends, and discussing recent developments in
the art world.

Prince Eugene was a landscape painter of unusual talent, who
would have made a name for himself had he been a poor man
without the prestige of his royal position.   He was very modest
and worked as hard at his art as if it had been the means of
earning his daily bread.

My strange composition called "The Cry of Poverty," which
was some years later purchased by the Swedish government for
the Gothenburg Museum, was created under almost as strange
circumstances as "Despair," while we lived on Via Manelli.

The writer, Per Hallstrom, a member of the Swedish Academy and a great man in Sweden, together with his family, was
among our most intimate friends in Firenze.   One evening,
after spending some hours with Hallstrom in his home at Villa
Giovanelli, discussing the deep and subtle vagaries of life along
devious and mystic routes known only to the truly Scandinavian
mind, I found myself drifting home still immersed in a
labyrinth of transcendental speculation when a great white hand

appeared before my eyes. I stopped stock-still with my heart pumping violently in apprehension. Wide awake in a moment, I saw in the dim light that it was not so big, but a real human hand. It was the hand of a beggar who, in the eloquent Italian fashion, without a word stretched it forth out of the dark for alms.

It gave me a great inspiration. I hurried home and lit all the lamps and candles I could find. Anna was asleep. On a modeling table I piled up a mass of clay and got to work. All humanity, yes! The very earth, like that beggar in the dark, stretched toward the heavens its hand for succor and nourishment. The very church steeples were mute fingers stretched toward God for rain, sunshine and life. I made a terrible face and a huge hand. I saw in my mind a sunset over a great city, out of which a half-blind face emerged in the blood of the sunset. It sent forth a silent shriek of woe to the unknown, unseen Lord of Life. At three o'clock this vision of terror—to me as beautiful as life itself—was finished. I had worked in a frenzy and accomplished what under normal conditions would have taken weeks. I then went up and awakened Anna.

"Anna," I said, "wake up, come down and look at it."

She shivered and yawned and answered:

"Won't tomorrow do as well? I am so sleepy."

"But, Anna," I continued, "it's the greatest thing ever created in the world. Do come, please."

"All right."

She came and looked, and looked—and being very conceited in those days, I accepted her silence as awe and admiration. Maybe it was—I don't know.

The next day I cast it in plaster and with tempera painted it in the colors of a red, violent sunset. Unfortunately this model in color is lost.

My three grotesques, "Pride," "Fear," and "Envy," were also created at Via Manelli and were purchased by the Marquis Riccardo Manelli at a private exhibition I held at the Vieusseux

Library. Prezzolini wrote in *Il Leonardo* about this show: "Edstrom reveals our most secret passions."

But there were incidents which lightened my unhappiness with Anna. One day Selma Lagerlöf came to Firenze at the end of a triumphal tour through Europe. She had been received and decorated by practically every crowned head on the Continent from Egypt to Sweden. The Pope had spent an hour talking with her. Perhaps no woman had ever been so honored as she was at this time. The entire group to which I belonged in Firenze looked forward eagerly to her coming and when she came swarmed around her as if she had been the queen bee in a hive.

Just as we were ready to settle down and enjoy her sweetness and genius, we realized that she had with her an unshakable companion named Mrs. Elkan. Mrs. Elkan was a writer of penny-liners and a queen of bores. She talked by the minute, by tens of minutes, by the hour. No one else could get in a word in her presence. With folded hands Selma Lagerlöf sat and listened and smiled like an obedient, modest child, while Elkan talked and talked. Soon everybody fled both of them. Wherever two or three of us were gathered together the burning question arose: "Why does Selma Lagerlöf live with that creature?" All kinds of surmises and reasons were suggested and thrown overboard. We simply could not fathom the puzzle. Lagerlöf was gentleness, sweetness and tact itself, and Elkan was loud-voiced, vulgar and rasping as a parrot. Neither wit, poetry nor narrative was evident in her chatter.

Then one day I met Selma Lagerlöf on the street. She seemed very nervous and upset as she told me Mrs. Elkan was very sick with erysipelas. At once I took Miss Lagerlöf in hand and for a period of a week we breakfasted, lunched and dined together. Of all the charming mentalities in the world, I have never known one more beautiful, whimsical and full of charm than that of this great writer. One evening at a concert she asked me a question.

"Supposing Mrs. Elkan should die," she said. "How in the world shall I manage to bury her?"

There was no sorrow or fear concerning Mrs. Elkan, but a revelation that Lagerlöf was childlike and helpless in any practical matter. She lived so much in the imagination that the most insignificant matters seemed ponderous to her.

I found later on that the buying of a railway ticket, learning the schedule of trains, the names of streets, or any minor practical issue, was to her difficult to master, and that Mrs. Elkan took care of all these things for her.

Quickly I reassured her.

"Oh, that is very easy. Here in Italy burials are practically a state monopoly. There are four classes of funerals, so as to fit every one's purse. All you have to do is to decide how much you want to spend on the performance."

She gave a sigh of relief.

"I didn't know that," she said. "It has bothered me a great deal."

Mrs. Elkan, however, did not die, and soon she took her ward north and continued to help Selma Lagerlöf in practical matters to the continued annoyance of every one else.

Another friend whom we enjoyed greatly was the Norwegian writer, Erik Lie, a member of a family of famous literary men. His father, Jonas Lie, was the first of the Scandinavian realists in literature. Erik Lie's greatest attribute was a constructive imagination. From mysterious intuitions he could evolve seemingly scientific facts. For a long time he had been unproductive so far as literary creativeness was concerned, but in personal conversation he painted pictures in words weird and colorful beyond many masterpieces of great authors. His whole life at this time was centered in the analysis and description of a tapeworm that was sapping his vitality. He was emaciated and his eyes shone out of great hollows in his skull like the fiery orbs of a prophet. He had traveled from country to country, trying all kinds of painful cures for his parasite without avail, until to his creative imagination the tapeworm had become not a worm but a demon of hellish wisdom and evil cunning. Fascinated, I listened to him by the hour as he enlarged upon the intelligence, subtlety and supernatural wisdom of the demon within him. Its instincts of self-preservation and tenacity of purpose were far deeper than those of the mind of man. It was as secretive and mysterious as life in the nethermost caverns at the bottom of the sea or the vegetation on a cooling planet. His elaboration of the life within himself was an epic of the terrible and awful beyond anything I have read in Dante's *Inferno*.

Clippings from the exhibition in Gothenburg commenced to come in. I had made a big success and was heralded as the most promising young sculptor who had exhibited his work for a long period. My "Caliban" was purchased for the Gothenburg Museum.

One winter day I met a strange man, Robert Barrett, the explorer. He was a son of the late Chicago millionaire manufacturer of patent roofing. Barrett and I became friends at once. He was a huge man, physically hard as nails and so untouched by dissipation that he looked like a boy in spite of his great dark beard. He was living at the fashionable mountain resort of Vallombrosa. One day I received a wire from him: "Snowing and blowing bully come my guest."

I packed at once and took the first train for Vallombrosa.

Barrett told me that he had not slept under a roof for ten years. He had a suite of ten or twelve rooms at the hotel where he was preparing for a new expedition into Tibet. At night he would sit and talk in front of a blazing fire until we were sleepy and then he would take a huge blanket of some kind of Russian felt and go out and sleep in some nook in the forest.

A few years previously he had met Horace Fletcher, who started the famous Fletcherizing craze of chewing food until it was reduced to a liquid. This reduces the quantity of one's food to a fraction of what one usually eats. Barrett had tried it on a year's trip into the Himalaya Mountains and had been able to carry enough provisions on two donkeys to last a year, whereas had he not Fletcherized, he would have been obliged to use eight donkeys to carry provisions.

He completely convinced me of the value of Fletcherizing. When I came home and Anna saw how I sat and chewed and chewed, she was greatly alarmed. Anna was not inclined toward new fads. She was hard-headed and practical. At that first meal she had a wonderful steak for me. Thick steaks were my favorite dish, and when she saw me nibbling little bits and chewing indefinitely, she at last put down her knife and fork and with a sob in her throat exclaimed:

"David—David, darling, what in the world has happened to you?"

Stammering and embarrassed, I did my best to explain and convince her of the wisdom of this great idea, but I felt defeated before I began.

We had had these encounters before. On ordinary matters I pretty much had my own way, but when it came to matters of life and health, Anna had the hard stubbornness of a mule. She snorted and shook her head very much the same as a donkey does when annoyed, and said:

"I knew that man was a nut the moment I set eyes on him."

However, I continued to chew for a time, but Anna gradually wore me out and I returned to my normal habit of gorging myself.

XXV

PARIS

WITH the coming of spring we followed the birds north-ward and stopped at Paris. At the Pension Vesqué where we lived was also Emil Sjögren, the Swedish composer, and his wife. Sjögren was a genial, childlike little fellow and his wife a man-of-war. She constantly tried to control her husband with a hand of iron, which annoyed me so much that I made a futile attempt to do something about it. One night I managed to get Emil loose and took him with me to the Café Versailles. The great Norwegian painter, Diriks, had sold a picture and he was buying champagne in magnums.

But Emil, unappreciative of my effort in his behalf, passed out after only a few drinks, and I had to carry him upstairs to his rooms. Not only had I been obliged to leave the party before it had fairly begun, but Mrs. Sjögren gave me a lecture which pretty effectively took the edge off the evening.

But that moment of freedom apparently went to Emil's head, for the next day he disappeared. For several days our group was loud in its excited, somewhat dramatic speculation. Emil was at the bottom of the Seine. Emil had gone off for good. We would never see Emil again. But in a remote part of Paris, kindly people had picked him up and in a few days brought him home, sobered, with a box of chocolates in one hand and a bunch of violets in the other, for his wife. Her name was Ebba or something like it, and he babbled, "Ebba, will you have some chocolates? Ebba, will you have some violets?"

One day Anna had a letter from George Brandes, the Danish

author, whom she had known all her life. Brandes is known
as the world's greatest Shakespearian authority. He was a
wizened, white-haired, rheumatic monkey of a man, but Anna
embraced him and cooed in his ears warm, affectionate froth.
As one at the shrine of Apollo, I waited to hear from his lips
golden words of poetry and wit. But instead of sparkling
bubbles from an overfull imagination he began in his screechy,
senile voice to talk about his women. The countess had sent
dahlias, the princess red roses, the baroness this, that and the
other, and famous beauties of all nations had given him tribute
on his return to Paris. Even the braggadocio of d'Annunzio
seemed tame compared to that of Brandes.

One of Sweden's most talented woman authors committed
suicide for love of this man. Geierstam published her memoirs,
in which she tells of her love over a period of years and up to
the fatal hour. What he had, to be able to stimulate such
fierce adoration, I don't know.

The real importance of this, my first visit to Paris, was the
renewed contact with Yrjo Hirn, the Finnish anthropologist.
In Florence he had been interested in my grotesques, "Fear,"
"Pride," and "Envy." During our separation he had found
in the library of the Salpêtrière Hospital for the Insane in Paris,
photographs made by the French psychiatrist, Charcot, of hysterical subjects during their seizures of unconsciousness. In
these photographs he had noted the same swelling up in states
of pride and the same contraction during states of fear. My
sketch of Anna that I had named "Despair" exhibited really the
third important and basic emotion, that of surprise, an arrested
state of mind. The statuette of "Envy" was not basic but rather
an illustration of a complex emotion, whereas pride, fear and
surprise have been quite generally accepted by psychologists as
basic emotions.

Hirn had at the time already published his *Origins of Art*
and was then working on *The Sacred Shrine*. His wife was
at the time working on her great translations of the works of

Lafcadio Hearn into Swedish.   Hirn ranks with Frazer, author of *The Golden Bough,* and Westermark, the other Finnish giant, among the anthropologists.   Although Hirn concentrates on Art, his writings on religious matters in his *The Sacred Shrine* are more profound than the writings of Westermark or Frazer. The splendor of Hirn's writings dims the light of all other writers on Art.

XXVI

THE END OF AN EPISODE

ONE of my wife's wealthy relatives gave us a big family homecoming dinner. As I looked down the long table and saw the dark-complexioned faces of the Josephsons, the Levins, the Levertins, Heymans, Davidsons, Jacobsons and Abrahamsons, I realized that through marriage I was related to half the wealth in Sweden. I had a tremor of both pleasure and fear. I felt myself to be at the beginning of things, a man on his way to a goal, but all these people glittering with jewels, smiling in smug complacency, had already arrived at their goal. In this lay my fearfulness, because I knew that their goal would never be my goal, their gods would never be my gods, their ideals my ideals. I had no prejudice against Jews; in fact, I was very fond of my mother-in-law and of Oscar, my wife's brother, as well as many others of her relatives. My fearfulness lay in the fact that these people had centuries of culture behind them, and were satiated and weary of the things that I stretched forward to with the eagerness of a primitive peasant. I was direct and explosive; they were sophisticated and self-contained.

However, I enjoyed keenly the feeling of being on top with them; of being one with wealth and power.

Without delay I secured a studio apartment and began work on commissions I had secured. One of the contracts I had signed was for a mighty fireplace in a house being built by the world-famous architect, Hagnar Ostberg, who later built the

City Hall in Stockholm—in my opinion by far the most beautiful edifice made in the world since the Renaissance.

What was significant about this piece of work of mine was
that in it I had combined a practical, useful construction with a
beautiful idea.   In my fireplace I had symbolized love as fire.
In the back, inside the fireplace, I had in relief two figures
flying up with the flames—modeled flames in relief merging
with the two young lovers.   The sides and top of the inside of
the fireplace were made as a vault or niche and in their surfaces
was represented a forest in which the dry treetops intertwined
in fantastic anguished forms.   At each side of the fireplace,
rising to the mantelpiece, were two female figures.   One of
them listened with voluptuous pleasure to the flames.   The
other had a shuddering fearful pose, covering her face with
her hands as she listened to the flames and the wind outside.
On the face of the mantelpiece I had a dragon and intertwined
with this decoration the sentence: "I am the will that wills that
all shall love and be consumed."

With the fireplace I had also designed a fire screen with a
wolf motive intertwined with pine trees.

I also worked on a portrait bust of Mrs. Anna Levin, one of
my wife's wealthy cousins.   She was the daughter of Jeanette
Jacobson, a famous opera singer of the nineteenth century.
Anna Levin was a dark, beautiful, magnificent creature, and as
warm and fine of character as she was in physical glory.   We
became very good friends.

The Jews in Stockholm treated me with the utmost consideration, and had it not been for my gnawing jealousy and conviction that my wife had put over some deviltry on me, I would
have been a very contented young man.   I was too proud to
spy on her and find evidence to confirm my suspicions, but at
the same time I could not get rid of them, with the result that
I was almost always in a mood of anger and revolt unless I was
with friends whom I liked.

With Anna I quarreled incessantly.   The following incident

with Thiel is typical of how raw my nerves were: Among the many other commissions I had received was an order for portrait busts of both Mr. and Mrs. Thiel. The work on both busts, which I was doing at their country home near Stockholm, was nearly finished and they were very pleased with my creations. In fact, they advised me to cast the portraits as they were. I also was satisfied and I continued to work on them only to accentuate and intensify a few points that no one understood but myself. It is often the last few touches that bring a work of art above the commonplace. Thiel and I, of course, always nagged and snarled at each other over one issue or another when we were in certain moods. One morning when he came for his sitting he was especially annoying.

"Do you know what kind of a character you've got, Edstrom?" he asked. "I've just reasoned out that there is absolutely nothing you might not do if you got mad enough. I'll give you an illustration of your tyranny. My wife and I have been posing here day in and day out for weeks, and always on edge for fear we might displease you. Every minute of my time is valuable, but I admire your work and I want to have these two portraits, therefore I've given you all the time you've asked, controlled myself, and agreed to pay you more than you asked for the work. Both you and I have much to gain for our sacrifices in time, labor and money, yet did you take the notion you would not hesitate for a minute to break those beautiful pieces of work to pieces. Are you never going to grow up, so that one can depend on you, be free and easy with you, and not on edge as to what you will do if you get mad?"

I did not answer a word, but continued to work. When the sitting was over he smiled and gazed admiringly for a few moments at my work before leaving; but I was seething with controlled fury.

As soon as he had gone out I did just what he had described as an extreme illustration of what I might do in anger. I smashed to pieces both his and Mrs. Thiel's bust. I simply could not bear the challenge of any man, and though I loved these two pieces of work as I did my very soul I could find no answer to his criticism save in their destruction.

Afterwards I packed my belongings ready for departure and then hunted him up as he was walking back and forth in a lane not far from the house, pondering over some matter. Very calmly I went up to him and said:

"Mr. Thiel, I have destroyed the two busts just as you suggested I should do."

Casting one horrified look at me, he ran as fast as he could away from me, acting as if he had suddenly taken some potent drug that had stimulated him to a quickness of movement beyond normal. I did not see either of the Thiels for months after that.

And then my relationship with Anna reached a climax.

My wife and I were at the great Nobel Festival when the year's prize in literature was to be awarded. We sat well up front in the great hall. The entire royal family were present and the élite of Sweden, as well as scores of distinguished visitors from other countries. Behind us sat two of Anna's cousins, the Misses Valentine, both well known as pianists. The hall was in a buzz of suppressed conversation. The ceremonies of the occasion were being delayed by the tardiness of old King Oscar, then ruler of Sweden. Presently I heard, above the buzz, one of the Valentine girls talking to Anna.

"Well," she said, "I'm glad he did get his concert after all. You surely must have worked hard to put it over so well."

"What?" I exclaimed.

I didn't know what they were talking about. So far as I knew Anna had had no connection with any one's concert. Then suddenly, in a flash, I remembered that she had been spending hours away from home every day saying that she had been to a dentist. All the time I had suspected that she had been going to see a lover, though I had had no idea who it was. But her sweet cousin, seeing that the shaft she had launched had gone home, was hastening to enlighten me.

"You ought to be pleased, David," she said archly. "Mr. Norris is a countryman of yours!"

For a moment I was speechless with shock and rage. Norris! A jubilee singer from one of the Southern States of America! So this was Anna's secret lover. This was the skeleton which she had so carefully concealed from me even before we were married. I had always known there was something. Now I knew what it was. Now I knew why she had wanted to marry me. Unable, because of racial prejudice, to marry him, she had fastened on me to solve the problem of marriage for her.

While I was still petrified with horror over the unbelievable degradation of my position, Anna took things into her own hands. The hall had became suddenly silent, because the tall, white-haired King Oscar was just then entering. Over the silence Anna's strident voice sounded like the crackling of sudden lightning.

"Don't you dare to abuse me here, David! I tell you, at least on an occasion like this I should be free from your crazy jealousy."

All eyes in the hall turned away from King Oscar to us while I sank low and silent, as deep in my seat as I could.

After the ceremonies were over, I left Anna at the door without a word and immediately took a train for the North to get my bearings. I stayed up there with my old friends for two weeks and then returned to Stockholm. Here I at once called on Mrs. Thiel and asked her if what the Valentine girl had told me was the truth or only a mean fabrication on her part.

"Yes, it is the truth," Mrs. Thiel told me.

I then went to Anna Levin, my wife's cousin, and asked her the same question.

"You poor boy, I am so sorry for you, but it is the truth."

In the meantime, through Oscar, my wife's brother, with

whom I was ever and always on the best of terms, Anna had been persuaded to go to Germany in company with her mother, so that I could finish my work in our studio home, for I refused to be under the same roof with her any longer. But I knew that I could not stay. I was mad with wounded pride and shame and I could not remain in Stockholm where every one knew what a cuckold had been made of me.

Norris had been a friend of my wife years before we met and the friendship had continued all the time uninterruptedly while she was moving heaven and earth to marry me. Now that I knew about it, I felt no anger or desire for revenge, only a deep shame. I was wounded to the quick—I was bewildered and didn't know what to do.

Then one day an old friend, a newspaper editor named Hugo Landen, called on me with a hard-luck story and wanted me to stake him for a passage to Cuba, where he had a brother who owned a plantation. His request gave me the answer I sought. Just as Ed Leonard years before had inspired me to tramp to Sweden with his offer: "Come with me to Africa," so Landen's: "For God's sake buy me a ticket to Cuba," inspired me to answer his question with: "Sure, I'll stake you to a ticket, but you will have to put up with my company on the way over there."

"Cuba," I mused, "no one will know me in Cuba."

I decided that I would spend a few months hunting and fishing on the island and then go up to New York and settle down. At once I went to Anna Levin, my wife's cousin, and told her of my plan. Mrs. Levin knew as much of my situation as it was possible for any one to know. When I had told her of Landen she encouraged me.

"It's a fine idea," she said, "but hurry off before Anna returns, because when she comes back to Stockholm anything is likely to happen."

Anna Levin was a shrewd, level-headed woman.

"David," she said, "do you know if you go to Thiel and tell

him you are leaving for Cuba and offer him all your sculptures at a bargain, he will buy the whole lot of them."

I went at once and called on him at his bank and he not only took my sculptures, but paid me what would have been a maximum market value at an exhibition.

I called up Ostberg and told him I would not finish the great fireplace for the Unander Scharin house because I was going to Cuba. In a few minutes he came around to my studio, bringing with him a contractor. He was desperate, but his face showed relief as he looked at my work.

"Why, it is finished," he said. Turning to the contractor, he continued: "We can cut that in marble just as it is, can't we?"

"Sure," replied the contractor.

I was absolutely amazed at this turn of affairs. To me there was a great deal to be done before it was ready to cast. Ostberg, after a few more flattering phrases about my achievement, left with the assurance that he would take care of the casting in plaster and everything, and all I had to do was to accept the money and give a receipt. But I was not convinced. The next day he telephoned that Unander Scharin, who was in Spain looking after some iron mines he owned there, had telegraphed that he would double his price for my fireplace—on Ostberg's advice. But I was beside myself. I could not see anything but a rotten, half-finished job, and before Ostberg had a chance to tempt me again I had some men reduce the whole model to fragments with axes and sledgehammers.

By way of Hamburg, Landen and I sailed on a Hamburg-American passenger ship for Havana in the early part of June, 1904.

I HAD a letter of introduction from a Señor Garcia, Cuban Consul-General at Hamburg, to General Menocal, who, years later, became President of Cuba, but who was at the time President of the Chaparra Sugar Plantations, owned by Rockefeller interests. I was, however, so sick of wealthy people and all the tension around money that I went straight into the country with Landen to a place called La Gloria. Here I became friendly with a young chap named Ostrand who had run away from home. His father was a millionaire rubber manufacturer and young Per wanted to be a farmer. But we did less farming than playing.

Before leaving Sweden I had bought a fine camping outfit, guns, rods, a tent for tropical climates, etc. I had left all my money and a power of attorney with Thiel. As soon as I decided to make La Gloria my headquarters, I wired him for a monthly remittance. This monthly remittance came in the form of drafts on New York. La Gloria had no banking facilities, and to get to Nuevitas, the nearest town, one had to travel almost two days in dinky, smelly sailboats through swamps teeming with mosquitoes and alligators.

One month I decided to try to get my draft cashed in La Gloria, and after some inquiry I was advised to try a certain saloonkeeper whom I did not know. He told me he had weekly contacts and would have my money in a few days, and so I gave my draft to him. In pioneer localities one does not use the same care with receipts and safeguards as in other places, and when after some ten days or more he had not received the money, I began to get suspicious. I did not have a line to show I had turned over my draft to him.

After more weeks and repeated visits I learned that he was a crook. My funds were low, the draft was ample, and my sudden anger knew no bounds. I was drinking heavily, and the influence of this, added to that of the hot climate and nights spent at poker and dice, had made my nerves a fertile soil for the seeds of my wrath. Without any thought of consequences, I decided that I must kill the saloonkeeper.

The machete was the favorite weapon, but I knew nothing about the use of this murderous jungle accessory. To bluff him I feared would not work. I was never much of a success at bluffing. I decided that I would go to him with a gun and get my money or shoot daylight into his guts. In my hunting trips I had learned the trail through the jungle to Las Minas, a small town in the mountains south of La Gloria. If I killed him I would have a fighting chance to get there and make connections by rail to the outside.

One day when there were a number of cowboys in town with their broncos tied up on the one street, I picked out a suitable mount and, gun in pocket, called on my man. But I had overdone my part. I was so overcome with awe at the thought that I was about to kill a man, that I found I could not speak aloud.

"Will you please give me my money?" I whispered tensely.

Disgusted at the tremulous insignificance of my own voice, I expected him to laugh at me, but to my surprise he turned deadly white and his hands trembled as he opened his cash drawer and got out the bills. Something in my expression must have impressed him more than my voice. As I took the bills I felt a furious wave of disappointment because he had robbed me of my excuse for shooting him.

Ostrand had a plantation at a place called Piloto not far from La Gloria. I moved down there and amused myself helping

him with his pineapples and bananas. My reward was that he
could take time to go with me on fishing and hunting trips over
Saturday and Sunday. He had an ex-sailor working for him
who took care of the place in our absence. I have seen few
men of such marvelous physique and manly beauty and strength
as Ostrand. He was fearless and absolutely without nerves.
Another Swede, Olson, had a crazy, leaky sailboat that was re-
paired with everything from barrel staves to hoopskirt wires.

It was a real Raggedy Ann of a boat and we sailed the mad
craft everywhere. On one of our week-end trips we ran into
a storm on a Saturday night which made us all believe that we
would never get back. We stripped to the skin, ready to swim
as long as we could after the wreck. One would bail while the
other sat at the tiller. The bailer could at times get a few seconds of sleep. All night we battled the storm, now and then
shouting and laughing to keep awake. What a man Ostrand
was! I was so supported by his courage that I felt no fear at
all.

Some time before dawn the wind calmed just as rapidly as it
had begun. We had been driven we didn't know where and it
was evening when we at last ran into an island. We pulled up
in the shallow water, got out some blankets, and threw ourselves on the sand and went to sleep.

I was awakened by what I thought was a wild pig and what
turned out to be a giant crab. Quietly I got coffee and bacon
and hard-tack from the half-submerged boat and cooked breakfast. Ostrand awoke with a grin as he smelled the coffee.
Then we both dived into the sea for lobsters. The coral reefs
around this island were full of them. You dive down and stick
your hand in the holes where they hide. The trick is to feel
around carefully and grab them over their backs so they can't
snap you with their claws. And in the holes are all kinds of
sticky creatures and crabs, and the sport means plenty of cuts;
but the thrill of living in the strange element of the water

through your fingers is of such rare quality that no one can know what it's like unless he has tried it.

We caught eighty lobsters on this trip and had a lot of excitement trying to shoot a giant shark that seemed to feel he owned the place. Our catch of lobsters, however, was a loss. It was Ostrand's turn to cook, the next day, and being too lazy to go a mile or so for fresh water he used sea water. Try boiling lobsters in sea water if you want to taste the nastiest stuff a tongue has ever touched.

I was having such a good time that after seven months I had so completely forgotten my troubles that I wanted to live in this Paradise forever.

"But when my money is gone, what then?" I thought. "I'll never be fit for civilization again unless I get out at once," and so I packed up and embarked for New York.

I arrived in the middle of winter in time for the winter exhibition of the National Academy. Watrous, the secretary, invited me to the opening and, with my clothes pressed, I met the élite of the world once more. But I didn't feel at home in New York.

I had heard of Elbert Hubbard and wrote him a letter and received an invitation to visit him at East Aurora. And then one of those coincidences which have so often influenced my life kept me from accepting the invitation.

One day, after seeing the Aquarium, I stood in the middle of Battery Park debating what to do next when I noticed someone walking all around me. I looked up and the man yelled "Edstrom!" and I yelled "Fallstrom!" It was one of my old shipmates from the *Allegro*. He was employed as mechanic at a motor factory, and nothing would do but that I go home with him and meet his wife in Brooklyn. He lived on Henry Street, and the next day I moved from the hotel to his house. After a few days I had made up my mind what to do and had bought passage for France with the intention of returning to Firenze after having bought some much-needed tools in Paris.

For a time I had been tempted to go to Ottumwa. My father was still alive. My good sense, however, told me that it might spoil his romance about me and be a waste of time and money. And so I embarked for France without seeing him.

Meanwhile I had received a silver medal at the World's Fair in St. Louis.

XXVIII

CONQUEST

I CAME back to Firenze like a whirlwind, determined to make the world my oyster. I would become in truth a great sculptor! I had not the slightest understanding of the value of publicity or of influential connections. To me success and great fame required but one thing and that was actual merit and achievement. The winning of a silver medal in St. Louis meant nothing to me as a token of actual achievement. It was just an evidence that I had talent and that as soon as I could really organize my powers and my production, something of real magnitude would eventuate.

My marriage and my entanglements with women had been tragic hindrances, but I felt that I had learned my lesson and was determined that such hindrances should never occur again. Woman, with her crooked, illogical ways, was for the propagation of the species, an instrument of pleasure at best, but a creature any one who wanted to reach the heights must evade like death itself.

Now that I had overcome the flesh and the devil, nothing seemed impossible. With complete self-control and a body kept in fine fettle, I laughed at obstacles. Confidently I set to work on a composition which was to be the proof of my greatness, a super-monument which would astonish the world through its power and beauty.

In my "Lucifer" I had shown defiance of all the gods of convention. All my childhood and youth I had been a slave to the rules of others, to the religion of my grandmother, to the fear of Loke and Skam, to the religion of my father, to the factory whistle which woke me at five in the morning, to the rules laid down by the foremen, to the needs and comforts of Father and Mother. Later on in school I became a slave to the discipline of the school. Hardly had I gotten out of restrictions of the Academy before I had been enslaved in marriage with all the sticky demands of a great, wealthy and cultured family.

Now I was the "master of my fate, the captain of my soul." From the time when I had begun to save my wages and deny myself pleasures for books and culture, the preparation for a great effort had become a habit. To break through the walls of difficulty, to forge ahead in any manner, had become associated in my mind with pain. To get to Europe I had tramped and stoked coal; in the schools I had starved and been sick. Will power had become my god.

Perhaps I would have been more lenient with myself had I heard the story of the farmer who tried to wean his horse from eating, only to find it dead one morning just when it had almost learned to live without food.

On Via Manelli 79 I secured the same studio in which I had lived with Anna. I had planned in Cuba to begin a Spartan mode of life upon my arrival in Firenze, and I set about following my plan at once. As a beginning I built myself an ample wooden platform to sleep on instead of a bed. I did not even allow myself a mattress. For a pillow I used a block of wood. To give tension to my nerves I began taking strychnin. I gradually increased the dosage until I was taking five milligrams a day. In the morning before going to work I took a walk of many miles. Up in the hills north of Fiesole was a beautiful waterfall, and here I would take an ice-cold shower bath. With an almost unbelievable ferocity I gave my body such discipline as the most brutal of men would not have inflicted upon a stubborn mule.

I rebelled against my body's gluttony, its erotic impulses, its love of basking leisurely in the sunshine, its craving for wine, cognac and whisky. There was no form of physical indulgence which it seemed to me my body did not hanker for just a little more than did that of any one else. But now my will culture had at last won out and I could do just as I pleased. I Fletcherized my food and organized my work in a rigid, methodical manner. There were periods of weeks when I left off my Spartan mode of life quite deliberately, knowing that I would again, when I so decided, return to it. These periods of relaxation were inspired by my need of stimulus from association with others. My creative work could not continue without human contact.

Firenze is a city where the foreign population comes and goes. When I looked around for old friends who had lived there when I left, I found many of them gone; strange faces greeted me when I knocked at familiar doors.

One of the first that I inquired about was a famous Belgian painter and sculptor, whom I shall call Peysan, for I do not care to give his real name. The Papini group of intellectuals had taken him in and he had left a deep impression on me, both because of his great genius and because of the tragic circumstances his erratic nature had created. When I had last seen him he told me that he had run away from his wife in Paris because she forced him to get up every morning before five to go to mass. But when he left Paris he incidentally took with him his pretty niece, some ten or fifteen years younger than himself. She was such a stunning, ravishing creature and he such a grotesque apparition that I could never get accustomed to seeing these two lovers together. Peysan looked more like a woman than any man I have ever known. His looks were accentuated by a mincing feminine mannerism and the wearing of his hair so long that it fell down on his shoulders. At home he delighted in going around in a woman's dressing gown, and when garbed thus no one who did not know him would have taken him for anything but a woman.

From Papini I finally learned what had happened to him. It

was a strange story he told me. Some time after I had left, a grandson of one of France's most renowned authors had come to Firenze and fallen violently in love with Peysan's sweetheart. Making no headway in his suit so long as Peysan was around, he put into operation a truly Machiavellian plot to get rid of the obstacle to his desires. Because of Peysan's many eccentricities, he managed to get him confined in a private sanitarium and soon afterward left for parts unknown with the delectable niece. Peysan was not insane by any manner of means, and after a time he was allowed to visit Firenze with a keeper. One day he slipped away and managed to walk to Genoa. At Genoa he eked out a living by drawing caricatures of sailors, and as a revenge on the man who had stolen his mistress, he signed these drawings with the latter's name. After a period he met a kind French captain, who gave him passage to France and at last he got back to Paris and his wife.

One of the stories of Peysan I have always liked is of the time when he sold a painting for a considerable sum and used the money to carry out an eccentric desire of his: to cover the walls of his studio with red velvet. To this end he secured the most costly velvet he could find. When the bill was presented he found he did not have money enough to pay for it. To make up the sum he cut down some of the velvet from the walls and pawned it.

After a period in Paris Peysan in some manner got in contact with the great Tolstoy. This exalted man invited him to his estates in Russia, where he stayed for a couple of years. After his visit he returned to Paris with a collection of paintings and sculptures so good that several rooms at the Paris Salon were allowed for their exhibition.

The fine quality and almost phenomenal quantity of his production while with Tolstoy are evidence of what a distracted, almost crazy genius may produce under the protection of a kind and genial friend. What Tolstoy did for this abnormal and haunted genius stands out to me as evidence of the depth and reality of Tolstoy's religious status more than his writings. Around Tolstoy life became more abundant and finer in quality; his was a healing influence.

At this time I had a distinct leaning toward Catholicism. I studied quite carefully the writings of Ignatius Loyola and gained a profound admiration for his Spiritual Exercises. Among the Papini group of intellectuals was a very distinguished priest-editor of a Catholic periodical. I told him of my interest in the Jesuits and expressed a desire to make the acquaintance of some eminent Jesuit father. He advised me not to seek any spiritual inspiration from the Italian Jesuits, because, he said, they were not ardent and would be a great disappointment to me. He advised me rather to wait until I could meet English or German Jesuits, because they were really conversant with the Loyola theology and tradition.

This priest himself made no pretense of religious depth. He belonged to that class of Catholic priests who have a worldly and intellectual attitude toward the church. Their interest is not spiritual but institutional. They look upon the church as a great social machine necessary for the weal of humanity. Ready to advise and direct in practical matters, they try to avoid as much as possible the office of spiritual advisor.

Ignatius Loyola had, previous to his religious experiences, been a soldier. After being permanently crippled from a wound in battle, he crowded into his religious pursuits the same discipline, courage and aggressiveness that had been peculiar to his character as a warrior. The rational premises and the rigid logic in the unfoldment of his spiritual exercises, in addition to the militant discipline he advocated in the training of the will to be able to execute the findings of the intellect, appealed to my own aggressive attitude toward the problems that confronted me. However, my priest friend at this time turned me away from my plan to adopt the Saint Ignatius system of subjugating the flesh by the spirit.

Another distinguished Italian who almost turned me away
from my work was the learned mathematician, Professor X.
He was famous for his knowledge of the higher mathematics
of the ancient Chinese. I still remember some beautiful and
quaint problems he taught me from these ancient and poetic
scholars of the Flowery Kingdom. He took it upon himself
to give me lessons in mathematics two or three times a week.
Soon, however, as I found myself getting deep into this fas-.
cinating, fantastic world of abstract development, I forced myself out of it as I had years ago forced myself back to the main
issue when I had been on the verge of losing my art in the study
of anatomy. I dared not try to excel in more than one thing.

Papini at this time published a book, the title of which I have
forgotten, to which William James, founder of the Pragmatic
School of Philosophy, had written a short introduction. The
aim of the Papini group was to study life from all angles in a
pragmatic way. Occultism, spiritualism, politics, orthodox religion and art were all taken into consideration. I remember
visiting a Christian Science meeting with Papini. Although he
posed as an agnostic, he was constantly engaged in religious
speculations and under the skin was a childlike, superstitious
Italian.

The group seemed to me at times oppressively serious. Like
a butterfly tossed and carried hither and thither by every gust
of wind, delighting in its buoyancy and freedom, so had I
learned to love a contact with every form of experience, but
abhorred staying with any group as soon as I felt that I had
thoroughly explored their minds.

And so, leaving the almost fanatic atmosphere of the intellectuals, I sought contrasting thrills in the fashionable international society for which Firenze is one of the continental strong-
holds. Among the many international figures of this world that
I met, I made lasting friendships with two men. One was Silas
McBee, then editor of *The Churchman* in New York. He was
an intimate friend and advisor to President Theodore Roose-

velt. Roosevelt, during his administration, sent him on many confidential missions to the various rulers of the world. Traveling with McBee was another eminent and learned man, Dr. Bevan, the historian. These two men, with whom I motored in an erratic automobile over dangerous roads, and rode on bicycles from Firenze over the Apennines to Bologna, later became important influences in my life.

XXIX

NOW BEFORE I DIE

I BELONGED to a very delightful Anglo-American club
that met every Saturday in a small restaurant. It was the
duty of every member of the club to bring as guest any available visitor of genius or standing who had come to Florence.
The result of this arrangement was that not a week went by in
which some distinguished visitor was not our guest.

At one of these Saturday nights I met a well-known
American writer whom I shall call Jenkins for the purposes of
this story. He had written the life-story of a criminal and
numerous studies of the leading anarchists of the Nineties.

It was after a very pleasant luncheon with Jenkins in his villa
that suddenly the noise of the electric tram in which I was
riding, grinding against the rails, became a terrible roar like that
of a mighty waterfall. A dizziness came over me. Forms and
distances seemed vague and distorted. I knew that I was seriously ill, but in what way I could not tell. I found that I could
scarcely move, but with an extreme exertion of will power I
managed to get off the car and walk to my studio.

But once there, I wanted to be alone in my illness. I told
Fanny, the concierge, that I was going to a friend's house. A
few blocks away there lived an old Italian lady who had rooms
for rent. I had often rented rooms from her temporarily for
uses of various sorts, and trusted her completely. I stumbled
into her apartment and she helped me undress and got me into
bed, where I immediately lost consciousness. How long I was
ill I do not know. I remember only that when I woke I longed

for a cigaret, but when I tried to get it, I found that I could not move my right arm. For a long time I lay there trembling in a cold sweat as I tried to face the extent of the calamity which had overtaken me. A sculptor without the use of his right arm! A sentence of death would be as easy to bear.

At last I managed to get up and to a mirror where I saw a veritable skeleton looking at me. My face looked like a death's head. As I stood there gazing in horror at my own face, such terrible pain set in in my paralyzed arm and shoulder that I staggered back to bed, where I thought I would go crazy if I did not get relief.

An Italian physician who had been taking care of me came shortly after my return to consciousness and gave me an injection of morphine that eased the pain. For weeks nothing but these injections would give me relief. He told me that I had neuritis, and that with proper treatment and care I could be cured. But as week followed week my arm and shoulder began to atrophy until the deltoid muscle and all the upper shoulder muscles seemed to have completely dried up and the skin seemed stretched tightly over the bone.

Thiel had been told of my illness and he not only sent me ample funds but promised me everything I needed until I was well.

Jenkins came to see me every day, and no one ever could have been a more tender and considerate friend. As soon as I was able to get around he went with me up to Vallombrosa, the famous mountain resort a few hours from Firenze. I have already described the beautiful forests of Vallombrosa, where I had previously spent two happy weeks with Robert Barrett, and learned that dangerous method of eating invented by Fletcher.

When I had last seen this wonderful place the ground was covered with snow; now it was gaily decked with luxurious green grass and millions of gay, sweet-smelling wildflowers. I was languid from weakness and constant dosing with morphine, and crushed with discouragement as I thought of the empty future. But between the terrible attacks of pain I lived, for the most part, in an agreeable daze induced by the narcotic.

There were many charming ladies there, the most beautiful of whom was the Princess Colonna from Naples. She took a kindly interest in me and we had many short walks and long conversations together. One day, when I became quite fervent in a discussion, I noticed a queer expression as if she were trying hard to control her emotions. I remarked:

"My Italian is not very eloquent, perhaps."

"Oh, yes—quite. Perhaps sometimes too eloquent!"

I then realized that my vocabulary had been gained mostly from my models and workmen, and was not the suave polite language used in cultured society. She understood perfectly, and when she saw that I also understood we both laughed happily.

It was a sweet, bitter, fantastic period. Life seemed to float around me like an exquisite mellow dream and nothing was quite real except the spasms of excruciating pain. The local physician, instead of giving me larger doses of morphine, had begun gradually to reduce them. Besides the narcotic, I had a salve of belladonna to rub on my arm, but this did not seem to do much good. I also began to drink, more than ever before, wine, cognac and liqueurs.

Jenkins was a fine companion, his smile that of a genial Pan. I have never known any one who to the same degree had the natural sensuousness of a wild animal. I was very fond of him, and when he became interested in helping me with an autobiography I was pleased. I was a broken man and I had no hope of recovery, but I nevertheless enjoyed the drama of being down and out just as condemned murderers are known to have enjoyed the fame of their anticipated hanging. The autobiography was to be a swan song, a deep and unexpurgated confession, such as none before had dared to write, a revelation of myself written "now before I die."

Jenkins, in his story of a criminal, portrays a broken thief, a man no longer able to make good at his trade. He no doubt saw in me a broken artist who never again would be able to function.

Immediately upon our return to Firenze we started on the autobiography with a vengeance. And I, still dramatizing myself, still thinking of myself as one about to die, resolved to enjoy what life was left to me.

There was at this time, as always in Firenze, an interesting foreign colony of young artists, writers and scholars. Perhaps never before or after have I so freely indulged in delicious drinks and food and good society. Jenkins did all the work on the book—I only answered his questions. When I was not doing this, I was talking with friends, drinking, enjoying whatever pleasure came along. Just as the consumptives in Davos who had no hope of living were willing to risk their lives for a fleeting hour of happiness, so did I recklessly take without hesitance what life offered.

One of the many cultured and interesting men I knew in Firenze was Berenson, the great critic of Renaissance art. It was he who gathered for Mrs. Jack Gardner the great collection of Renaissance art which she gave to the City of Boston upon her death. I had many delightful quarrels with this clever, militant little fellow.

I remember in particular having dinner one night with him at his delightful villa in Settignano, when our discussion about Rembrandt ended in a noisy row. For Berenson there was only one great art period in the history of the world, and that was the Italian Renaissance. I do not remember all our bitter words, but I shall never forget his parting shot after I was half-way down to the outside portal of his garden. He stood in the doorway, allowing the light from the room to illuminate the path until I got out to the road, and then in a loud voice he sped me on my way with a last word.

"Remember, Rembrandt is a pig!"

With that he slammed the door so that I should not have the opportunity to throw back an answer.

The difference between my artist friends and the Papini group was that most of us now and then went on a debauch. I cherish fondly the memory of one night with Maurice Stern, the now famous artist, when we both became gorgeously drunk. Stern insisted that I was too far gone to go home alone, and that he absolutely could not allow me to risk life and safety without his protection. I just had to go home with him. After reeling along for a block or two, Stern came to the conclusion that drinking was a nasty, nasty business.

"Tish awful nasty, David," he said earnestly. "David, shay, when we get to the next corner under the light we'll do something!"

When we got there Stern outlined what we should do. He would count slowly to three, raise his walking stick, and when he brought it down we were to yell at the top of our voices a foul, unprintable word. We did, and at every corner we came to we repeated the act. The ritual was to make us remember forever that we were in a foul condition of swinery and we were never, never as long as we lived, to get drunk again.

Rollshofen, the famous, dignified Rollshofen, I remember with amusement. He had a magnificent studio and gave elaborate parties. He was a social lion striving to be an old master. With infinite labor he had tried to discover the technique of the old masters. He had learned that they painted with very small brushes, and this had inspired him to paint his huge, pretentious canvases with very small brushes, hoping, futilely, to get the same result. Fortunately he had married a lady of wealth and could indulge his notions without restraint.

Bit by bit I felt my strength returning and there came a day when I viewed with horror the things that I was telling Jenkins about myself. "It is all wrong," I said to myself, and began to worry about it, night and day.

Jenkins had in his home all the notes from my confessions. Only vaguely did I remember the details I had told him, and one day I asked him to bring all the notes for me to go over. He objected and said that it would be much better if I waited until the whole story of my life had been told, but at my insistence he yielded.

As I read here and there the notes he had made, I received a shock that it is impossible for me to describe. Even to this day the mere memory of those notes disturbs me and makes me blush with shame and humiliation. Not only had I told things about myself and others which I should never have let pass my lips, but I seemed to have enlarged and exaggerated circumstances and characteristics and even fabricated evil things about myself. I seemed to have reveled in the desire to make myself an unspeakable beast. The picture was that of a Caligula or Cæsar. The most exquisite experiences had been made to seem vulgar, trivial and uncouth.

In my art I believe most fervently in a truthful rendering of any one I model, but if I do not believe in idealization, neither do I believe in the accentuation of what is ugly, trivial, dirty and repugnant. Jenkins had pictured and synthesized what was tangible and clear to himself, but ignored what was essential and interesting to me.

I tried to work it out with him but we could not understand each other and could not agree. He was a skilful writer and I did not object to his picturing me in a manner that was not quite pleasing; I was eager to compromise with him. I wanted the book done. After two or three conferences, however, I realized that a compromise was impossible.

Suddenly I decided that the best thing I could do was to go to Paris, where, at a distance, I could reason things out. Taking the manuscript with me, I went.

I secured a studio on the Rue des Volontaires. In the same building I made the acquaintance of Frederic Lees, a well-known English journalist and writer, who wrote a great deal on scientific subjects. He knew most of the scientists in England and France, and was especially intimate with the president of the Pasteur Institute.

One day I took to him the notes Jenkins had written down from my dictation. I told him the whole story and said I was not in a mental state to decide rationally on the merits of the manuscript or my moral rights in the matter. In substance I put the matter to him in these words:

"You are an experienced writer of scientific matters and you are trained in cool, deliberate judgment. Take no consideration of what my feelings might be in this issue but give me an opinion as to the value of this material from a literary and scientific point of view."

Lees took several days to read the stuff and then asked me to come for his answer. We sat in his living room before an open fireplace and for a long time we were both silent. When he spoke his voice was full of concern and compassion.

"Edstrom," he said gently, "let me throw this mess on the fire right away. The stuff is all bunk, foul and valueless from any angle. Let us burn it now and forget all about it."

I looked at him gratefully.

"I would give anything I have in the world," I said, "if it had never been written, and if you think I am justified in burning it, nothing would please me more."

"All right, here it goes," he said, and threw the bunch of notes on the flames without waiting for me to change my mind.

If I could as easily have burned up the sense of having been violated, turned inside out, how happy I would have been! But a conviction that I had been mentally ravished, that another will than my own had stretched its hands into the delicate machinery of my brain and seemingly scraped the nerve fibers for stuff that should never have been brought to the level of consciousness, would not leave me.

What I had said or not said was not what mattered. What really mattered was that *anything* had been said which I would not have said freely and voluntarily. Was I a subject that any one could sway? Had I been hypnotized? Had I been hypnotized before by others? Had I run off to Cuba through suggestion and not of my own volition? Had I started out to be an artist through the influence of Schiewe and not through an inner and imperative urge from my own nature? Had I, who had begun my journey on earth under the terrifying influence of Odin, Loke and Skam, been a plaything of outside influences all through life, and not a strong, sovereign, proud male, courageous and self-determined, as I had believed myself to be?

XXX

TERROR

A FEW years before, when I had made my grotesque "Terror" I did not expect ever to find myself a model for it. Now I was in a state of fear more agonizing than my puny creation ever could express. My composition had been the result of cold observation of an artist friend, Ghiglia, a man of exceptionally sensitive and high-strung nerves. Ghiglia was afraid of ghosts and people and, observing his blanched cheeks and cringing movements even over a story, I analyzed the biological functions connected with fear.

When, with the great anthropologist Hirn, I studied the voluminous material on acute emotional reactions gathered by Charcot at the Salpêtrière Hospital for the insane, and found that the photographs taken by Charcot of girl subjects in acute fear showed, in general, the same movements as my grotesques, it thrilled me with pride.

Now I was afflicted with a terror similar to that of these poor girls in their hysterical attacks. The hysterics, however, were more blessed than I, because after the attack was gone they had no memory of their terror. My state of fear, however, had been created in much the same manner as theirs, that is, by a deep shock.

Some of the most characteristic hysterics had developed from the shock of violation by brutal men. It is not the shock of physical pain that creates hysteria. Any human being may stand the most prolonged and terrible anguish from physical pain without suffering permanent mental injury, but if there is a vio-

lation of the moral sensibilities that ruptures the inner consciousness of coordination, so that the central, determinate sense of
I am is violated, permanent injury may be done to the mental
health of an individual without even a scratch of the body.

"Had I been hypnotized or had I not been hypnotized?" was
the phantom of terror that haunted me night and day. My
terror told me that I would never have said the things I had
found in Jenkins' notes, save under hypnotism. Yet my good
sense told me if that had been the case I would never have been
able to pack my things, get out of Firenze and go to Paris.

As I began to feel better and the pain left me and I was able
to sleep without morphine, I became more and more self-
assertive. But an ague, a trembling, would seize me in the
middle of the day in the brightest sunlight. Just as a child in
the dark is seized with terror, so was I driven into these moods
at the slightest provocation. Ideas of persecution of every imaginable kind began to haunt me, and only my strong will
power made it possible to associate with others. I was mentally
more desperately ill than I had ever been physically.

One day I discovered that the boarding house connected with
the Pasteur Institute took in outside boarders. The price was
reasonable, and I thought that by living every day in the presence of great scientists, in the atmosphere of their work, I
might gain dignity of being and clarity of mind. And so I
moved in.

A great deal of the work at the Institute consisted of vivisec-
tion in its thousand and one phases. Across the yard from my
window were the stables where all the animals used in research
work were kept. All night long roosters would crow in a way
I thought no normal rooster could crow. Sometimes it seemed
that there were hens that cackled and crowed alternately. The
barking, moaning and whimpering of dogs was awful.

There were monkeys and cats screaming and yowling with an
apparent anguish beyond description. Cows, horses, guinea
pigs, squirrels, rats and mice! For hours I would sit at the

window listening, often trembling with terror, while the calm, serene moon bathed the buildings in a flood of cold light. The horrors which I felt and imagined were antagonized by the outward calm of the night. But still I sat and listened, seeking the terror of other creatures in a more awful state than mine.

One of the ideas of persecution that tortured me was an exaggeration of the degree to which my work had been plagiarized. Imagine a man who has had a chicken stolen and then begins to believe that he has had a hundred chickens stolen. From a hundred the number grows to be a thousand, until he believes he is a veritable fountain of wealth being tapped by sinister forces. I pictured half the world of lesser artists stealing the wealth of my genius.

Among several traits that saved me from going to pieces was my thorough artistic training. With a compass and square I had gained the ability to determine exactly the physical measurements of a body through the laws of geometry. Also I had a memory which was not only good but critically analytical, a memory and a sense of critical analysis which constantly challenged the imagination.

My ability to correct optimism and face facts now came to good use in my pessimistic state. Perhaps it was that, more than anything else, which saved me from complete oblivion. At last this system of elimination, from within myself, of what was unreal, brought me to the state of humility of a human worm. I crawled instead of walked. I would not trust myself to anything except the simplest kind of facts. If I joked or discussed any subject, it was with an air doubt and reserve instead of with my old self-assurance. I gave myself no credit for ability of judgment in any subtle or astute line of reasoning. From the most humble premise I began to reconstruct my personality along new lines.

In this mood I began to model my first statue after my illness. It illustrated, in a way, my desire regarding myself. Later on I called this piece of work "First Rhapsody," still

later, "Aspiration." At the time of its making I had no name
for it. The motive was simply an expression of the beginning
of my reconstruction, my method of resurrection. If I had
been an architect I might have built a pyramid. The first
"Aspiration" had the feeling of a pyramid in its construction.

Lees, in seeing the first model, said: "Why haven't you made
any feet on the statue?"

At first this gave me a shock, and then I replied:

"She has no feet; they are covered with the drapery. Showing the feet would take away what I mean."

It was the line-on-line building up into a mood of resurrection, ascension, a movement upward from a positive, solid beginning.

In years to come I was to make several models of the idea,
but never have I been able to achieve the greatness that I
touched in the first faltering, naive creation by which I saved
my own reason. It was a prayer by one who no longer dared
to believe himself. It was a prayer, saying in sculpture only
one thing: "From the ground I aspire upward." Over and
over again in the lines and expression of this model is repeated:
"Upward, upward—I move upward. The sun is warm. The
sun gives light. I open my arms, my hands, my heart to that
which is from above. I am on the ground. I am of the earth.
I am a worm. I believe only in the earth. One is one. One
and one are two. I will not let myself aspire more than that.
One and one are two. Of two one looks upward. There is an
above. I love thee, O Sun-and-Rain, I, the one on the ground.
I turn myself toward thee, O Sun-and-Rain that quickeneth all
things."

At the time I was not conscious of the fact that my "Aspiration" had the same movement, the same general position as my
"Soul Triumphant," the figure that I had seen in the coal
bunker on the *Allegro* and later on sketched while a student at
the Academy. There was one primary difference. The figure

I had seen in the coal bunker was a male figure. My "Aspiration" was the figure of a woman.

And then came one of the greatest shocks of the entire period of my collapse. My brother-in-law was at this time working as clerk for a clothing man named Olson in Minneapolis, Minnesota. This chap Olson, during a visit to Paris, called on me. He was very courteous and invited me out with him on several occasions. After his return to America I received a letter from my niece in Uarda, telling me that Olson would give me a job at fifteen dollars a week to travel around in the country among the farmers and take orders for clothing. This letter, as nothing else had done, brought me to a full realization of what a complete failure I seemed to others. This kindly man could not see in me even material for a clerk in his store, but I would do to travel among the farmers. The great David Edstrom was indeed brought down from the heights.

Close on the heels of this offer, Anna secured a divorce from me on the ground of desertion.

XXXI

PARIS IS KIND

NO city, no place in the world, is so kind to the artist as is Paris. Surely I would have perished had I not gone to Paris in the hour of my great debasement and sickness. At Rue Belloni No. 4, near the Montparnasse Station, I rented a studio with a sleeping balcony. Here I again began to struggle upward. I will not tell of the many haunting terrors that still pursued me, but rather of the kindness of Paris that soothed and comforted me.

Sick or well, I have always had a love for taking walks as long as my time or strength permitted. In Paris I made it a habit to walk out the Boulevard Pasteur and the Invalides until I came to the Alexander Bridge. On the Boulevard Pasteur, not far from my studio, an old couple ran a small restaurant, which I passed every day, and here I gradually began to take my meals. Sometimes, however, I would eat at other places. When this happened, the old lady and gentleman seemed as concerned over my unannounced absence as if I had been their son. At last, thinking they had found the reason for my non-appearance, they talked to me about it. After a number of typical French compliments and polite introductions to the momentous question they were about to enter into with me. they came to the point.

"Monsieur Rodin, when he was a poor young man, used to take his meals with us," they said. "Sometimes—isn't it droll? —he would not have any money, but what did that matter? He was our friend and customer, so we said: 'Never mind, mon-

sieur, when you make the sale then you pay for the meals.'
Sometimes it was one day, sometimes two or three, yes, sometimes it was many weeks, and then he would make the sale and
he would pay and we would drink the champagne and be very
happy together. Yes, and Monsieur Bourdelle—with him it
was the same way. It would be a day, two days, three, or perhaps many, many weeks, and then he would make the sale and
we would always drink the champagne and be very happy together. Do not take it ill, monsieur, or misunderstand, because
we have the grand love for the arts, so if monsieur has not the
silver for a day, two days, three, or for the many weeks, what
does it matter with friends and lovers of the art? We give the
food and when monsieur makes the sale he pays us, we drink
the champagne and become happy together. Is it not so?"

Dozens of similar stories could be told of the kindness of the
people of Paris to their artists.

In Firenze I had met Leo and Gertrude Stein through Jenkins, who, with Mike and Sarah Stein, were the first protag-
onists of Matisse and other modernists. This was before Gertrude Stein had gained international fame through her modernistic writing. The Steins kept open house for all writers, musicians and artists. I do not suppose Gertrude could guess how
many times I came into their large studio with my nerves raw
with anguish and gained relief at just seeing her, stolid, fat,
Buddha-like, sitting in a corner with a grin on her face. Gertrude Stein seemed to be fermenting inside all the time with
some mirthful idea. Her voice had a deep contralto quality
unlike any voice I've ever heard. She was the only out-and-
out fat woman whose every ounce of avoirdupois seemed precious and lovable. Do not misunderstand me—I did not have
any feeling of romantic love for her. One did not fall in love
with Gertrude Stein; at least I never heard of any one doing so.

Leo Stein was bewhiskered and had a never-satisfied question
mark in his expression. I found the whole family most friendly
and charming, but Gertrude alone had any unusual degree of

intelligence. Even at this time she amused herself with writing short sketches of her friends. The one she wrote about me was not very pleasing to my vanity. I cannot remember the whole content of it nor adequately imitate her style, but it went something like this:

"He was thin, then he became fat, and then thin. He became very, very fat and he felt—yes, he felt. He became thin, he became fat, and he always felt very deeply."

Some hair-trigger condition of my glandular system caused the changes in my weight. I would fall in love and get thin; fall out and get fat—and then I always felt—felt.

Gertrude was an impressionist—or should I say expressionist? However, it was good for my soul to be near a life without too much subtlety. The modernist art, though to the layman it might seem transcendental, is in fact the most materialistic of all art in the history of mankind. It springs from experimental study and analysis of nature, not from dreaming or fabulation. There is less imagination about modernistic art than about any of the schools preceding it. If a Picasso shows a flare of fancy he juggles with the most inane and childish facts that he has seen and observed, not with allegorical conceptions or abstract philosophical musings or even historical personages. The modernists are of the earth earthy and in the same boat with the modern scientists. Picasso, Nagelman, Matisse, and all the followers of modernism passed in and out of the Stein homes as if they had been members of the two households.

Although I found great comfort and heartsease with the Steins I could never unburden my fears or anguish to them. I was as lonely as if I had been the man in the moon. The outward, material things of life were sweet enough, but inside of me was a core of terror and foretaste of doom. I think it was this loneliness which led me to a study of palmistry.

Sarah Stein dabbled in it and awakened my interest in the art. I took the study quite seriously and haunted all the old bookshops on the Seine and elsewhere to gather together a library on the subject. At last I had quite a collection of books and started to study with great concentration. When I had absorbed all the theoretical knowledge I could find I began to try it out.

Demi-mondaines are almost always addicts to fortune-telling and so I went to one of the cafés frequented by the better class and in a day I was famous. I charged nothing for a reading— I was only curious to see whether I could read palms successfully. For a few weeks I thought it was fine to be called on any time of the night or day by some frantic man or woman, from the highest to the lowest, for advice. People of distinction would blurt out things about themselves that I don't believe they'd tell to their doctor or confessor—and I was even more astounded than they over my ability to find truths in their palms. I will give an example no more unusual than a score of others.

I was at a memorial banquet given to the great epic poet of Finland, Runeberg. After all the speeches were over, most of the guests lingered on, talking and drinking, and a number surrounded me insisting that I tell them something. "Tell me, tell me," was the thing that rang in my ears wherever I went. Among those who stuck their hands in front of me was a charming, to me unknown, young woman. I looked at her hand and spoke objectively.

"A terrible tragedy—a murder has seared your soul," I said, "and cast gloom over your life."

At once there burst forth a stream of angry protestations against me.

"You know who she is and you have the tactlessness to say a thing like that," was one of the accusations flung at me. In a gentle voice the lady herself took up my defense.

"He does not know me—he is a fine truthful man—please let him go on. I know he can help me."

The lady was Miss Schauman, sister of young Schauman, who one day on the Senate stairs at Helsingfors shot Bobrikoff, the hated Governor of Finland, and then killed himself. The Czar, as was the custom in those barbaric days, had instituted a perfect orgy of revenge on the family and its friends, but Miss Schauman had escaped to Paris. I knew nothing about the whole affair except what I had read in the papers, and I did not know who she was when I read her hand. The whole story was written in the lines of her palm.

At last I became so hounded with people waking me up at all times of the night and stopping me on the street or pushing themselves into my studio, that I quit the whole business. It was also perturbing to see tragedies ahead—unmerited rewards and then sometimes a hodge-podge of facts which I could not understand. Great concentration was necessary and constant practise to get good results. I do not believe one person in a million has the ability to read a hand rationally, and then even with the most skilful it is a hit-or-miss affair.

One evening I read the hand of a friend, and it showed death within a few months so absolutely that it made me very unhappy. Luckily I did not have the courage to tell him the bad news, because this man is still alive—healthy, wealthy, and the father of many children. Something in that hand I could not understand counterbalanced every bad sign there. The same thing happens with doctors in their diagnoses—men who should, according to all the laws of biology, die, do not always die.

Henning Berger, the late Swedish writer, in a book dealing with Paris, describes me somewhat as follows: "A Swedish-American sculptor is sitting in a corner telling fortunes in a high falsetto voice."

One day, while calling at the Steins, I met Jenkins there. What my face showed I don't know, but within I felt wilted and sick at heart. Our conversation was on the surface pleasant enough and we did not refer to my autobiography at all.

In a few days, however, I was told by Gertrude that he had written a book about me. She had read the manuscript. I do not remember her comment on it, but I do remember that she told me she had persuaded him not to publish it. In a way it acted like a terrible whiplash on me. I felt just as I did over my first marriage, a sense of shame and self-condemnation for being a fool.

Fortunately I did not at this time get a chance to read Jenkins' manuscript about me and was thus blessedly in ignorance of the ghastly picture he had painted of me. Later I read it to my infinite horror.

He had described me as "a man with a huge face, with two small, restless eyes, the lids of which had that curious fall at the corners denoting an impaired nervous system often resulting in what is loosely called criminal tendencies. His flabby cheeks had a two-days' growth of scanty beard—pale in color, thin, but not so intended, apparently, by nature. It seemed as though it constituted the remains of a once luxurious growth. His head was covered with hair, and yet the effect was strangely one of baldness. It seemed as if that head must once have had something far richer in hirsute development. As he stood, with his hand outstretched, his big frame seemed like the trunk of a tree that had been struck by lightning. As he took a step in advance there was a stiffness, a deadness, in the expression of his heavy lips."

In the exaggerated state of my sensitiveness, even when I finally read this, it seemed horrible to me beyond words. And had I seen it at the time when it was written, a time during which I was close to the edge of madness anyway, I think it would have completely broken me. I am convinced that I owe my life, whatever it may be worth, to Gertrude Stein for having kept the manuscript out of my hands.

XXXII

THE FOURTH DIMENSION

FOR a snail all existence is length and breadth. To him the mystery of mysteries must be height. He knows nothing of a third dimension. If he were able to believe in a supreme being he would undoubtedly conceive one with the power to deliver him from the limitations of his two-dimensional world. And similarly human beings, having risen a step higher than the snail, seek a four-dimensional existence. Our various approaches to God are largely inspired by a desire to escape the limitations of time and space in what the religious of all times have called eternal life. And I, feeling that I had fallen as low as a snail, yet retaining that human aspiration which would not let me die or quite lose hope, turned to religious thought for help.

I have defined Firenze as the City of our Lady; Paris might be defined as the city of all gods. Here there is a god for every race, every individual. And I needed God in a new form, one in which I had not lost faith—a dream of the miraculous in new dress. In my walks to the Alexander Bridge I found such a god on the western bridgehead—a large statue of Pallas Athene, which gently began to supply that need.

One day in looking at it I remembered the legend of how this goddess saved Ulysses, also that Orestes, when he was pursued by the Furies, was saved by Pallas Athene, and I began to pray to the statue:

"Oh, goddess of wisdom, thou that knowest all things, is there not some sweet subtle power that could restore my arm and give me again power to work and create? I am through with all my foolishness and wickedness and violence. Oh, serene and all-wise lady of wisdom, give me a revelation which will tell me what to do. Lead me the right way to health and freedom. I adore life and every creeping thing on earth. Not even in my greatest pain have I wanted to die. I am thoroughly humble. Give me one more chance."

I made it a habit to walk down to Pallas Athene every morning. I invented scores of subtle and beautiful prayers, in fact used all the ingenuity and cleverness I was capable of to prove to her that I was worthy of another chance.

In the height of inspiration I had often touched upon the miraculous in my art, finding myself, without explanation, in a state of mind so lucid that I could see a piece of work I was doing as a whole, a unit from below, above, back and front at the same time. It is a state of mind impossible for any one but a sculptor who has experienced it to understand.

If there is a miraculous power in sculpture, why should there not be an actual power in all things that might even heal the sick and the poor? I mused.

And then, without my knowing that it was happening, my prayers seemed to be heard and I entered into the way of healing.

At the studio of Leo and Gertrude Stein I heard a discussion one evening concerning a series of articles in *McClure's Magazine* about Mrs. Mary Baker Eddy. The articles were the source of great merriment and disparaging criticism by the various persons in the studio. I remembered that I had attended a Christian Science meeting with Giovanni Papini in Florence, Italy, and that we found it at the time both ludicrous and boresome.

But that had been before my illness. Extreme and bitter ridicule has always stimulated my interest in the subject ridiculed. From experience I had found that such ridicule seldom occurred except with reference to persons who are worth knowing.

That evening when I departed from the Steins' studio I had with me all the back numbers of *McClure's* which contained the series of articles, and the study of these was my introduction to Christian Science, which was from then on to play such an important rôle in my life.

With a paralyzed arm and engulfed in the gloom of a shattered nervous system I was grasping at straws to be saved from oblivion. After reading the articles, which reeked with contempt, I was converted much more deeply than I could have been by any kind of praise of Mrs. Eddy. I saw before me this hysterical, middle-aged woman struggling down lonely lanes carrying her pitiful belongings, an object of laughter as she told of her wonderful revelation. When openly abused she tossed her head in defiance with a "You'll see one of these days!" However, as in the time of Jesus, simple-minded people here and there, engulfed by despair, had tried her cure and were helped.

Moved to believe, I hunted up a practitioner and happened to get a Miss B., who was one of the most stupid and superstitious old maids I have ever met. However, if you are dying from thirst you do not refuse a drink because the saving angel has a wart on her nose. I read Mrs. Eddy's writings, I attended church and went for treatments, but I received no aid. Nevertheless, I still believed the principle of the doctrine and was sure that sooner or later there would be results.

I had a friend in Paris, a young Swedish nobleman and artist named Gyllenhammar. He had lived in Paris so long that he had acquired the Frenchman's exquisite cynicism toward things unproved. He gibed me in a friendly way about my enthusiasm for the new doctrine and one day he suggested satirically:

"Why don't you try your Christian Science on Whisky Bill?"

Few people in the Quarter knew Bill's real name. At the time Gyllenhammar told me of him, Bill was in the throes of delirium tremens and was about to be sent to an asylum again. He was close to middle-age and, as he himself declared proudly, he had been nine times in asylums for the insane from drink. Years before coming to Paris he had been a famous illustrator and at one time had gained national fame in America through a painting entitled "Cleopatra Coming Out of the Bath." This fame, however, did not result from any excellence of the painting, but grew out of the fact that it had hung in the Anheuser-Busch Saloon in St. Louis and Carry Nation in one of her crusades had thrown a brickbat right through the middle of Cleopatra's beautiful nude body. A promoter bought the mutilated painting and exhibited it all over America.

Bill was under the control of a guardian. His wealthy family in Texas sent a monthly allowance to the Reverend Mr. Van Winkle, Rector of St. Luke's Chapel in Paris, to pay for Bill's board, rent and clothes. For drinks Bill borrowed "funds," as we called money in the Quarter.

Gyllenhammar's suggestion that I try Christian Science on this unregenerate seemed a good one. It occurred to me, regardless of any missionary impulse, that if I could help Bill perhaps I might also be helped. I had often before found that by helping others in more material matters I had found help in my own problems.

Without delay, and notwithstanding the fact that we were only casually acquainted, I went that very day to Bill's studio.

The place was filthy beyond description and I had to fight an overwhelming nausea from the stench that met me there. I found my patient lying motionless on his bed. Sores and eruptions covered his face. His eyes, wide open in a fixed stare of terror, seemed bloody from inflammation. There were black and blue spots here and there where he had injured himself.

I had been there only a few minutes when the Reverend Mr. Van Winkle arrived with two husky attendants from an asylum to take Bill away. I pleaded fervently with Van Winkle to let me try to help the poor fellow. He objected, but at last my ardor won out and his own faith in the power of God to heal was touched. After I had promised him most solemnly not to leave my patient night or day until he was well, he departed with a "God bless you." The men with him shrugged their shoulders contemptuously, thus expressing their opinion of vacillating foreigners.

For twelve nights and days I never left Bill for a moment. At night I slept on the floor at his side, sometimes holding his hands by the hour and helping him to fight the terrors that beset him. As soon as he was able to walk about I took him to my practitioner, the silly Miss B. She gave him one look and refused to take the case. She was afraid and passed me on to the famous singing teacher, C. C. Clark, who was an ardent Christian Scientist. Clark said:

"There is only one person who can help him, and that is Miss Downer."

Accordingly we went to Miss Downer, and at once, without a moment's hesitation, she agreed to take the case.

And thus I met Cora Downer, by far the most interesting woman I have ever known. Both her parents were born in County Cork, Ireland. Her mother, born a Raymond, was related to such famous families as the Beresfords, Donegals and Wyndenhams. Her father was a distiller and manufacturer in Dubuque, Iowa, at the time of Cora's birth. As a child she was healed by Christian Science and at fifteen years of age became a healer in the sect. Later on she studied with Kimball, one of the greatest men in the organization. At the time I met her, on the occasion of the Whisky Bill episode, she had an international reputation among all classes of society. She numbered her students by the hundreds and she had both healed and taught members of aristocracy, and great leaders in the financial world both in America and Europe. Several well-known physicians were her students and patients. She was a woman of unusual culture in all lines.

As soon as I saw her I was thrilled. She was beautifully gowned and her surroundings precious and exquisite. Well-chosen paintings hung on her walls and every piece of furniture was a masterpiece of ancient workmanship. A profusion of flowers arranged with taste gave her home an air of brightness and joy. I fell in love with her at first sight.

Every day I took Whisky Bill to her home, and under her treatments he improved rapidly. Never have I seen such a transformation. Soon there emerged one of the sweetest personalities I have ever known. He became careful about his appearance, swept and cleaned up his studio and began to work. His smile had a whimsical sweetness of rare charm. The miracle had happened. He was completely and permanently healed and is today one of the world's most famous painters. Just as at the time I did not know his real name, so but very few in his circle of admirers remember now that at one time he was known in Paris as Whisky Bill.

One day when I went to see Cora Downer with Bill I took with me three pieces of my own work. I told her I also was in great need of help and asked her if she would not give me a few treatments in consideration of these objects of my art. They were of a symbolic nature, and, encouraged by her immediate interest in them, I expatiated upon their meaning. The first of them I described as "A Prayer in Sculpture—a movement outward and upward to connect, touch, and affiliate with a greater power."

"This little group of two figures," I continued, describing the second object, "is my conception of love, which I call 'Clouds.' Just as two clouds on different air currents suddenly merge, so the two figures, a boy and a girl, swaying like clouds, meet for a moment or for a lifetime in the vault of eternity.

"This other figure," I said, "is my Sphinx. It combines the cruel mechanistic existence of life such as Time with organic life, circumscribing all life by mathematical limitations. All the warmth and joy of organic life seem to be measured and ordered within a rigid mathematical law of limitations. The heavenly bodies themselves move through space under irrevocable laws and the span of human life and endeavor is likewise circumscribed. In the forms of my Sphinx I show the cruel outlines of the circle, geometrical angles and the ellipse, yet within these forms there breathes forth the sensuousness of organic life. To me this is the great riddle, the sphinx of existence, that the immutable laws of geometry govern the transient fragrance of the rose, the joy of youth, and the recurrence of the seasons here and with the stars."

"I'll help you," she replied; "be quiet; I'll give you a treatment now."

Just as an artist in drawing a straight line has pictured in his mind the perfect straight line metaphysically, so Mrs. Eddy instructs the seeker after truth to understand man as being perfect in the one Mind. Now there may be a million straight lines drawn by a million different beings, in stone, on paper, scratched on the surface of a diamond, cut in wood, etc., but none of these lines can be perfect. The only perfectly straight line in existence is the one line, the metaphysical line, in Mind. The same applies to figures—there is only one one, there is only one two, etc. Such a complicated thing as a human being we cannot visualize as perfect, but we can declare that in the one universal Mind man is conceived perfect, and it is the holding of this thought that effectuates the healing.

These are truths which are evident in art. The best artist is he who is able to hold his mental picture so vividly that it embodies itself in the material symbol he draws, paints or models; and the most successful healer is he who so persistently and firmly holds the thought that man in nature is perfect, that the evidence of fever, ill-smelling sores, or other evidences of disease do not overwhelm him. The patient's fear and belief of illness are then also eliminated and hope springs forth in the same way as a promise of financial aid by a wealthy man brings hope and courage to an impoverished individual. However, only practise can give a real understanding of the subject, just as the theory of swimming is not fully understood until one has actually learned how to swim in practise.

Day after day I went to her for treatments. At first I noticed no change, but bit by bit I took up my work again and suddenly one day I found myself working quite freely with my right arm. It was no longer paralyzed! How long I had been working with it I don't know. I had been so interested in my work that I had gone ahead naturally without noticing that I was able to use both arms as I had in the past. No words can describe my joy or my gratitude to Cora Downer. I adored her, with a sort of reverence I had never accorded a woman before.

I plunged into my work again. Never have I had greater vigor, intensity, and persistence than I developed in that period which followed recovery from my paralysis. I produced many new works and, fired by my happiness at what seemed to me almost a return from the dead, and a new understanding of many things which had come out of my knowledge of Christian Science, I opened a school of sculpture. In my teaching I used a great many of the methods of Christian Science.

My school was a success at once and gained some little fame. I charged high tuition fees and had as pupils a number of men who were quite well established before coming to me. A well-known German sculptor, whose name I have forgotten, came for private lessons, paying me ten dollars for a half hour's instruction, which was a great deal for that time in Paris. Elof Kruger, a grandson of old Oom Paul Kruger, President of the Transvaal, was one of my pupils. After six months' study the Salon accepted a piece of his sculpture, and he had never worked at any form of art previously. It was a unique case, as Elof did not have exceptional talent. A nephew of the great Russian sculptor Antakolsky, named Wolkewisky, was in one of my classes.

I awakened such enthusiasm in my students that often I

found them waiting impatiently at the school a half-hour before time, in the hope of getting in earlier.   Their intensity of
interest and their jealousy of one another were at times exhaust-
ing to me, because I had to devise means of holding them back
instead of urging them on.   My method was as follows:

I never corrected a fault, but would sit down in front of the
model of the student and on a piece of paper draw from the
live model—bits here and there in any old fashion, talking all
the time.

"Now let's imagine I am a caterpillar crawling over the form,
like this," I would say.   And I'd draw a line such as the caterpillar might make.   Or, "Let's imagine I am a sled and am slid-
ing down a slope the same steepness as that back; or we might
think of that head as a melon and feel it with both hands like
this"; and I'd rapidly draw a melon.   "Or we might imagine
we had no lead pencil," and I'd tear out a silhouette of the
figure.   After a few minutes the pupil would be moving, stamp-
ing and sighing behind me, restless to get to work.   By that
time he would have seen the faults in his model in his own way
—and the next day the work would be much further advanced
than if I'd helped him by calling his attention to defects in his
model.

The most difficult thing, when I had developed a degree of
originality in a pupil, was to get him to give real value to his
work.   Few persons have the moral or intellectual courage to
believe in themselves.   They want something outside of themselves to cheer for.   It is cowardice that makes imitators, not
necessity.   Most persons could be original if they had the courage.   The combativeness of the social enemy, the criminal, who
must have an opponent, is the same mental cowardice that
makes Mrs. Grundy a fool.   Both are afraid to use their intel-
ligences as lights on their way.

At this period Matisse, whom I knew very well, also had a
school and was driven to distraction because he couldn't keep his
pupils from imitating his work.   He had been a teacher of

anatomy under the great Richet at the Beaux Arts Academy and was thoroughly trained in the academic method of teaching. But his pupils did not come to him to learn but to imitate. Matisse eventually gave up his school in disgust.

"They think they understand me, and they don't even know anatomy," he wailed, rolling his eyes in distraction.

I myself went for awhile to the Academy Colarossi to draw under Steinlen, one of the very best of modern teachers in drawing. In his class were many American illustrators of great skill; they had developed styles of their own, but under Steinlen they worked up to greater skill. He was a great teacher because he could appraise a pupil's merits and weaknesses from the pupil's own point of view, and help him find himself. I also went to classes under Injalbert to correct certain habits in my modeling. For a period I attended sketch classes in company with Matisse.

In Paris you find the greatest and most famous artists in the world studying side by side not only with their peers, but with the veriest beginners. In Paris artists never boast, as they do in America, that they are "finished masters." I've seen some of the greatest of them tear their hair and wail like children because "it is so difficult to get things right!"

In the spring of 1908 I had a number of pieces at the Independent Salon. Apollinaire, the great French critic, gave me a few complimentary lines in his paper on my exhibit. Here I exhibited a cubistic head, and I am sure it was the first cubistic piece of sculpture exhibited in Paris. My "Sphinx," made in 1900, contained an inkling of the same rhythm of form, but was more traditional. Cézanne is the only artist who had deeply felt the cubistic approach to form at this time. No modern artist, except Bourdelle, has to my mind reached his intensity in form. In developing plastic form through the medium of color units, Matisse is greater.

I believe it was in 1908, at the Independent Salon, that I saw one of the most tragic and dramatic pieces of art I'd ever seen.

It was a statue of Christ on the cross. The only, to me, truly dramatic crucifixion I had ever encountered before was Mantegna's "Crucifixion" at the Louvre. Mantegna gave drama to the event by showing the primitive greed and stupidity of the Roman soldiers as they threw dice for the mantle of our Lord. They were so absorbed in their game that they had not a thought about the job just completed. It was only routine— this business of crucifying a man. Now the to me unknown artist of the "Crucifixion" in the Independent Salon arrived at dramatic rendering in another manner. At the foot of the cross, beneath the crucified Lord, he had strewn broken bottles, bits of rusty wire, nails, rags and refuse of all kinds, such as might be found in an alley or a city dump. Almost all other crucifixions have the taint of church snobbishness, so that a crucifixion becomes something elegant, dignified and ritualistic. This man's Christ was a humble corpse.

Bourdelle, who at this time had not reached great fame, was a very good friend of mine. I considered him the greatest sculptor in the world, and since then the leading critics have accorded him the same rating. But at this time he was struggling desperately to make a living through his art for himself and family. One day while I was working on a portrait bust of a Mr. F., a rich American, a Mr. X, one of the great steel masters from Pittsburgh, who was a friend of my sitter, came to watch me work. During the sitting Mr. X happened to mention that he was going to buy $100,000 worth of Rodin sculptures for his private gallery in Pittsburgh. At once I saw an opportunity to help my friend Bourdelle. I succeeded in getting the steel magnate to accompany me to Bourdelle's studio a few days later. At the time Bourdelle had several small models and studies for a figure of Hercules pulling a bow, which I believed would some day be considered the greatest piece of sculpture of modern times. This figure I praised with all the eloquence I could command and told Mr. X that if he bought a copy it would in a few years be worth perhaps a hundred times more than the sum for which he could now purchase it. Bourdelle was so poor that a thousand dollars would have seemed a fortune to him. Mr. X laughed scornfully at my fervor and with a smug attitude, implying that he was from Missouri and could not be taken in, left the studio with arrogant rudeness.

Both before and after this disappointing episode I told Bourdelle over and over again, during a period of months, that if he would execute his Hercules in heroic size for the Salon it would make a great sensation. A few years later he did so and almost overnight he became world-famous. To me Bourdelle's Hercules surpasses anything made by Rodin—or by any other sculptor, for that matter, since the time of Phidias.

Thus, through healing thought, through work, through learning anew and teaching, I came back into life.

XXXIII

PALLAS ATHENE

DURING all this time I had been seeing Cora Downer every day. But my relationship with her was different from that which I had known with any other woman. Through her influence and Christian Science I had regained my health and will to live and work. In this new life she had given me the most precious gift I had ever received from any one. I held her in the deepest awe, loved her with a kind of worshiping love I had never accorded any other woman. In the summer of 1908 I asked her to marry me, and she consented; but it was not until a week after this that I dared to kiss her for the first time.

After we had become engaged I became an Orlando Furioso in my work and ambitions. I was like a new-made man, one who could not be stopped by any difficulties. By the spring of 1909 I had made enough new statues to warrant the acceptance of an invitation to give a one-man show with the Allied Artists in London. On the spur of the moment, as I was preparing to leave for London, I proposed to Cora that she accompany me and that we get married during my exhibition. We had become so in need of seeing each other every day that she yielded readily to my entreaty.

The exhibition was a success. Among the things I sold was a small bronze to Whitelaw Reid, our Ambassador to the Court of St. James's at the time. But as a whole I neglected the affair in order to be with Cora, whom I married immediately upon our reaching London.   We played around and let the world go hang.

Returning to Paris, we established ourselves on the Quai de Béthune on the Isle St. Louis.   The old palace in which we rented an apartment was supposed to have been the one-time home of Richelieu.   It was one of the quaintest and most beautiful old houses in Paris, and Cora furnished the whole apartment in Louis XIII antiques.   We bought the lease to our home from the French Minister of Foreign Affairs, Pichon.   The apartment was equipped with a bath, which was very unusual for a French home, a fact vividly illustrated by a letter we received from Madame Pichon.   In this letter she informed us that she had installed the bath herself and that it did not go with the apartment, for which reason she wanted us to pay for it.   She concluded her letter with: "You must not consider the price exorbitant, because, although the bath is two years old, it has only been used twice and is as good as new."

In Paris it seemed that a bath was something quite serious and dangerous, not to be indulged in promiscuously nor with impunity.   When a French doctor has given up all hope for a patient he sometimes prescribes a bath as a last resort, apparently believing that it will kill or cure.   Professional bath attendants on huge vans carry bathtubs and all the needed paraphernalia to the patients' homes and give baths in accordance with the doctor's prescriptions.   Drafts and bathing are dangers the Frenchman avoids if possible.   Girls brought up in convents are taught that it is sinful, when engaged in their ablutions, to expose the whole body at one time, even when alone.   This was exemplified in a famous French divorce suit in which a well-known Prince sued his wife for separation on the ground that she refused to bathe.   In her defense she sought to justify this refusal on the basis of religious scruples, the details of which were given in court to the amusement and glee of the public in general.

Both I and the world at large believed my wife to be a lady

of great wealth. She told me that her income, as soon as certain affairs of hers were concluded, would be between fifty and one hundred thousand dollars a year. Her beautiful gowns, the magnificence of the old authentic antiques with which she furnished our home, and the proud dignity and self-assurance of her bearing all combined to suggest great wealth and standing.

As my marriage became publicized, the rumors of her wealth grew. In Sweden it was reported that she owned a palace on the Place de la Concorde and was worth a hundred million dollars. My mail brought me scores of begging letters—some from people I knew and many from others of whom I had never heard. One individual whom I had considered a friend even tried to blackmail me. He wrote me a letter referring to an escapade we had indulged in together and ending with a request for a loan. I answered him by going into still more picturesque details of our adventure, and this letter fell into his own wife's hands and made him no end of trouble. I showed both letters to Cora and she thought the matter a huge joke.

We were extremely happy for a time. I remember sitting with her in front of our old open fireplace, talking by the hour. She was the best-read person, as well as the most brilliant conversationalist, I have ever known; not a continuous talker, but witty and full of information and fancy. She was also a wonderful listener, and those who had sensitiveness and intelligence expanded and were at their best with her. She was to me the incarnation of Pallas Athene. No words can express the depth and intensity of my devotion to her. Everything I had ever imagined of virtue in any woman I found more rich and more wonderful as a reality in her.

But under her self-control and dignity, her charm, culture and learning, there throbbed a crazy Celtic heart, unable to reason or act logically in practical and worldly matters. Her good income as a practitioner and teacher, together with an inheritance of about ten thousand dollars, combined with her aristocratic bearing, had made her the victim of a ruthless

schemer and promoter, a certain Count de X. To him, in response to promises of great wealth, had gone her inheritance,
her earnings and over a hundred thousand dollars she had
borrowed from wealthy patients and students.

My discovery of this situation was a tremendous shock to me.
As an adoring lover I felt that she was a victim to be pitied and
commiserated, but as a narrow-minded peasant I regarded her
as an inexcusable sucker and gambler. A large dressmaking
establishment in Paris had bills against her running into five
figures. She had kept things going by borrowing from Peter
to pay Paul.

For a time the day-by-day revelations of the situation almost
drove me crazy. To add to my utter consternation came a terrible disappointment in her basic integrity—the discovery that
she had no faith in Christian Science. In anger, when I repri-
manded her, she scoffed at the organization and told me intimate secrets about prominent men and women in the organization that fairly appalled me.

But what power has anything under the sun over love? The
most heartbreaking facts I condoned and became a party to her
every fault. "We must keep up our front or we are lost," I
reasoned. Through her, for the first time in my life, I was in
debt. For the first time in my life I did things that I must
keep secret. I began also, like her, to live a double life and
encouraged her to continue in duplicity. The only difference
between us in the whole sordid matter was that she, through
her imagination, believed in a miraculous solution; she seemed
to feel that somehow she was quite honest and good and the
rest of the world bad. She suffered terribly as I made her see
the shamefulness of her attitude.

As a result of this she decided in her impulsive way to
abandon Christian Science, but by this time I had gone so far
in my own duplicity and negativism that I insisted she continue
her practise and our most bitter quarrels centered around this
subject. I continued steadfast in my faith and reasoned that

her bitterness and unbelief resulted from her disappointment in the Count and others who had robbed her and deceived her, and not because of a deep change of heart toward Christian Science.

No Swede can ever describe a Celt. Cæsar says somewhere in his writings: "It was no unusual thing to find a Celt accepting a note for debt to be paid in a life to come." There are such strange contradictions in the truly Celtic temperament that it defies rational classification. Words are inadequate, my intelligence is inadequate even to this day, to clarify Cora's character. All I know is that I was deeply and incurably in love with her. I could not leave her; and I saw no solution except to dig through—to work and make much money, stave off creditors, and fight every one who tried to break up our union. Our life was like a boat wildly bucking on the erratic waters of a tumultuous mountain stream. We fought and quarreled but mostly we laughed and enjoyed the frenzied pace we had adopted.

However, after having accepted the new order and made an almost incredibly difficult *salto mortale* in adjusting the Cora in fact with the Cora of my dreams, I sensed a danger of sooner or later having to face eventualities of an even more sinister nature than those which had already come upon me. There were times when something would happen in a crowd, that made Cora's cheeks turn chalky white from emotions I could not understand. Subtle evasions, mysterious occurrences, familiar greetings from men and women of such repulsive appearance that even a rustic must have realized they belonged to the underworld, filled me with vague fear and forebodings. In my strenuous optimism I argued that as a practitioner Cora must have met all kinds of people. However, at times I felt as if I walked in the shadow of death. Was I interfering, through my protection of Cora, with the plans of dark, sinister forces that would eventually annihilate us both?

In the summer of 1909 I made the first model of my "Triumph of Labor" for entry in a competition in Sweden for an industrial monument. In the competition I called my model "Industry, the Conqueror of Loke." I had not yet lost the magnificent and unspeakably sinful god who had filled my childhood with desire and terror.

In a previous chapter I have described the beginning of my efforts to portray Man the Conqueror. A wealthy bookbinder in Stockholm had donated a large sum of money for a monument glorifying industry, and I saw in the present competition an opportunity to express my idea. I used the same group, as before described, depicting three Titans overcoming a giant serpent. On the base of my model I showed four groups in relief, picturing (1) the primitive trades, (2) modern industry, (3) the toilers at evening, and (4) a home scene.

Through questionable official procedure I lost out in the competition and Milles received the first prize. But there was such a hue and cry that the committee was forced to ask Milles and me to submit new models on a larger scale. With this second model I failed completely. I had secured a mediocre assistant to carry out my plans, while I went about other work to keep money coming in. My creation was awful, and Milles received the commission with a composition that was neither original nor beautiful.

In some way, through some one—I don't remember how or who—the late Pierpont Morgan had asked me to see him upon his arrival in Paris. Morgan was on his way from Egypt, a much sicker man than the world in general suspected. I was in hopes that his desire to see me indicated that he wanted to order a bust of himself.

Morgan had a huge bulbous nose, and if there was anything I enjoyed modeling it was a man of strength with a big nose. However, what it was that he desired of me I never learned, for when I called at his hotel upon his arrival I was told he had canceled all engagements because of the sinking of the *Titanic*. The *Titanic* was one of the big assets of his newly and loosely organized International Steamship Trust. In his weakened condition the sinking of this great ship was a great blow. Henry Harris, the theatrical producer, and other of my friends were on the ship, and the anxiety and worry over their fate caused me completely to forget my disappointment at not meeting Morgan. In fact, I do not think I have ever again thought of the incident until now as I come to write of the events leading up to my going to Vienna.

Edna Aug, the distinguished vaudeville star, who was living with us while fulfilling an engagement in one of the Paris theaters, had been introduced to me by Will Harris, Henry's brother, and it was she who secured for me the commission that sent me off for a time to the city of the Merry Widow. Miss Aug was greatly interested in my art; and having one day in Paris met Ben Tieber, the owner of the Apollo Theater in Vienna, where she had previously appeared, she suggested to him that he have me make a portrait bust of him. Edna advised me to be on the lookout for him, but she did not prepare me for the kind of man I was to meet when he called to see me. He was one of the biggest and ugliest persons I had ever seen; and with a naive directness he began at once, as soon as he had entered my studio to tell me what an important person he was.

"I have," he told me among other things, "bought one of the finest palaces in Vienna. Wagner, our greatest architect, built it for himself. I also bought his art collection, including several original life-sized Canova statues in marble. Realize, young man, what an honor for you to have a piece of your work side by side with the immortal Canova."

As I abhor Canova's sculpture beyond anything, this peroration of Tieber's made me desire above all else not to work for him. However, before I had time to formulate a polite phrase of refusal, I saw his monumental nose. It fascinated me and I began at once to study him more closely and in detail. His jaw was that of a brute, his eyes small, shrewd and piggy, his neck like that of a bull. His skull was round and well formed, adding to the fierce strength of the whole. He was tall and broad, but his hugeness was the result of tremendously developed muscles and not of fat. The general impression of the man was one of extraordinary power and aggressiveness. Next to Papini he was, according to conventional standards, the ugliest man I had ever seen, but at the same time the best-looking and most fascinating, according to my standard of appraisal.

Ben Tieber had a peculiarity of wanting to pay in gold for whatever he bought. Later on I learned that he had accumulated his great fortune in the gold fields of Africa and it was perhaps here that he had acquired a love for metal and abhorred its mere symbols as embodied in checks and paper money. The man amused me greatly, and when he took out a huge chamois-skin bag bursting with gold coins and proceeded to count out two thousand francs as a retainer on our contract, I had to control myself in order not to betray how much I was beginning to like him.

The first thing he showed me in his ostentatious home, when I arrived in Vienna to begin my work for him, was an almost finished painting of himself by a famous court painter of the Austrian capital. As soon as I saw this picture I was shaken with fear and apprehension as to what would come to me after I had made my bust. On the canvas I saw, not the crude, powerful Levantine Jew living on our planet under the name of Ben Tieber, but a sweet-faced Apollo. His grand proboscis had been straightened out with classical refinements, his small restless eyes were enlarged and given a dreamy, far-away look, his iron-like jaw had been emasculated, and his lips given a sensitive refinement.

I gasped over the audacity of the artist who had dared so completely to reconstruct a face. There was no doubt about it, Ben Tieber had secured a real court painter. I knew at once that hell would be popping when in my work he should stand revealed as he actually looked. But the stakes were too high for me to falter, and I resolved, come what might, that I would finish that bust as I saw fit and he was going to pay me in full whether he liked it or not. I foresaw that he would not actually reject the work but that as soon as it was nearing completion he would make himself completely disagreeable in an effort to make me feel obliged to break the contract. And that is exactly what he undertook to do before the first week was over.

The finishing of the bust after the first week hinged on the outcome of a conflict of wills. I was determined to create a masterpiece and receive my reward in money and fame, and he, I knew, was just as determined that no damned artist should make such a frightfully ugly thing of him and collect real gold for it. It was a battle between a stubborn, square-head Swede and a Levantine Jew.

One day Baron Jochum Beck-Friis, the Swedish Minister to Vienna, noted my strained looks and inquired what was worrying me. I told him of my battle with Ben Tieber. This gay, human and talented aristocrat in a most spontaneous and charming manner replied, after hearing my tale of woe:

"Come over and live with me at the Legation. I have a comfortable big guest room and a gorgeous bed in which two kings have slept. We will have a good time and that will help to make your task with Ben Tieber less arduous."

I accepted his invitation, and to top it all the baron also gave me an order for his own bust. When I told Ben Tieber of this he became a little more human for a day or two, but then returned to his old tactics. However, I won out, and now comes the humorous part of the tale. I exhibited the bust to "The Hagenbund," the most exclusive Art Association in Austria, and it was so well received by the critics that Tieber ordered an extra replica of it for his theater. He was, after all, a man of sense and intelligence. When he understood that I had given him the best there was in me and had not sought to ridicule him through my work, he did the gracious thing by me after making me suffer. That magnificent painting of himself I never did see again.

My host, Baron Beck-Friis, was one of the most popular bachelors in Vienna. He played the piano well, had a fine voice, loved fun and had a great deal of charm. He was between thirty and forty years old, just the age when a man has learned discretion and refinement in pleasant pursuits, and still has the vitality to react intensely to delicious foods, rare wines, and things exquisite and beautiful. He was, indeed, one of the most charming companions with whom I have ever shared a period of play and gaiety.

What season of the year I was in Vienna I have forgotten, but I remember it was carnival time. There remains a hazy memory of meeting men of distinction in art, literature, and music, and gaily uniformed officers, but my memories of them are like images in floating soap bubbles. Of every other city where I have lived, I have definite memories of people, their names and characteristics; I can recall principal buildings, industries, customs, and in general I have retained a very accurate synthesis of them; but my memories of old Vienna live like a crazy cubistic moving picture in my mind—a complicated maze of hundreds of mirrors reflecting warm, laughing faces, while I hear delightful music, laughter, treading feet on polished floors. There is also the brightly colored blur of confetti and the vision of fragrant red hair cascading over my face. There must have been a girl with red hair, a throaty vibrant voice talking in a strange tongue, because I remember also such a voice. Yes, I almost forgot—lips that were very warm.

Instead of coming home flush with gold I arrived almost penniless, and under cross-examination I did with honesty reply to almost all questions: "I don't remember." What astounds me is that during this blank in my life I produced two of the best pieces of sculpture I have ever made. Some critics have even placed my Beck-Friis bust as the most significant work of my whole career. And as I think of this bust I also remem-

ber terrible headaches and ice packs from too much champagne
and fitful hours of sleep in that most magnificent of beds—a bed
perhaps made for a Turk, it was so ample. Beck-Friis had
for many years been minister to Turkey and it might really have
been a Turkish interpretation of a bed.

XXXIV

HIS ROYAL HIGHNESS

DURING the spring of 1910 I was invited to exhibit in Berlin at the Secession Society with a group of Swedish artists, Zorn, Carl Larson, Janson, Richard Bergh, and others. Cora went with me to Berlin, where we put up at a very modest hotel, the Bismarck. We were almost completely without money. After paying our first week's bill we had one carfare between us and no immediate prospects of more. I had to do some hard and fast thinking. After a few moments I got a flash from the father of all inspiration, grim necessity.

"Darling," I said to my wife, "you take the carfare and go down to the Kaiserhof Hotel. But don't start right away. Give me time to get there before you do. Ask me no questions; it might jinx my hunch."

The Kaiserhof was then the most fashionable hotel of Berlin. Its manager was a Swede named Trulson. I did not know him, but he was reputed to be one of the smartest hotel men in Europe. I asked to see Trulson and was admitted to his office. After we had performed bows and engaged in the amenities of the occasion, I pitched into the subject.

"Mr. Trulson," I said, "I am to exhibit at the Secession Society with the Konstnärsförbundet. I have no money. I don't know when or how I will get any. Will you trust me and give me and my wife a room, food and drinks until there is a change for the better or a permanent worse?"

"Why, certainly," he answered without the least indication of surprise or hesitance.

Accordingly we moved into the Kaiserhof, and the next day my luck changed. A buying committee for the Swedish government bought my "Athlete" at the exhibition for the National Museum at Stockholm. The great banker, Robert von Mendelssohn, a descendant of the composer, bought a bronze for several thousand marks. At this exhibition I also sold my statue "Aspiration" to a doctor in Stettin whose name I have forgotten.

Portrait orders, social events, bookings for future exhibitions, and good things in general followed so rapidly that I felt as if I had caught a dragon by the tail and was flying into space unable any longer to control or guide my own fate.

One day, as I approached the Secession Palace on my way to the exhibition, I saw a carriage with royal trappings drive up. A flunky jumped down from the back of the vehicle and opened the door. Unwinding like a huge anaconda, the giant-like Swedish Minister, Eric Trolle, squeezed out of the carriage. After him sprang the Crown Prince of Sweden, Gustav Adolf. I knew that all the Swedish artists were out of town on some trip for the day and that there was no one in authority to receive the royal guest. Trolle looked anxiously around and saw me. Responding to his imperative gesture I came up and was introduced to His Royal Highness.

With a movement of the eyes Trolle invested me with the office of royal guide and reception committee. I could feel myself blushing to the roots of my hair with embarrassment.

Vaguely I had a feeling of having expected something like this to happen, but it was not until months later, when I chanced to come across an old astrological horoscope of my life, that I became aware of the fact that the event had been foretold.

After that the prince became one of my stanchest friends. A mysterious influence seemed at once to publicize me all over the Continent, in England, and in America as a man in royal favor. The notes and articles about me, sent me by my clipping bureau, doubled and trebled after I had been seen for a couple of hours with H.R.H. Gustav Adolf at the exhibition.

Eric Trolle, the minister, and his Countess, both sat for portraits during my Berlin stay. These portraits were cast in bronze and later placed in Trolleholm, the ancestral castle of the Trolle family. This family dates back to pre-Christian, heathen days. The name was given by one of the early chieftains because a member of the family had slain a Troll.

One night at the Royal Opera I saw Kaiser Wilhelm for the first time. Farrar sang Marguerite in *Faust* that evening. I have always disliked both this opera and Farrar, but I was so fascinated as I watched Wilhelm that this particular performance has remained one of the most thrilling memories of this period.

Cora and I sat well up front in the orchestra with our party. The Emperor's box was to the left, well in view. His whole body seemed to be moving all the time, his eyes darting here and there. His talk seemed rapid and terse. He never smiled. He was rather gaunt and as stiff as a ramrod.

I never met the Emperor. I belonged to what was then the most radical movement in art, a movement he detested. The Sieges Allee, which he created with its hundreds of elaborate, pretentious marble groups and statues immortalizing the kings and emperors of Germany, was a never-ending subject for ridicule by the group of artists to which I belonged. Here in America it has never been known how bitterly and persistently the Kaiser was ridiculed, both privately and in print, before the war. No modern country in the world has enjoyed such freedom of speech as Germany did in those days. No President of the United States was ever so openly and brutally attacked as was the Kaiser day by day in pre-war Germany. I remember that one issue of *Simplicissimus* was so vile in its abuse of the Kaiser, the royal family and the army, that even to describe its contents in print would constitute a penal offense in America.

There was one dominating note running through the writings of the German critics regarding my work. That was, that my art was vigorous and healthy, without affectation or morbidness. Later in the year I exhibited with Casirer, who, next to Duveen, was perhaps the greatest art dealer at that time in Europe. Later still in the season I had a show, together with the famous Norwegian landscape painter, Diriks, in the galleries of Keller and Reiner.

Cora and I remained for more than a year in the Kaiserhof. It was a fine year. Among famous men I modeled there were the great Jew, Franz Oppenheimer, and Frederic Van Eeden, the Dutch poet and writer. Franz Oppenheimer was a grand and learned man. His face was a network of terrible scars from the many duels he had fought during a time when a Jew was anathema in Germany. He hated blood. He told me he vomited at the sight of it. He was the gentlest man I have ever known, yet he had fought like a tiger with a heart bleeding in compassion for his foes. Though nauseated and trembling at the beginning of each duel, he nevertheless became such a formidable foe that at last none dared to challenge him, and he was allowed to rise to the pinnacle of fame and honor.

Van Eeden was a strange dreamer. The only time in my life that I have had an oral delusion was while I was working on his bust. Mine was the top studio in the building where I was located. One day I heard plainly the most heavenly instrumental music. I went to the window to assure myself it did not come from somewhere outside. No, it was right there in the room and persisted. A cold sweat of fear seized me, but I controlled myself while the cadences and undulations of the music kept on. Of course, I believed firmly that I was going insane. The next day I told Van Eeden all about it, because I heard the music again when he started to pose. He laughed in his quiet way and said:

"Oh, that is a common occurrence with people who are close to me. My wife often hears the music."

A few weeks later, at the People's Theater, I attended the première of a play by Van Eeden called *Eisbraun*. As the play unfolded I found to my surprise that this phenomenon of hearing and seeing things by a young dreamer was the main theme of the tragedy. But the hero of Van Eeden's drama ends in an asylum, although it is intimated that he is sane.

Van Eeden has since become a Catholic. In his book, *Der Kleine Johannes*, he reaches his greatest depth in the portrayal of the adventures of the human soul in a world of mystery below or above our waking state. In one of his novels he tells the story of his second wife, whom I met a year later at his home in Bussum, Holland. He was at the time he met her one of the famous psychiatrists in the hospital for the insane, the Salpêtrière in Paris, and she was a hopelessly insane inmate of the institution. He healed her with hypnotism and then married her. There was a weird undercurrent in his nature that in spite of his exquisite humor and gentleness gave me a sense of the uncanny.

Dr. Oppenheimer and Van Eeden were intimate and warm friends, yet two greater opposites I have never known. Oppenheimer was as loud and boisterous as Van Eeden was reserved and low of voice. One was a religious man, the other a materialist. Oppenheimer loved women, wine, song and sports of all kind; Van Eeden lived in a dream world and touched life with gentle, saint-like hands.

After my year in Berlin I put on a private exhibition in Stockholm. My enemies gave me a warm reception, but I was strong and the opposition they gave me added to the zest of life. The world, at last, seemed mine.

XXXV

IN SWEDEN WITH CORA

AFTER my exhibition in Stockholm I received one commission after another. One of these came through my old patron, Ernest Thiel. He had made a bet with a great ironmaster and financier, Judge Tillverg, the conditions of which were that the loser should pay for a portrait bust in bronze of each of the men. The judge lost and I began a bust of him and one of Thiel.

Judge Tillverg became so interested in me that he gave me orders for busts of two other friends of his. Then he conceived the idea of building my "Sphinx" in Swedish granite, larger in proportion than the Sphinx of Egypt, on the great military maneuvering grounds adjoining Stockholm. I began to get bids on the project and we were ready to sign the contract when the judge suddenly developed a deadly fear of me. He accused me of having hypnotized him, saying, in proof, that he had told me the innermost secrets of his life, which he could not have done had I not hypnotized him. It seemed a joke to me and I could only laugh at him. I am so notoriously bad as a salesman and so lacking in persuasive power that I even lose friends by my abruptness; yet this man thought I had hypnotized him! If I had been a little patient with him, I might have convinced him that I was not dangerous, but as the weakness of his character became apparent, I expressed such contempt and derision for him that his fear of me increased, and after paying me for all work contracted for, he never wanted to be in my presence again.

Later I was told that an enemy of mine, aware of his neurotic nature, had given him his wild idea of my baneful influence in order to keep me from having the "Sphinx" commission.

Another strange patron of the arts with whom I became acquainted was Klas Faehreus. This great collector had built a magnificent art gallery rivaling in beauty and scope the gallery created by Ernest Thiel. Faehreus made a contract with me to model two groups directly in the mortar covering the end walls of the main gallery. I made sketches of two motives that he approved. For one wall I made a design showing Venus posing in front of a mirror held in position by two cupids. For the other wall I designed Hercules in the throes of love. His hands tied with a chain of roses, and with a woful expression on his face, he is dancing to the tune of a flute a cupid is playing behind him, while at the same time imitating the clumsy dance step of Hercules. Another cupid has a firm hold on the rose chain, pulling Hercules ahead.

Faehreus was delighted with the compositions and I began the work. The wall was very high. Consequently the figures, to be in proportion to the huge wall space, had to be about ten feet tall. Working directly on the wall, I was obliged to climb up and down incessantly. It was the kind of work I enjoyed, but hardly had I commenced when Faehreus undertook to tell me how to make the reliefs.

"Make them thin and airy."

Soon I gave in and lost all interest in the work.

One evening, after he had made his daily visit, I decided for my own pleasure to make the Venus as I thought she should have been made and then scrape her down to his way of thinking before he could see my change. Summer nights in Sweden last only about two hours, and I worked until eleven o'clock. I was then so tired I decided to wait until next morning to change my Venus. I had made the relief about ten inches in thickness and treated it in a new and novel manner unlike any relief I have ever seen, but it just suited the lighting of the room and the material used for the walls.

Unfortunately, I met some friends that night and got into the most interesting of all card games, "Vira." The party was wet and long. I did not go to my quarters to rest but stayed with my host and slept until noon the following day.

Faehreus had in the meantime seen my relief and started out to find me and tell me what was on his mind. However, he failed at the time to locate me, and when he finally did so I had already changed the Venus back to the conventional style he had forced me to use. When he saw this he became violently angry.

"Why have you changed her?" he cried. He jumped like a spider and blew like a sea lion. "Why, that relief was the most beautiful thing I have ever seen. And now you have destroyed it!"

He insisted that I restore the Venus, which I attempted to do, but with indifferent success.

I was by this time so tired of his rantings and his desire to direct my work without knowing a thing about the process, that I could never get the fire into it again. He was a great connoisseur, but was wholly ignorant of the methods an artist uses in achieving his ends. An artist to be at his best must be absolutely free from any restrictions or even a suspicion of being watched.

By this time Thiel and I had become bosom friends. My bust of him became internationally known. It is one of the finest pieces of work I have ever done and was the result of his fine understanding and appreciation of my art. No artist can be an artist unto himself alone. A work of art is always made for some one or to some one. The artist without a sympathetic audience is only half an artist.

One morning my wife noted in the papers that Countess Casa di Miranda (Christine Nilsson, the Swedish singer) had arrived in Stockholm from the Riviera.

"David," said Cora, "Christine Nilsson was born not far from the same place in Smaland that you were. Why don't you call her up and propose making a bust of her?"

"Fine idea, darling. I'll call her up on the instant."

Within a few hours the Countess was in our apartment and a verbal arrangement made for sittings, price, etc., of a bust in Carrara marble. About six-thirty that evening I suddenly became worried.

"Cora," I said, "do you know that Christine Nilsson is going to decide that she doesn't want that bust? She is a woman of good sense, and now that she has had time to reflect she has lost the delusion of again being beautiful and young and sought after by artists. She is by this time feeling her sixty-odd years and her heavy flesh and triple chin. Unless I beat her to it she is going to call up and say she has been called away or is very ill."

Cora replied:

"I believe you are right, David, but what are you going to do about it?"

Looking at my watch, I replied:

"If I can get down to the art shop and get some modeling stuff before closing time I am going to work all night and make an Ophelia as I imagine she played Ophelia in Paris when a young girl. You remember she was just a country girl with a great voice and a wonderful genius for music when Paris went crazy over her."

I called down to the office to have a car ready for me and I got to the store just before it closed. All night I worked on the Ophelia, and at eight o'clock the next morning the Countess called up and told me, as I had anticipated, that she had been tragically called away just when she was so happy looking forward to our sittings. I replied that since talking with her I had conceived the idea of making her as Ophelia and that I had worked all night to have the model ready for her this very morning.

The Countess came over almost immediately and was delighted by what she saw. Right then and there a new agreement was made, this time in writing and with a substantial retainer. This "Ophelia" has since had a romance of its own and gained me much fame.

The Faehreus Gallery was eventually finished and a great housewarming party planned by the owner. Faehreus was by this time so angry at me that Cora and I were not invited, although I had worked on the building. Later on, when I saw the interior, I found that he had hung two magnificent cutglass chandeliers in such a way that my reliefs could not be seen to advantage. Later he tried to compensate for his nastiness by buying some smaller bronzes from me at exorbitant prices. There was one little group of some naked cupids carrying a pumpkin that he bought with the understanding that I destroy the plaster model and make only one bronze, so that his copy would be the only one in the world.

Of the many famous and great men I met, there was not one who did not admire Cora. My old friend, Gustav Steffen, Professor of Political Economy at the Gothenburg University and a member of the Upper House of the Swedish Senate, said to me:

"Edstrom, I cannot quite understand how some one like you could win such a woman. She is too great for you."

They were rude, but to me sweet, words.

Gosta Forssell, head of the Cancer Institute of Stockholm and a woman of international fame, became devoted to her. In Berlin Dr. Oppenheimer, Van Eeden, His Excellency Eric Trolle, and every other man of distinction I met became fascinated with her wit, learning and exquisite charm. Mrs. Thiel said to me one day:

"Are you not aware that my husband is in love with your wife?"

This was to me most amusing. Through all the years I had

"OPHELIA"

Bronze statue in the Thiel Gallery at Stockholm. Replicas owned by several private collectors

"THE HUNCHBACK"
Terra cotta in the Thiel Collection at Stockholm

been interested in Mrs. Thiel in just the way that Thiel became interested in Cora.

I was not jealous of my wife, though I did watch her like a hawk, to guard against the sinister shadows I felt around her, threatening us both; but these shadows had nothing to do with the conventional, decent people with whom we mingled.

While Cora was still with me in Sweden, we made a trip to Dalsheda, the place of my birth. Strange to say, I had never before been there since leaving it when I was seven years of age. It was February when we arrived. Cora had a dreadful toothache, and the first thing I did after we put up at a small hotel in Hvetlands, the small town near Dalsheda, was to send for a dentist. He insisted that the aching tooth should be pulled; but he was afraid to do so without putting Cora under an anesthetic, and I was obliged to call in a physician to aid in the operation. It was a harrowing experience and several days went by before I could leave Cora to drive out and visit the place described in the first chapter of this narrative.

When I eventually did again rove over the same hills, listen to the same little brook, look at the same blue hill, I found that my memory of the place was most accurate, except as to the width, breadth and height of objects in the landscape. It was a miniature of the grand memories of childhood.

At last Cora became bored and tired of living in Sweden. Her health also seemed to suffer from the harsh climate. I was negotiating with the City of Gothenburg to aid in the planning of a public square and the making of a large fountain. There were also other big things in view, and as my stay in Sweden seemed to become more and more indefinite, I at last reluctantly consented to let her return to Paris alone and open up our apartment there. After she left me I became very lonely in Sweden; so that when I received an invitation to exhibit on Bond Street in London, I gladly accepted and, hurrying through with the commissions I had under way, I left for England via Paris.

XXXVI

PRINCESS PAT

MY success in Vienna, Berlin, and Stockholm was cast in the shade by the glamour of events starting from the time of my exhibition in Old Bond Street at the Patterson Gallery in London during the spring of 1913. Paul Konody, one of the most influential critics in London, wrote an impassioned article in the *Observer* about my work, of which I give a short extract:

> After the barrenness of the two sculpture rooms at the Royal Academy, it is a delightful experience to stroll into the little Patterson Gallery in Old Bond Street, and to spend an hour or so among the fascinating creations of a sculptor who not only has something to say that is worth saying, but who also expresses himself in a language as forcible as it is personal. Mr. David Edstrom is Swedish by birth, American by bringing up, and cosmopolitan in his art. He studied at Stockholm, Florence and Paris, but, to judge from the examples of his work now shown, he owes little or nothing to any particular master or modern school. He has assimilated the teaching of the ages, of the great periods of glyptic art, following invariably the spirit rather than the letter, and adopting this spirit to his very individual conception. As his introducer, Axel L. Romdahl, has it, he has passed "through all the crises of searching, but has always searched inwardly, ignoring the formulas of fashion and popular taste."
>
> . . . An impressionist like Medardo Rosso allows the light to play so important a function that some of his works become positively meaningless or unintelligible unless they are seen with the light falling upon them at one particular angle—so little does he depend upon positive definition of form. Considered

from this point of view, Mr. Edstrom is not an impressionist, except in some few works like his very remarkable bust of His Excellency Baron Beck-Friis, with which I have already dealt at length on the occasion of its appearance at last year's "London Salon," and to a minor degree in the very characteristic head of an "Old Italian Soldier," although in this case he already reveals his tendency toward making the individual impression subordinate to the type. But nearly all his other busts have a constructional basis. They are built up, each from scores of preliminary drawings, in the accentuation of the angles. And nothing could be further removed from the impressionist point of view, which is more concerned with the transitory effect under certain conditions of light.

Among the most interesting portrait busts shown at the Patterson Gallery is the one of "Ernest Thiel"—a head that in its curious mingling of fierceness and cultured taste suggests a man of the Cesare Borgia type, some condottiere of the Italian Renaissance. Equally remarkable are the busts of Countess Alice Trolle, Francisco d'Andrade, and Dr. Franz Oppenheimer, with a face of rude strength all askew as the result of gashes received by him in his duels.

The Observer, London, May 11, 1913.

Sir Claude Philips, curator of the Wallace Collection, also gave me enthusiastic praise in the *Telegraph*. Collins Baker, another eminent critic, was even more enthusiastic in the *Saturday Review*. Haldane Macfall, famous as art historian, novelist and critic, perhaps reaches the highest degree of praise, first in an article in the *Daily Express* and later in *The Academy*, of which the following excerpts give an idea of the tenor of his praise.

. . . The power of the imagination, and the capacity to achieve the things of the imagination are his; and it is for the world of men to encourage and enable such a genius to bring forth the splendor that is in him, and thereby enrich mankind. . . . It is for us to encourage genius—and this man is a genius.

The Express, London, May 16, 1913.

The Swedish sculptor Edstrom has shown London his astounding powers—I remember writing of Rodin in this wise not so many years ago. . . . If we have had a sculptor of genius in our midst of recent years, here is the man.

The Academy, London, July 26, 1913.

The Duke of Connaught, who at the time was Lieutenant Governor of Canada, was in London with his family seeking medical aid for his Duchess. As a serious operation was contemplated, the Swedish Crown Prince, with his wife, Margaret of Connaught, came to London to be near the Duchess, the Princess's mother, during the period of anxiety over the latter's health. The Crown Prince looked me up almost immediately upon his arrival and, with the same wholehearted friendship he had shown me in Berlin, backed my interests.

First of all he gave me a commission to model a portrait bust of himself. Mrs. Francis Leggett, of New York, whose elder daughter was married to George Montague, later Earl of Sandwich, had a large house on Bruton Street only a few blocks away from my exhibition. She offered me the use of her stable as a studio for my work on the bust of H.R.H., which I accepted gladly.

Prince Gustav Adolf came here every day and posed, and if I had rented the most fashionable studio in London it could not have given me the publicity this did. Members of the English royal family and visiting royalties, as well as leaders in English and continental circles of the élite, visited my stable studio.

One evening, as our sitting was about over, I remembered that the Crown Prince and I were expected to go that evening to an official banquet in his honor. I reminded him that it was getting late, but as they could not start before "we" arrived, we need not worry.

At the time I was living at the Arundel Hotel, not far from the Savoy, where the affair was staged, and as the Crown Prince lived at the Clarence House, I felt sure I would be on time.

I did not realize, however, that a prince has two or three valets to help him change, and that royal vehicles are not tied up in traffic. To my horror, when I came to the banquet, every one was seated—and I was extremely embarrassed before I finally found my place. His Royal Highness showed great amusement over the fact that they did really start the banquet before "we" got there.

Some time after beginning the bust of the Swedish Crown Prince it was arranged that I also make a bust of Princess Patricia, sister of the Swedish Crown Princess. "Princess Pat," as she was affectionately nicknamed by the world, was the most romantic, popular and publicized young woman of the day. Her beauty, her talents and democratic temperament had endeared her to the great masses of the empire and, for that matter, to the whole world.

To avoid having a horde of news reporters and curious people haunting the now famous studio on Bruton Street, we decided that I must make her bust at some other place, so a large room in Clarence House, where the Duke of Connaught and his family resided while in London, was put at my disposal.

In Vienna, living in the Swedish Legation with the gay bachelor, Baron Beck-Friis, I had entered into Viennese society through the unconventional back door of the bohemian fringe of the élite, but here in London my entry was through one of the most punctilious, strait-laced families of all the courts in Europe.

I have never known two more well-brought-up girls than the two Connaught sisters, Margaret and Patricia. The elder, Princess Margaret, I did not learn to know well until after the beginning of the war, when she entered my life during a sinister and trying period.

Patricia, with whom at this time I spent an hour every day, was more charming. As I learned to know her intimately, I found her a girl with an astounding imagination and passion for art.

One day she invited me to her apartment in the palace. In a room which must have measured sixty by forty feet, she had brought her treasures together in delightfully artistic confusion: not only her own artistic creations, consisting of embroideries, tapestry work, lace, drawings and oil paintings of surprising merit, but odds and ends from all parts of the world—including a most impudent parrot.

The quantity of Patricia's own work was so great that it seemed incredible to me that so young a girl could have had the time to produce it. However, I found that she detested court life and had a habit of getting up at five in the morning to get more hours for her artistic pursuits. This was her play; the routine of social and official life she considered work.

Princess Pat was very discreet and loyal to her caste and family, but her ardor for painting, her love of music and art in every form, told me more than anything else why no outward pressure had been able to force her into a conventional royal marriage in a foreign court.

Her beauty, her slender girlish figure, her sense of humor and vivacity, gave her a charm seldom found anywhere in the world, and, outside of all political considerations, made her very desirable to eligible princes on the Continent.

I sensed in my contact with her (and my intuition later was confirmed by others more close to her than myself), that her greatest fear was that in some way, through political pressure, she might be forced to marry into a certain reigning house, the friendship of which England was anxious to cultivate. Not only did she fear the deadly routine of being a queen, but, more than that, she was not in accord with the nation's moral tone and lack of regard for the sensibilities of womanhood.

Emil Fuchs, the famous English painter and sculptor, persuaded me to use Italian plasteline for the Patricia bust. I had never used this material but had seen splendid work done with it by Prince Troubetzkoy and other noted sculptors, and therefore accepted from Fuchs a batch of the stuff.

It was a great mistake. Day by day I found myself unable to make any headway in the soft mess. Patricia posed like an angel. Never once did she break an appointment. Her mother's Canadian physician, a man with an inexhaustible supply of droll stories, came in almost every day for a short visit during our sittings and contributed toward making them sparkling and gay. However, as the fear grew in me that the bust would be a failure, all the enjoyment I felt at the beginning of the work was changed to anguish.

At last I was forced to admit defeat and told Patricia the bad news. Instead of showing disappointment, she became all sympathy and proposed that I begin another bust in clay. As she was going on a yachting cruise in the North Sea in a few days, we decided to postpone doing the new bust until she returned. The bust of her brother-in-law, Crown Prince Gustav Adolf, that I modeled in clay, was successful, however, and met with his unqualified approval.

When the Connaughts left London I accepted an invitation from Mrs. Leggett to her house at Stratford-on-Avon to be her guest during the Shakespearian Festival at that place. Walter Hines Page, the new American ambassador, succeeding Whitelaw Reid, had just arrived in England, and he and his family were guests at Mrs. Leggett's house for a few days during the four weeks I was there.

Sir Frank Benson, creator of a new tradition in Shakespearian production, and the manager of the Shakespeare Theater in Stratford-on-Avon, breakfasted every morning at the Leggett house. Never have I seen such a day-by-day stream of notables as was entertained by this splendid and hospitable woman.

Breakfast was a kind of open table for everybody of note visiting the town during the festivals. Besides Sir Frank and the leading members of the cast, there were actors, writers, poets, musicians, leaders in all manner of pursuits from all the corners of the world. J. J. Burns, the American detective, on business which his agency was handling for the American Bankers Association in Europe, was entertained by Mrs. Leggett.

Marie Corelli, whose mystical and fantastic novels I had read years before, had a magnificent house at Stratford-on-Avon. I always had imagined her as a mysterious superwoman, with a Rossetti face and a spiritual, pre-Raphaelite atmosphere enveloping her. Instead I met a fat, roly-poly, common-looking little woman, appearing more like a cockney servant than the creator of majestic, satanic villains and resplendent angels battling over the eternal welfare of the hero and heroine.

At a famous vicarage near Stratford-on-Avon there was an oil painting of the girl Shakespeare is credited with having used as his model for Ophelia. What interested me about the picture in particular was that it showed the same anemic, psychopathic type of girl as I had portrayed in my own statue of Ophelia. I felt pleased over this because every Ophelia I ever had seen, painted or sculptured by other artists, always had shown an effort by these artists to picture a pretty girl, not the mentally-frail character that became insane under pressure.

Every twenty-four hours in Stratford-on-Avon was a cycle of events as exciting as life in London. Nottingham was planning a great World's Fair to be held in 1915, and I had been made commissioner for the Scandinavian countries. It was a great honor, with an ample salary from the time I began to work on it. Just as I was about to leave for London on business for the exposition I received a wire from Princess Patricia that she would be back in England in a week or so and would be pleased if I could then come to Bagshot Castle and make the new bust we had planned.

I hurried up to London to finish all my business there before she arrived in England. On my arrival I noticed in a bookstore a large display of Ellen Key's book *Love and Marriage* just out in an English translation. I went into the store and bought a copy, which I sent to a lady in Stratford-on-Avon, enclosing in the book my visiting card on which was engraved my Paris address. This little courtesy came near having disastrous consequences. The lady in question had entertained me in her palatial home a number of times. She was very wealthy and one of the most beautiful women in England; in fact so strikingly magnificent that I was taken off my feet. But I was not at all interested in her. She had no warmth or brains, but it was quite natural that I should express admiration for her superb beauty. While a guest at her house she had led the conversation to a discussion of anecdotes about Miss Key, and it was this fact that had inspired me to send her a copy of *Love and Marriage.*

In Paris my wife had instructions to open all my mail and send me only letters that it was necessary for me to look after personally. When the beautiful lady in Stratford-on-Avon had received my book *Love and Marriage* she had immediately sent me one of the most open love declarations I have ever received from any one. In it she referred to what a wonderful race would be developed when humanity learned to know more about love and eugenics, and suggested an early intimate rendezvous in London. This letter had been sent to my Paris address. When I was ready to leave for Bagshot I received a letter from my wife enclosing the one from the beautiful lady in Stratford-on-Avon. My wife's letter read about as follows:

DEAR DAVID:
I am enclosing a letter from a friend of yours in Stratford. I have written the lady that your letter has been forwarded to you so that she may not be overanxious because of any delay in hearing from you.
Your loving wife,
CORA.

Instead of going to Bagshot and my work on the Princess's bust, I hurried over to Paris as fast as I could. Cora was furious at me and was deaf to all my pleas that I had not made love to the lady of the eugenic letter. She would not believe me at all. In the letter the lady had not mentioned her receipt of Miss Key's book, but in my explanations to my wife I happened to mention my innocent present of this book as being the only expression of friendship I had shown. When I spoke of *Love and Marriage* my wife looked at me with something like understanding for the first time.

"Have you read the book?" she asked.

"You know I never read Ellen Key's twaddle," I answered.

She then burst out laughing and said: "David, never send a lady a book without first reading it. That book to any lady is equivalent to a declaration of love."

I was saved and we kissed and made up. I hurried back to London and then to Bagshot to begin Princess Patricia's bust. There was so much work to do in connection with the exposition, and other matters, that I could allot only three or four days to the Patricia bust. This made me very unhappy. I liked her so much that I was most anxious to do a really good bust of her, but I knew it was impossible in this short time, particularly with my mind filled with all kinds of hard-boiled, practical matters.

However, as a sketch it was not so bad. Prince Arthur, Patricia's brother, had just been engaged to the Princess of Fife, and there was bustle and fever around the place. The last day I worked on the bust I had to make a train for Paris the same day. In my shirt sleeves I hustled like a demon, and the Duchess, Prince Arthur, his fiancée and some other people were in the room during the last half-hour. The coachman was at the door waiting to drive me to the station. They served tea to Princess Pat and me in our working room so that I should not lose any time.

Suddenly I needed some water to moisten the clay and in my hurry I took the teapot and poured some tea on it instead. The Duchess exclaimed:

"But, my dear sir, we have water on the place!"

Every one else laughed.

Without putting on my coat I rushed out of the room when

I had finished, a flunky having deposited my baggage in the carriage. I did not have time to wash my hands, so the best I could do as a farewell was to wave my dirty hands and laugh, and as many as could crowd into the door also waved and laughed with me as the carriage rolled away.

XXXVII

THE BATTLEGROUND OF LIFE

AFTER accepting the Scandinavian commission to the Nottingham World's Fair I was delighted with the luncheon the British Consul General in Paris gave in order to have me meet the English bankers and business men in Paris who were interested in that exposition. Nottingham was the industrial center of about seventeen million people, and I had to master a knowledge of the volume, nature and markets of this area. My work was not only to gather a representative Scandinavian art exhibit but also to manage the sale of exposition space to Scandinavian industries. My excellent memory and ability to grasp any subject rapidly made the task seem rather easy, large as it really was; to cultivate connections with people necessary for the enterprise, was the real difficulty. I was obliged to meet many persons who were utterly of no interest to me.

During these busy times, occupied with my exposition work and my many social activities, I would often have to go from London to Paris or from Paris to London on a moment's notice. Prestige had carried with it a bondage to men and conditions to which I had previously never dreamt it possible for my unruly nature to submit. One day I would be floating on the pleasing surface of social events and the next be facing crude ugly realities with business men or politicians.

This hard life brought me into many strange situations which at times touched upon major political events. The Entente and the Triple Alliance ruled the world, each ruthlessly fighting against the other for new colonies and world trade. Old con-

servative England hated Germany for her new and modern
methods and wanted to crush her through military force; pro-
gressive England wanted to make friends with Germany and
modernize production and trade exploitation.

Both in England and Germany were powerful interests that
strove for a secret understanding that would lessen the danger
of war between these two groups of nations. On the other
hand, both in England and Germany were virulent chauvinists
who saw war as the only means to attain their various objectives.

In the wild scramble of the great powers to gain influence
over the smaller nations, England had invited twelve of the
leading editors-in-chief of Sweden as guests of the City of
London. It was a major political move to further her propa-
ganda with Sweden. Among the twelve guests was Branting,
the great Socialist leader, a man of powerful political influence.
Branting was committed to the Entente and was quite aware
of the war danger, but had no interest in diminishing it. From
conversations with him, and from other sources of information,
I was convinced that he wanted to see Germany crushed.

The French Socialists, with their eminent leader Jaurès, and
leading Belgian and German Socialists, were all fanatical
pacifists and did not want to commit themselves either to the
Triple Alliance or to the Entente. I, with my partizans, hoped
against hope that England and Germany would come to friendly
terms before hell broke loose. Branting was more of an obstacle in the way than I believe is generally understood. A
very shrewd political friend of mine had secured proof that
Branting, during this London visit, would endeavor to convince
the English chauvinists of Sweden's neutrality or even friendliness to the Entente in case of war. My friend reasoned that
if a meeting of eminent Socialists in London at this time could
be brought about and Branting be exposed to his fellow Socialists as a chauvinist and not a pacifist, it would weaken his
political influence.

The twelve Swedish publicists were booked to stay at the

Hotel Metropole while in London, and to be near the center
of activity my friend advised me that I register at the Metropole
a few days before their arrival. It was decided that I should
give a tea party for Branting, inviting the leading radicals in
London to meet him. My late friend, Gaylord Wilshire, the
American syndicalist and for twenty years owner and editor of
Wilshire's Weekly, promised to aid me in getting the guests
together. He did this as a personal favor to give me prestige
with radical intellectuals without a suspicion of any ulterior
motive on my part. Price Collier, the eminent American writer,
and a few other non-radicals were included in the list of invited
guests. Among these were Bernard Shaw and H. G. Wells,
who, however, were unable to attend; but Hyndman, the leader
of the Socialist Party in England, was there, and altogether the
event brought together a very representative crowd.

The wily Branting accepted the honor of the occasion with
warmth and then came very late. When he did put in his be-
lated appearance he filibustered by making endless excuses for
his tardiness, telling stories, indulging in badinage, and then,
as dinner time was at hand, excused himself and left in a burst
of small talk. Thus there was no opportunity to ask him questions which had been prepared for him to answer and not a word
was forthcoming that could be used to publicize his tie-up with
the Entente.

Some time previously, through a general strike in Sweden,
Branting had forced his way to great power. He was generally
accused of having financed this strike with funds received from
abroad, though this was never proved.

Next to the Russian Isvolsky, I believe Branting was the most
adroit and shifty, and the fastest-thinking politician in Europe
—but he was a man of big ideals and true to his principles as
he saw them, whereas Isvolsky was a crook, a scamp, a villain,
and blandly callous to the sinister consequences of his machina-
tions. There was a somber depth to Branting that gave me
chills when I talked with him. He had a far-visioned look

about him, as though he were seeing things invisible to ordinary eyes. Yet he was hard, evasive, and smooth as a snake.

I also became acquainted with Charles Ferguson, whom Wilson had delegated to study the trust systems of Europe, and through Ferguson I attempted to realize one of my dearest ambitions.

After my failure to have my monument "The Triumph of Labor" erected in Sweden, I was always alert for connections elsewhere that might lead to a consummation of my great project. My patience with men of affairs was largely inspired by the hope that sooner or later I would meet some one who would aid me in erecting this monument.

Ellen Key and Ferguson were the two most brilliant and eloquent talkers I have ever known, but both had a vague something in their looks that made you aware they never observed facts acutely. Like buoyant boats their minds seemed to float on an undulating river of words. In their conversation there were never any quick stops of harsh analysis or questioning of their own ideas, no slowing up or faltering to arrange facts or seek more specific words, but a smooth flow of words where thoughts seemed to evolve from the words themselves instead of being vehicles of practical ideas or facts.

In disciplined minds aware of realities, minds alert to concrete and specific and fearful generalizations, great eloquence is seldom evident. Scientists and men of affairs find words annoying and inadequate to carry their ideas.

Ferguson talked fervently about Wilson and Colonel House, who was also in London at this time. My "Triumph of Labor" interested Ferguson immensely and he soon talked about it more eloquently than I was able to do. He wrote a very enthusiastic article about it for an American newspaper syndicate from which I quote the following:

> Edstrom has studios in Stockholm and Paris, but just now he is here in London. The London newspapers have much to say of him, and their art critics are unstinting in their praise of his

works. Perhaps they are assisted in their perspicacity by the fact
that Edstrom came to London in company with the Crown
Prince of Sweden, is making a portrait of the little English Princess Patricia, and has otherwise proved himself to be a man accepted of the mighty.

It was to be expected that this man would confound the
critics, for his ways in art are the ways of discovery and fresh
adventure. He is as bold and original as Rodin. But he is not
conceited or fantastic—as Rodin is. His works stand for what
he really thinks about life, and his thoughts are orderly and self-
consistent.

Europe has not yet accepted and acclaimed the part of Edstrom's art that lies nearest the meaning and purpose of the
man. It remains for America to do that.

I found the sculptor in a stable in Bruton Mews, off Berkeley
Square—an extemporized studio lent him by an American lady
as an act of hospitality and an overture of American appreciation.

Edstrom was working over the clay model of a monumental
composition designed for a public square. This work is his in-
most inspiration—the passion of his life. He turns aside from
the patronage of princes and prime ministers to fondle this clay.

Europe does not thrill to Edstrom's "Triumph of Labor."
Perhaps it is because the people in Europe who buy the creations
of artists are still feudal and aristocratic. America should understand. The United States should stretch out its hands and
lay hold of Edstrom's magnum opus.

There are some Americans here in London—people with influence at Washington—who say that there is in the world only
one perfectly suitable place for the setting up of this "Triumph
of Labor," and that is on the terrace at the east front of the
Capitol, where the crowd gathers when a President is inaugu-
rated.

The central figure of the design is a heroic group of three
workingmen wrestling in the toils of gigantic serpents. One is
reminded at once of the celebrated antique marble at the Capitol
in Rome—the Laocoon. But in Edstrom's work the struggle
of man against the sinister and brutal forces of nature is not
despairing, but triumphant.

Of course the meaning of this sculpture is that modern democracy has found a way—through the organization of indus-

try—to master the natural forces and the base passions which worked together to destroy the Roman Empire and all the ancient feudal states.

Could there be any fitter symbol to set before the eyes of democratic politics in the United States? Have we not in the public squares in Washington an ample sufficiency of prancing horses and waving swords? Is it not time to establish in some conspicuous place there a work of art to represent that creative force which is the real glory of the Republic—the all-conquering power of organized work?

"Democratic art," says Edstrom, "is the art that celebrates the task of the real world and the valor of ordinary men. Art becomes an agency of privilege and monopoly when it weakens the will of the earth-wrestler and makes him yearn toward an unreal world of loveliness and a light that never was."

The idea of placing the monument in front of the Capitol in Washington was suggested by Colonel House, although the Colonel's name is not used in the article. Ferguson arranged to have me meet House, but before the date set for our meeting I was obliged to hurry over to Paris on some matter. When I returned House had left for America and never again did opportunity open the door for a consummation of my enterprise through the Wilson administration.

Some of the outer fringes of international life in London were very strange. One day I sat next to an Irish girl who posed as a fortune-teller, and overheard her telling Edehm Pasha, the Albanian Prime Minister, that it was in the cards that Prince Wilhelm was to be King of Albania. He seemed to take the prediction most seriously. Astrologers, mediums and seers of all kinds dabbled in world affairs. At the house of the Greek poet Drakoules I met scores of this fortune-telling tribe. One of his receptions was like a madhouse, yet mingled with the fanatics, the frenzied ones, were men of real power in world politics. At his house I met Miss Scatcherd, one of the late W. T. Stead's intimate friends. Stead, one of the greatest journalists of his time, was among the first to make spiritualism a fad in England. Miss Scatcherd talked to me constantly about a new method of getting spirit photographs. It must have been at a party similar to one at the home of Drakoules that Lewis Carroll conceived the Mad Hatter's Tea Party. The more absurd and incomprehensible the statements made, the more they were applauded as deep, wise and masterly.

The third wife of Strindberg, a fat, good-natured Austrian woman, ran a night club in London at this time. Here I met many men of distinction, but also bohemians that for eccentricity outdid those of Paris. I remember meeting here one night a young poet with his little sweetheart. Both had bobbed hair of the same length. She was the first woman I had ever seen with bobbed hair. They were both dark-complexioned, dressed in very fine soft velvet, exquisitely groomed, and very, very pretty. The young man recited one of his poems with the sweet lisp of a child. I remember to my regret only a couple of lines from his poem:

> Lavender and roses,
> Lavender and roses,
> Put your hand upon my hair—

I was damaging my health with delicious wines, rich foods and feverish activity night and day. And then one day, at the home of Gaylord Wilshire on Hampstead Heath, I met the *bête noir* of American conservatives, Upton Sinclair, who gave me a new method of getting rid of autointoxication. He had the rosy cheeks of a young farmer boy, but when I saw the expression in his eyes I knew that he was old and wise in knowledge of the world. The contrast gave me a surprise and a shock. Some criminals, even of mature age, have youthful, unwrinkled faces, but this man I saw at once was not a criminal. He was just clean of blood. I did not know he was a famous author. Bluntly and without preface I asked for an explanation.

"How did you get that youthful skin? Your ears are as

transparent as those of a young girl, yet you are a man of many ups and downs."

He seemed as pleased at my remark as I would have been over a ten-thousand-dollar check and immediately explained that his physical condition was the result of a system of fasting. He told me all about it. He must have talked on for an hour or more. I was so impressed that I at once began a four days' fast. The result was true magic. My red, bloated face cleared up and my vitality increased a hundred per cent. Ever since that time I have fasted off and on when I have needed to.

I have seldom met a man who knew more interesting people than did Gaylord Wilshire. He was generous, gentle, full of the milk of human kindness. I would like to say a great deal about him, but his life was such a crazy patchwork that I have not the skill to go into it intimately and at the same time do him justice. Tolerance and kindliness were his most marked characteristics, but a lack of practical ability involved him in conditions for which he was severely criticized. I may be mistaken, but I believe he sincerely believed in his various fads and enterprises, however queer they may have seemed to a cold-hearted world. He and his wife Mary, who in later years became a practitioner of psychoanalysis, did more nice things for others than any two persons I have ever known.

The Wilshire house lay right on Hampstead Heath and on Sundays I saw there a strange sight. Thousands of lovers from London lay on the grass caressing each other without embarrassment. Couple lay by couple so close that it was difficult to pick your way between them in crossing the heath. One could observe the most intimate situations yet no couple paid any attention to the others around them nor to the passing pedestrians. If I had not seen this spectacle myself I would never have believed it possible.

I cannot leave London without saying something of the artists living there whom I learned to know. During the flowering of Greek art and during the Renaissance, a definite cohesive style or tradition encircled every artistic endeavor. There were never any violent innovations from decade to decade, from master to pupil, but there was a definite tradition that was steadfastly adhered to in the evolving movement. Not so in modern times. In London at this period, just as in Paris, Berlin and Stockholm, the art world seemed like a tower of Babel where one spoke a language not understood except by the few in his particular group. I, like the rest of the artists, had very little sympathy except for the few that were congenial to my point of view. In speaking of London artists whom I knew I must therefore speak in accents of aggressive criticism. My voice in the general babble is a cry for my point of view.

Sargent was at this time working on his huge decorations for the Boston Library. I had never been enthusiastic about his portraits. To me he seemed a fine painter but far from the dazzling star he had been proclaimed.

I saw him a number of times and spent hours in his studio studying his work and listening to him describe it. I was only more disappointed than before. Genius unappreciated and talent overestimated have always been to me bitter disappointments wherever I have met them. Most people can tell an alloy from gold; why can't they take the time to understand the most precious thing the gods have given to mankind—beauty —the pearl of pearls—the *magnum bonum* of existence?

Sargent tried to get a sum total to fit his ambitions without having the content to create that sum total. Magnificence, great symbolic truths, power, movement, color, beauty—did he achieve these? He did not! The tragedy of such a man—and he characterizes American artistic culture—is that as a whole he starts to build without first accumulating the material necessary. He decides to be original, he decides to do something beautiful, he decides to be vigorous, noble, delicate, refined— whatever he may decide is the proper thing to be.

Although I never met him, I cannot but mention Gilbert, the only great English sculptor of modern times, in connection with Sargent. Gilbert was a sculptor by the grace of God, a true genius, and he was at the time living an exile in Belgium. He had been obliged to leave England because of financial difficulties. England, like America, does not excuse an artist or a man of genius in any line for involving himself in financial irregularities. Even Macfall, that broad-minded and great man, replied, when I bitterly accused England of Philistinism for treating a man like Gilbert the way it did:

"Edstrom, Gilbert is a bad citizen."

It made me sick. Gilbert had been a Royal Academician and that stupid body had even taken away this honor from him. Gilbert had become—just as had Benvenuto, Phidias and other great artists of the past—a little mad over the joy of making precious works of art out of precious metals. The income from his commissions was not sufficient to warrant what he spent on materials, and he became involved. I asked Macfall, in connection with Gilbert, how it was I was so nicely treated when a man like Gilbert was allowed to perish, and he answered:

"We Englishmen put personality ahead of art. It is your personality more than your art that has made you friends in England."

I gasped with surprise, because I held my personality in low esteem but had high respect for my artistic ability.

But, coming back to Sargent, imagine what wonders could have been presented to the world had Gilbert been given the opportunity that was given Sargent?

And then there was Gemito, who at this time was languishing in an asylum for the insane, put there by jealous rivals. Gemito is the only great Italian sculptor of modern times. When he was finally released, an old man of eighty, it was made apparent that he had been, not insane, but the object of cruel persecution.

More obnoxious than the greatest honor that might be lavished upon a man like Sargent, who, though overestimated, was all in all a great artist, is the undeserved reputation of such a woman as Mrs. Harry Payne Vanderbilt Whitney, a woman

of mediocre talent, yet, through wealth and social prestige, able
to gain international fame and influence.

Of men of interest I must mention Lovat Frazer, a lovely
genial youth, who died a few years later. Drinkwater wrote
his life after a bitter controversy with Macfall, Frazer's most
intimate friend. Macfall owned so many letters, drawings and
other materials connected with Lovat Frazer's life that he was
the logical man to have written the book.

At the home of my friends, Mr. and Mrs. Sidney Schiff, I
met many of the world's greatest musicians. When Caruso
was in London he was often the guest of the Schiffs. The season
I was there Tosti, the great Italian composer, lived in the Schiff
home. Mrs. Schiff had a beautiful but small soprano voice
and was a delightful artist.

A curious and painful episode occurred to me in connection
with them. Madame X, a very great Swedish singer, who had
lost her voice temporarily, was at the time in London working
with an Italian maestro to regain her powers. She was traveling with a young and beautiful Swedish Countess whom I knew.
This lady told me the voice of Madame X was now as good
as ever, but what she needed was to sing for some sympathetic
musical people of note to regain her confidence. I spoke to
Mrs. Schiff about it, and she, with the spontaneous kindness
peculiar to her character, at once agreed to arrange an exclusive
soirée for her. At the recital were the élite of the musical
world in London at the time. Tosti himself accompanied the
Swedish lady at the piano. She sang very well indeed, though
nervously, but after the *soirée* was over Tosti unfortunately
remarked that she should concentrate on the task of breathing
more smoothly. For this little remark Madame X blamed me
and became abusive. She had made a favorable impression on
her audience, yet she accused me of having ruined her career.
What she needed was a nerve specialist, not a singing teacher.

Epstein, the only man of great strength among the sculptors
living in London, I did not meet. He was, from what I

gathered through Lewis Hind, a kind of modern Pan worshiper. His statue of Oscar Wilde made for the Père La Chaise Cemetery in Paris was indescribable and shocked even Paris as that city had never been shocked before. The statue had to be modified. The sculptures from old Pompeii, not shown to the general public, are not more frank than Epstein's original model of his Oscar Wilde.

Besides those heretofore mentioned, I met Brangwyn, Ezra Pound, John Dillon, Benrimo, Austin Harrison, Felix Moscheles, Sir George Frampton, Littlejohn, Gaudier-Breszdska, John Tweed, Wells, Edmund Gosse, and scores of other notables. I often saw my old friend from earlier days, Caley Robinson, who had now risen to fame. We had, however, both changed so that there had been created a barrier between us through which we could not break. He had become more the dreamer and the artist, and I had become, I imagine, to his point of view hard-boiled and unartistic. In his presence my heart ached with longing to bring back our old relationship, but everything I said seemed to make the gap between us wider.

The greatest honor I received in London was an invitation to exhibit with a little group of artists calling themselves the Internationalists, exhibiting at Knoedler's, a few doors from the Patterson Gallery in Old Bond Street. Among this group Rodin was the dominating figure. It was also interesting to me that they chose, among other things, my "Clouds" for this show. I had always been in doubt myself as to the merits of this piece of work.

Before the hectic season was over, something occurred that nearly gave me another nervous breakdown. Had it not been for the friendship of Maurice Hewlett, the great English novelist, and others, I believe I would have blown up completely. One day I received from André Tridon, an American writer and psychoanalyst living in New York, two copies of an American magazine containing the first two chapters of a biography of myself by Jenkins. In spite of our previous diffi-

culties over it, he had begun the publication of a story of my
life. The first chapter was humiliating beyond description,
and I walked the streets of London in utter despair for many
hours. Then Maurice Hewlett got my mind active again by
getting me to begin an autobiography to counteract the influence
the Jenkins story might have on the world.

To place me in a happy, congenial atmosphere, my friends
arranged quarters for me at the Savage Club. It is on the
Thames in the center of the newspaper world, a club of world
travelers, writers, great hunters and men of prominence who
have a taste for spirited intellectual contacts. Here I wrote
about fifteen thousand words of an autobiography. Hewlett
read these chapters and was enthusiastic over them. He took
me to Heinemann, the English publisher, who read my manuscript while we waited, and said that he would publish my book.

"Make it as long as you like," he said, "but don't let any one
help you with it. I want your life just as you tell it."

I had not gone far in the work before I learned that some
of my friends had persuaded Jenkins again to stop publication
of the story, as a result of which I dropped the whole undertaking. I had a big commission in Sweden and my exposition
to look after, and I was glad to forget myself and my unhappy
past for the thrilling events at hand.

At this time my studio in Paris was located in a remodeled
machine shop on a quaint little street called Rue Tournefort,
behind the Pantheon, in old, old Paris. The original building
must have accrued from the inventive notions of successive
owners—part after part added from time to time, rambling this
way and that, as convenience had suggested. I made of it a
unique and romantic place, and it was so large that I could
easily entertain three hundred people at a reception.

Here I had many interesting social affairs. The acoustics
were good and many fine musicians played and sang at my
soirées. William Guard, secretary to the Metropolitan Opera,
and other scouts for eminent musical talents, came to my place

to hear young men and women who promised to become musical favorites. Among the interesting political figures I met were some of the leaders of the Young Turks.

The late Max Nordau, who was perhaps the most learned man in the world on politics in the countries touching upon the Mediterranean and Adriatic, though seemingly neutral, gave the young Jews who composed the leadership of the Young Turks a great deal of advice. Nordau was a charming man and I never learned so much about international affairs and the characteristics of various races as I did from him. He was married to a Swedish woman. He was known to the world in general as the author of a much-discussed book, *Degeneration*, but to the political world as a man whom it was wise to consult. He gave me the impression of a world citizen with few prejudices—a man of fine moral integrity who believed in the ultimate solution of all problems through knowledge.

I remember once, in talking with Nordau, how he enlarged upon the sanctity and beauty of marriage. He recited the whole poem "John Anderson, My Jo" to me. At the time it struck me as funny, because he was so obviously the real international Jew, seemingly unsentimental in everything.

Max Nordau created in me a deep feeling of sympathy for the Jews who had created the Young Turk party. I became especially fond of Santo Semo Bey, one of the leaders of this group which had overthrown the bogy-man and star villain of Europe, the Sultan Abdul Hamid. As Santo Semo Bey told it to me, the tale of this conspiracy was the most thrilling I've ever heard or read in history or fiction. He said plot after plot to overthrow Abdul Hamid had been thwarted through the discovery of the secret documents of the conspirators by spies of the Sultan, and each effort had ended with wholesale executions. In Turkey or abroad, never could the successive and persistent revolutionary forces that sought the downfall of the old scamp keep their records and documents hidden from these secret agents, until one bright young Jew hit upon the idea of penetrating the harem of a certain high official, winning over his harem ladies to the revolution, and getting them to be the keepers of the documents.

To further the work of these Oriental idealists, I arranged a big *soirée* at which the Bey gave an illustrated lecture on the revolt. Several beautiful runaway harem ladies were there to give visual evidence of what wonderful specimens of feminine pulchritude had been cruelly imprisoned and watched over by cold-hearted eunuchs. Among these harem ladies was a Circassian blonde, as slender as a willow and as beautiful as a houri from Paradise. She was so modest she almost seemed like a young girl just out of a convent, but I could not but feel that she enjoyed the hurly-burly of western freedom.

Santo Semo Bey, however, sold me on the virtues of polygamy. He described harem life as something very fine, and against this custom his party had no quarrel. He convinced me of the soundness of his argument. I am sure there will come a time in the history of the world when polygamy will be considered from a more scientific and intelligent angle than it is now.

XXXVIII

I REFUSE A QUEEN

THE Laremche Kunsthandel of Amsterdam, Holland, had for some time been urging me to have a one-man exhibition with them. The painter, Carl Larson, who next to Zorn I believe is the best-known artist of modern times among Swedish artists, was a very good friend of mine. It occurred to me that if I could persuade the Laremche Kunsthandel to include him in their invitation and make it a two-man show, and Larson also was willing, it would be very much to my advantage. After a great deal of correspondence back and forth the matter was arranged.

Larson sent about fifty paintings and the exhibition looked very fine in the rooms of this splendid Art Gallery. To my great chagrin the Dutch critics did not like Carl Larson's works, and one paper wrote an article saying I was a great joker and had taken Carl Larson with me only as a foil to show the depth of my work against a background of Larson's superficial stuff. This was most unjust, as I was and am a great admirer of Larson, and my reason for asking him was to have a truly great and acknowledged man to give my own show dignity. In fact I believe his murals in the National Museum to be the greatest of their kind painted since the time of the Renaissance.

Most distinguished among these paintings is his mural called "Midwinter's Blood." Here Larson shows how, at the high-winter's feast—the terrible rite of which my grandmother had told me so effectively during my earliest childhood—when the northerners feel most severely the cruelty of the arctic gods, the king himself offers his body to bleed and burn that the tribe may survive because of his sacrifice. Larson saw deeper into the dark abyss of the pagan nature of the Swede than any other artist of the North. His small water-colors were gay and often superficial, but his monumental works had a power and pathos unknown in any other mural painter since the time of Michelangelo. Untoward circumstances hindered me from ever showing this great man my profound admiration. He had cultivated a gay, playful mask that made it almost impossible to have a serious word with him.

My exhibit was a success, yet the whole affair was not a happy one for me because Larson became quite bitter over the criticisms the Dutch gave him, and somehow blamed me for them.

Then another matter caused a stir. I was approached by royal representatives and asked to make a bust of the Queen of Holland. My technique is not adapted to portraits of women unless they are extremely beautiful. My realism is so unrelenting and revealing that any portrait by me of a woman is a shock to the subject. I knew that any bust which I would have made of the queen would have caused a scandal and angered the whole Dutch nation. And so I declined the honor. Somehow the papers got hold of my refusal without giving my point of view at all, rather making me out an artist who scorned the official world, and the news caused bad feeling among people whom I wanted very much to have as friends.

My portrait of Countess Trolle had been reproduced in the Dutch papers and magazines and was also reproduced in my catalogue. It was a successful portrait but it was popular because the countess was a woman of great distinction. My technique accentuated all these qualities but a portrait of the queen made in the same intense, truthful and simple way would have revealed a woman—not the idealized figure a queen must have. There are scores of official painters and sculptors who have developed a technique and an insincerity that enable them to re-create and give a certain distinction to any figure. If a woman

I model is dull-looking, she will seem still more dull in my portrait, because I unmask and bring forth in clarity what nature has produced. I have not trained myself to flattery and untruth. If there is a fine quality in an ugly face I will get it out and reveal the nobility of the character, but humanity does not like to have its ugly features revealed even if a fine character is also accentuated. Men of great individual achievement laugh at their warts and crooked noses, skinny necks or whatever peculiarities they may have, but the greatest woman in the world cannot bear to have her natural features revealed unless she is a rare beauty.

From early history portraiture has been a political matter, not an artistic one, with emperors and rulers. Napoleon enforced a certain dignity and conventionality in all portraits made of him, but look at his death mask! Here we have a face with powerful cheekbones, a ruthless physical brutality that is in keeping with his robust autocratic life. Our George Washington is also portrayed in the same sweet manner; luminous large eyes and tender flesh. But in life his eyes were small, his cheekbones high and powerful, his chin round, stubborn and wilful.

Artists who live around the great and the near-great are mostly pussyfooters and artistic prevaricators. There have been only two periods in art where the great have loved ruthless sincerity in portraiture. The Romans imported artists from Greece and had themselves portrayed in a manner unequaled, save by the Renaissance artists, in sincerity and truthfulness. The Stoic philosophy was the backbone of Roman culture, and stoicism demands first of all that one face facts. The Renaissance, in spite of all its idealism in art, also was frank and simple in its portraiture. Even Raphael in his portraits is virile and direct.

Woman's only power lies in her sex appeal, and therefore successful painters of women must take the woman's point of view. I have never been able to model women—even old women, or the most sensible—without posing them on a revolving model stand. By always avoiding the lady's eyes, working from the sides and from behind so that she cannot catch my glance, I can work undisturbed by the sitter's determination to impose on me her conception of herself, or rather of the way she wants the world to see her.

A woman is conscious of every little peculiarity that adds to or detracts from her charm. She begins in childhood to learn what attracts and what repels. A woman's first action when she decides to sit for you is to ensnare you in the glamour of her charm; that is, to project herself as she has through years of experience made herself seem to others. The successful painter of women accepts her attitude, follows it to the limit, and accentuates her charms as she has developed them.

Had I had the fame of Rodin and been able to ask a retainer of twenty-five thousand dollars, I would have made Queen Wilhelmina and would have enjoyed it. The bust would, of course, have been refused, and I would have kept it for myself.

XXXIX

IN A MAN'S HEART

IT was nearly Christmas when I had exhausted all possibilities in Holland, and I decided to spend the holidays with Cora and begin the execution of a contract with the City of Gothenburg after New Year's. When I arrived in Paris, I went to the bank to replenish my traveling funds and found my account, to which Cora had free access, down almost to nothing. Only a couple of weeks before this I had deposited four thousand crowns. Our apartment was modest and Cora spent little on herself except for clothes and I never objected to that. To be beautifully gowned was her nature and I adored her for it. But she had nothing new now and her state of health convinced me that she had been spending too little, rather than too much, for food.

Her reception of me was not as warm as usual. She was evasive and nervous. I tried to be sympathetic and gay to give her a chance to tell me what had happened. But she avoided being alone with me as much as possible. In a low voice at breakfast, lunch, and dinner, however, I asked her over and over again:

"Where has the money gone? Where? Where?"

And then one morning, in the midst of it, she gave a piercing, terrifying scream, and dug her manicured nails into her face, gave a pull downward and furrowed her cheeks so that the blood ran. Thoroughly frightened, I hurried out and called in the neighbors. As we entered she pointed at me and accused me.

307

"Look what he has done to me," she cried.

Shocked beyond words at her charge, I sent a messenger at once to her best friend, a Miss Williams whom I liked very much, a splendid English girl, the orphan of an English general. As soon as "Billy" arrived, I began to pack, for I knew I could never live with Cora again. From the moment she had accused me of hurting her she had cut me out of her life forever.

I loved her, I have always loved her. I loved her then and have loved her through all the years since. I loved her when she died in Vermont alone and deserted. I love her to this day. One of the most famous international physicians of our time, Dr. Lidin of Stockholm, whose bust I modeled, had observed Cora for a number of weeks, and he had told me that sooner or later I would find our union impossible because of her neurosis and the drugs he felt sure she indulged in. What mean blackmailers, crooks and drug vendors ruined her life I don't know. Yet even my good friend, Gertrude Stein, in her autobiography says I destroyed her.

It was impossible for me to explain my love to the world and accuse her to her Christian Science followers, although years later prominent Christian Scientists advised me to write out a full report of my life with Cora for the Board of Directors of the Christian Science Church in Boston. Such things can, however, never be adequately explained. I feel with Shakespeare, as he expresses himself in Antony's speech over the bier of Cæsar, that it is best to remember the good and bury the faults. To me Cora was the greatest personality that I have ever known, and her faults were small in comparison with her virtues. Her life was blasted before I met her, and had it not been so she would never have married such a one as myself.

Thus I must be grateful for her faults, since because of them she was mine for a time. They leveled off the difference in culture between us.

PROPOSED MEMORIAL TO JOHN ERICSSON

Congress appropriated funds for this monument to the inventor of the *Monitor*, but Edstrom refused to make it because the committee wanted to put it near the Lincoln Memorial where it would be dwarfed

MARGARET, LATE CROWN PRINCESS OF SWEDEN

XL

LOVE AND TANGO

LEAVING Paris I went north again, determined to throw off all the chains of respectability, to be carefree and gay and taste whatever delights dissipation had to offer me.

With the best dancing teacher of Gothenburg, an expert physical-culture trainer and dietician, I was soon ready for a flying start in my planned life of self-indulgence. I became also a student of the rich Oriental literature of sex on its higher levels. I had been too busy to give much intelligent thought to the possibilities of sex as a means to pleasure. As with most decent men, sex was a burden when not the expression of real love and affection.

After a time, when I had mastered thirty-two movements of the tango and all the new things in jazz dancing, I was ready to begin my life of deliberate sin. Then I flowered with spats, a new wardrobe and a monocle, which Paul Konody had told me were great assets in sophisticated style. Paris gowns gave the ladies a mean advantage that was offset by a monocle and spats.

Besides the job with Ericsson on the square and the fountain design, I began a portrait bust of Dr. Axel Romdahl, Director of the Gothenburg Museum. In this work I applied for the first time the modernist forms I had invented in the year 1900 in the making of my "Sphinx."

It was Romdahl who brought to one of my parties a woman whom I shall call Lady X, and his honest, stolid soul must have been rumpled terribly by what followed. After two minutes of my first tango with Lady X I could have used George Sand's perennial phrase when she met a new lover:

"I love you as I have never loved before."

After that first night I saw her constantly. And always we danced; our bodies became as one as we moved across the dance floor in perfect coordination. We composed and improvised as we danced, left out measures and gave new interpretations to suit our moods. Sometimes we hardly moved, and our rhythms and passions were mere inner pulsations, it seemed. Gay, sad, mad, humorous, affectionate, satirical—there seemed to be nothing that we could not convey and carry on in rhythm together. We made works of art out of waltzes and fox trots, and introduced mazurka moods into the mellow tango rhythms from the Argentine.

We went to obscure common dance halls, where no one knew us, to indulge our dance madness. In society here, there and everywhere we danced together, and scandal-loving minds began to make clacking tongues wag. But we paid no attention to them. Together we reached the heights of great ecstasies. She was a great poet and musician. Culture, wealth and position had been hers from childhood. She was twenty-two and, like her father, a famous physician, was an agnostic. The here and now was all she believed in. Better to die than to miss the ecstasies of real life now. I was then forty-two, and it was at times a great effort to keep up the pace with her. She was irresistible and I could never refuse her. I was *semper paratus* when she called, even though it took my last bit of vitality.

Before coming North I had contracted to make a portrait bust of Ellen Key, and during the latter part of July I had to leave Gothenburg for her villa "Strand" near Alvastra on Lake Vettern in order to work. As soon as I was with her she began to scold me.

"That affair with Lady X is going to ruin you," she said. "She is twenty years younger than you are, wealthy, popular, and her powerful friends and family have already undermined your position."

"I know they've tried to," I replied. "But as soon as I get through here, I am to do Princess Margaret. That doesn't look as if their little souls had achieved much."

"Don't fool yourself. The Princess, like myself, is one of these loyal fools who never desert a friend in trouble. But she is no gage by which to measure the rest of the world. Unless you break with Lady X at once you will be ruined."

Of course, I knew that she was giving me good advice, but every day with Lady X was worth dying for, and I would not give her up.

Ellen's house was full of guests from all parts of the world. Some came only for a few hours to worship her or consult her on the feminist movement far and near. When Germany declared war, however, every one fled. Those last few days the place was a veritable tower of Babel. All friendliness flew away and nationalistic hatreds came to the surface. Ellen was a pacifist and we soon began to quarrel. I hastened the job as much as I could, and returned to Gothenburg for a short meeting with my sweetheart before going North.

Kings, queens, princes and princesses are just people, and yet in my career there was a time when, like the bee following the scent of the nectar-laden flower, the magic incense enclouding royalty attracted me more than fame or wealth.

The time agreed upon between Gustav Adolf and myself to model his wife's bust arrived and I left for Stockholm. Crown Princess Margaret was one of the most considerate, kind, and self-sacrificing women I have ever known. She never postponed sittings, never became impatient or argumentative, and even sacrificed other interests in order to meet with my convenience. Yet the making of her bust almost ended in disaster.

In a way I least expected, she almost drove me to distraction. From the moment she sat down on the model's table she began to knit socks. In and out, back and forth, flashed and clacked the long needles in a wild jerky rhythm that made me wiggle my toes in time with each clack, and turn my eyes at the insistence of their hypnotic power.

One day I couldn't stand it any longer and in a fierce whisper exploded. "Please, Your Royal Highness, please, will you put that knitting away for awhile?"

She never answered a word, nor did the needles cease their infernal speed. Silently she bowed her head so I could not see her face, but her flush of anger spread to her ears and down the neck.

"Ah," I reflected, "one must not ask a Royal Highness not to knit."

I was terribly worried over this job. My friend Fülop de Laszio had painted both Margaret and Patricia as raving beauties. In painting it was possible to show these two sisters thus and preserve some likeness, but in sculpture, which is three-dimensional, it was necessary to tell the exact sculptural truth and nothing but the truth or lose all character and likeness. It is absolutely impossible to fake portrait sculpture successfully.

I did not worry over what Margaret would think of the bust. She was just as free from vanity as her sister. What made me uneasy, as I molded the high cheekbones and rather dumpy German form inherited from her mother, was what her husband would think of it.

Gustav Adolf was madly in love with his wife. And a husband in love is a man in love, be he prince or plebeian, and to a man in love his beloved is a composite in feature and soul of Aphrodite and Titania in one—of feminine perfection.

For this reason my tenseness and fear made me again put forth a plea against the terrible knitting orgy. Again the princess remained silent. After a few days' interval, for a third time I asked to be spared the crucifixion of being a party to sock knitting. This time Margaret laid down her knitting and with tear-filled eyes told me the socks were for her brother, Prince

Arthur, who was in the trenches. Both Margaret and "Pat" had the dark eyes with black lashes peculiar to the Irish, and tearful Irish blue eyes are impossible to resist. Also that wistful lame boy, her brother, limping in cold slushy mud, came to my vision. A realization that not only his but most of Margaret's childhood friends were being destroyed came to consciousness.

The King, the army and the aristocracy of Sweden were all pro-German. I had also on several occasions given utterance to German sympathies in both the Swedish and German press. Margaret, far from people of her kind, alone in the drab inclement North, in the midst of hostile people, went her way calmly and unperturbed.

During one of my off days, while I was struggling with a light fever, Otto Wrething, my old friend from Umea, came to visit me.

"Where have you been?" I cried out at him.

"Out on a masonry job," he replied.

"I thought you were a painter."

"I don't mean the same kind of masonry you mean," he answered.

Ever since I had been twelve years old I had wanted to be a Mason and now I took advantage of the fact that he was active in Masonry and asked him whether I could get in.

"I think it could be arranged," he said, "if you will get a special dispensation from King Gustav. The fact that you are an American citizen is the only thing in the way."

The next time the Crown Prince came in to see me work I asked if he would introduce me to his father for this purpose. He told me that would not be necessary but he would arrange the matter for me. He did this within a few days, and as soon as my work was finished I made the forty-eight-hour journey north to Umea.

The initiations were a tremendous surprise to me. The ordeal of the first degree in Sweden is an unforgettable event in any man's life.   Many never proceed any farther and at times wish later they had never gone as far as that.   To get members, American Masonry has deleted many of the old rituals.   I was thoroughly shocked out of my self-complacency and looked with new eyes at my conduct during the preceding year.   I am not ashamed to say that not since I was a lad had I wept such hot tears of both remorse and happiness.   In Umea under the flare of the Aurora Borealis I entered the gates of a new concept of life.

XLI

NEW YORK CITY

YOU begin living in a place after you have begun in secret to foresee and visualize your intention. You are separated from some one when you cease to love, and that is the reason it is said marriages are made in heaven. The pattern of events is always made before the events happen.

During all the years abroad I had had no desire to return home, not because I did not love America but because I was so busy living day by day. I was in the midst of art and politics from one end of Europe to the other. I wrote satires and articles on politics and art for three different publications constantly, *Veckojournalen, Nya Dagligt Allehnda* and *Goteborgs Morgon Post.*

I had enemies in every walk of life. At the Baltic Exhibition of Germany, Russia, Denmark and Sweden, the Academy group tried to oust me. Being an Academician, I had a right to pass my stuff without jury, and being recognized by the modernist group named Konstnärsförbundet I was invited to their shows. The Academicians resented this, and so, when I came to Malmö before the show, no place had been allotted to me. No stands had been made for my works. They had reckoned I would, because of my notoriously violent temper, pull out my exhibit. Instead I met the director, Professor Bjork, and made him so angry that he gave me a splendid place. I made friends with the carpenters and they worked all one night to get my stands ready. Dressed like a diplomat, with monocle and white spats, I marched in with seventeen men in military formation carrying

my stands and set up my show just before the press and royalty
and the cream of society arrived. As usual, I was successful.

But my affair with Lady X gave my enemies ammunition
which they used skilfully, and before spring I was ready to
admit that Ellen Key had been right when she told me I must
drop it or be ruined. My sweetheart was a woman of great culture, and after long and pertinent discussions we decided that
the only solution was for me to go to America. All the reasons
for this decision are not for public knowledge. They involved
the happiness and rights of some very fine people. We had had
a year of supreme happiness and decided that we could not take
more. I sailed on the *Bergensfjord* for New York in the summer of 1915.

In New York I had many friends and acquaintances. Silas
McBee, publisher of *The Churchman,* and his editor, Dr. Lloyd
Bevan, with both of whom I had had such happy meetings in
Italy and Paris, were among the first I looked up.

Through Dr. Goddard Leach, now editor of *The Forum,* I
met Hamilton Holt, William H. Short, a protégé of Carnegie,
and others interested in the League to Enforce Peace. Short,
subsidized by Carnegie, had years before the war created the
New York Peace Society, the nucleus around which the League
to Enforce Peace was built. Though a Puritan and the least
artistic man I have ever known, he became the most stanch and
intimate friend I have ever had. Though we fought more bitterly and constantly than I believe either of us had ever fought
with any one else, our friendship held out without interruption
until his death. I believed in an ultimate peace but did not
believe in the success of his plans except as a beginning of things
that would eventually be realized.

Philadelphia was then planning the building of its Museum
and the great layout of a cultural center and a wide avenue. I
was invited to visit the place and express myself on the plans.
These have since been carried out at tremendous cost and in
grand style. The project involved demolishing miles of old

houses, and, appalled by the cost, I had nothing to contribute. I could not think in American terms of vastness.

My contacts, however, led me into political, social and economic problems and away from my art. American art at that time bored me. It meant nothing to me. I met Jonas Lie, who then posed as an advanced crusader, painting skyscrapers. He seemed very amusing. I found the same old "stuntism" I had seen in Europe during the past years among the American artists, saw mental gyration over whether to paint in a high or low key, whom to follow, what to imitate, and never any authentic yearning for self-expression.

For years I lived off and on at the National Arts Club in Gramercy Square. As a home it was delightful; artistically it was a morgue. But of evenings I found relaxation playing billiards and pool with the dead souls I met there and listening to their childish patter. They were so much better billiard players than artists that there was no incentive to discuss art and we were really free to enjoy the games.

More and more, as time went on, I wondered what place I could find in this, the country of my adoption. And then I had a brilliant idea.

My earliest awareness of the world at large as a child had come to me through the reform farm in Dalsheda, of which my father had charge. Even more than art the problem of evil and crime had always interested me. Temperamentally I was a sucker, a believer in the good of human nature. Sensitive because an artist, I hated despotism and cruelty. How to make men live decently without treating them like beasts was always in my thought. My father had succeeded; my good friend, the Earl of Sandwich, through his George Junior Republic, was doing wonderful work. When I heard of what Thomas Mott Osborne was trying out in Sing Sing I secured letters to him and left for Ossining to see for myself. Through his cooperation I was admitted to Sing Sing Prison as a voluntary prisoner.

XLII

SING SING

PERIODICALLY I am a misogynist. The memory of the peaceful Franciscan Monastery on the crest of Fiesole only a few minutes' climb from my villa always came to me when the misogynist mood was on. My misogyny arose, not from actual hatred of, but from a too terrible desire for, women. Monasteries are the refuge of many such men. The atmosphere of Sing Sing gave me the same strange shock as I had received when I used to visit the Fathers in Fiesole. Men isolated from women for years become different; strange psychic currents are uncovered. They develop characteristics that unfit them for life later on. They are not unhappy, but stunted. Like wild animals in a cage, they live on and on, but they are of no use in the economy of existence. The bright eyes, the hungry, eager magnetism of these men I met in Sing Sing awakened a sympathetic response in me.

Osborne's Mutual Welfare League created from the model of the George Junior Republic had its court to judge on infringements of prison rules. One of the judges was a yegg. He was tall, muscular, erect, poised and vital. Not since I had gone with those loggers down the Umea River had I seen such a specimen of a man. I would have liked to be in a logging crew with him. He was wild, untutored, and saw life only seconds ahead.

"Time—what is it? God alone knows," says Eddington in one of his books. "Time—what is it?" asks Einstein. "Time—what is it?" asks Millikan. "Time—what is it?" has been asked by all the seekers of truth from the beginning of thinking men.

Tell us what time is and we shall know what good or bad men are. While Christ prayed in Gethsemane, the disciples slept. He reproved them that they could not stay awake for such a little time.

"Doing time" is the slang for imprisonment. Three score years and ten—a man's allotment of time. Time gallops for the man who is waiting to be hanged and drags for the maiden awaiting her lover, says Shakespeare. Prisons kill time, make it useless to its inhabitants. Would it not be more sensible to make prisons schools and teach the use of time?

The terrible old buildings of Sing Sing in 1915 seemed to me nasty and evidence of a depraved public morale. Narrow, cold, concrete boxes without proper ventilation, with an iron bucket as the only sanitary arrangement, could only create a desire not to think, not to be, not to remember, not to love or hate, but to die, or hibernate until freedom came. What possibilities has a prisoner when freedom does come? He is not free but a prisoner, kept away from life because the knowledge of how to use time has been taken away from him.

To make a beautiful work of art takes time. There is never quite enough. The days are too short, the strength of eye, hand and body never enough for the desire of the heart and soul. Thomas Mott Osborne was a sentimentalist and in many ways impractical, but his vision was right. Intelligence and culture are needed, not cruelty and punishment, to make life safe. Smug, cowardly men cheating within the law seemed to me less worthy of friendship than many of the men I met at Sing Sing. But there were the same types as out in the world. The difference lay in how they had been taught in childhood to spend their time.

For the first time in my life I yearned to create an art class. I asked Osborne if it were possible. "Yes, at your own expense," he said. What would the politicians say if I taught the prisoners to make statues?

It was with regret that I left Sing Sing, not yet having found a place in America.

XLIII

SAINT IGNATIUS

I HAD credentials from both the *Goteborgs Morgon Post* and the *Veckojournalen* as correspondent. The *Veckojournalen* is Sweden's leading weekly and the *Morgon Post* a daily, politically very well informed. As a result of these connections, I was given what in detective parlance is called "rough shadowing." It began on the ship on the way to America. I would arrange certain papers in a certain way and later find that they had been tampered with while I was out of my stateroom. Clothes were moved from one suitcase to another. Since the beginning of the war Sweden had been a center for foreign spies and my Swedish connections laid me open to the gravest suspicions.

In Sweden a friend stole for me a private state paper in which was outlined a plan by which the officials of a certain power were to use me. As a curiosity I still keep it. Its tenor was that I was more or less of a boob, weak, susceptible to flattery and eager to pose as an insider. My position and talkativeness might thus be used to advantage.

I was frightened and ill at ease. And then I was eating my heart out with longing for both my wife and Lady X. Both were infinitely dear to me without inner conflict. I loved in one her Irish soul and charm, her humor, wit and mad courage; the other I loved for her youth, beauty, vitality, a creature such as the Greeks conceive of in the goddess Aphrodite. Cora, I always addressed as Pallas Athene. She could in posture and dignity have been a model for Phidias when he made his statue of that goddess. In her contest in Olympus with Aphrodite and Juno, however, Aphrodite and not Pallas Athene was awarded the prize by young Paris. In life also, Aphrodite generally has the last inning. Lady X was my Aphrodite.

I decided to go to the World's Fair in San Francisco, where I had a large exhibition. And then a friend sent me an interview about my coming and plans for my entertainment. It was my first meeting with sensational American journalism since Hearst's *American Magazine* had featured me in colors on its two middle pages. It had taken me years to recover from that atrocity, and this stuff was in the same genre. Disgusted and sick at heart, I decided that I could not face that kind of romance just then.

Needing advice, I went to my old friend Dr. Bevan, who for a long time had been a professor of history in the University of the South, at Sewanee, Tennessee. When I told him of my heartaches and weariness, he advised me to go to Sewanee for a time until I got rested. I took his advice, and without ever having begun work in New York, I entrained for the Cumberlands and Sewanee.

Before getting there I discovered that I was suspected of being a German spy with seventeen trunks, and posing as an artist. Because I was wearing beautiful enamel and gold Masonic insignia, I was approached by a number of the brethren on the way down. The emblem was made in the form of a little mason's trowel and was the only one I have ever seen in this country. Letters from both Bevan and McBee guaranteed a warm reception in this old stronghold of Southern culture. The professors, students and old families residing in Sewanee proceeded to make me very happy and at home. The Southerner is the only type of American I have ever learned to love, save members of the working classes in the North.

In a sense it was like entering an American Stratford-on-Avon as that delightful birthplace of Shakespeare might have been a hundred years ago. The soft Southern drawl soothed and calmed me. The boys introduced me to football and gave me something to cheer for. They had a championship team holding its own at that time with big schools like Vanderbilt, Alabama, Ames, and other great universities. One year they had even beat Yale. They had about four hundred students, little money, meager equipment, but all were gentlemen.

I had a beautiful collection of pipes, some many hundreds of years old. A young chap named Scheider, later on an aide to Pershing, invited me to the lovely fraternity house of the A. T. O.'s. I felt my collection would grace their house and give more pleasure to them than it could to me, so I gave them my collection and they promptly gave me the privileges of their homes. My knowledge of anatomy also made me an efficient masseur, enabling me to help the overworked doctor, and I spent a lot of time rubbing and bandaging sprains and bruises. I followed them to many of their games and developed a capacity for howling, bellowing, squawking and whooping with glee that I had never had before. At one game I crushed a brand new derby and sent it sailing out to the field as a demonstration to the boys after they had made a terrific fight for a touchdown.

The Faculty Club took me in. A rocky, sporty golf course gave me many happy hours when spring came.

Four Episcopalian bishops lived in Sewanee. The great American theologian, Du Bose, lived there. Gradually, stimulated by contact with them, I took up again the study of philosophy and theology. One day I mentioned to Bishop Guery from Charleston, South Carolina, that sooner or later I was going to enter a Jesuit monastery for a time. Guery was a true religious and was immediately interested and encouraging.

"But," he said, "we have a house of the Holy Cross Fathers only a few miles from here at St. Andrews. If you are interested in the monastic life, I'll give you a letter to Father Harrison, the Prior."

Thus it came about that I became an inmate of St. Andrews

for over a year. During this time I had secured a contract for a Civil War monument in my home town of Ottumwa. My visit there was short and had only one major interest, that of meeting many of the boys and girls who had worked in the factories with me as boy and youth. Some of the best families in Ottumwa entertained me, but what is more smug than Iowa society, and what could be more repugnant to Iowa society than one such as I?

At the monastery I built a studio where I made the big eagle for the shaft of the monument. The cold froze the bird several times and I had a difficult time. At the monastery we followed the rule of silence all the time except during the noonday meal on Sunday. It was a relief from day to day not to hear my own voice. As a layman, I was obliged to take part in only five religious exercises a day. These were a source of great spiritual and esthetic joy. As the Psalms of David were uttered in chanting and responses, repeated over and over again, they lived for me as nothing else could make them.

After my terrible illness I had studied the exercises of St. Ignatius with great ardor. They are often named the "Manresa Exercises" because of the place where he had the religious experience and revelations that brought them forth. It was here that he conceived the Society of Jesus, the most wonderful religious society in the world. St. Ignatius has always been to me the greatest religious of all time.

After some persuasion, and after I had given evidence of my familiarity with the Loyola theology, Father Harrison consented to aid me in going through the exercises. Absolute seclusion in my cell was required except for the visits of the priest who watched over me and helped me. The first exercise is this: "Who made me?" For twenty-four hours you may ask the air, the wind, the sky, who made you. It is an exercise that will never be forgotten. Ask it a thousand times alone in silence: "Who made me? Who made me? Who made me?" Feel of your blanket, ask the stars, whisper it to the moon. "Silvery, silent moon, tell me, tell me who made me."

If you desire to read the true St. Ignatius exercises, ask a Jesuit friend to lend them to you. They are not, for some reason or other, to be had at bookstores. The books sold are not the Manresa exercises given the members of the Order. The logic of Loyola is as unmerciful as mathematics. When you have come to a conclusion as to who made you, whatever it may be, you will never again be the same person.

Here at St. Andrews I arranged with Masonic brethren in Sewanee to gain entry to the Scottish Rite lodge. In Nashville I took the degrees from the third to the thirty-second. If there is a heaven that my mortal consciousness can picture, no place more near to it exists than the thirty-second degree as the Tennessee brethren gave it.

After perhaps the happiest year in my life in the monastery I realized that I must leave. Turmoil, battle, hot, bruising contacts with life are my mission. There is a monastic loneliness in the midst of chaos far greater than monastic isolation. When you strike where you desire to be kind, smile when you want to strike, hide your thoughts deep and carry on, you live in a great solitude.

In 1917 I was back in New York with a studio on Broadway near Fifty-ninth Street.

XLIV

NEW YORK—1917

THIS period I consider the most uninteresting of my whole life. I wrote many articles for the *Saturday Evening Post*, *Physical Culture*, *Psychology* (now extinct), Swedish papers, and free publicity for the League to Enforce Peace. I made many monuments. I gave great parties. I made Liberty Loan talks here and there. I visited Canada to study the political situation with Short. I met some great Jesuits in Montreal. One was a true saint teaching at St. Joseph's.

With the then Sovereign Grand Commander Judge Fleming Moore I did a great deal of studying of the rising evils that later culminated in the Ku Klux madness. He worked in harmony with the Catholic Knights of Columbus. A truly great Mason of profound knowledge. In Sweden the Master of the Umea Lodge had been a student of the ancient Egyptian rites of which Pythagoras had been an adept. I also was given opportunity to read some of the correspondence of the late King Oscar with General Pike, the greatest Mason of the modern era or of all history so far as we know.

I want to forget the making of much money, of many meetings with the great during this time. Wilson's stupid running over to Paris, the billions spent in making airplanes that could not fly, ships that would not float, the squandering of something like forty billion dollars and the evidence of the stupidity of my people that made such waste possible are not pleasant to remember. I met President Taft, the heads of British and Belgian war missions. With Sir Frederic Bach, head of the British war mission, I had long confidential talks, and he foresaw that the war would result in a fizzle because of American weakness and French fear. A stalemate had been the best ending and not a crushed Germany.

Many reasons that I do not care to discuss at last inspired me to go West. To make monuments is not to make art. Public monuments are seldom works of art either here or elsewhere. St. Gaudens made a few exceptions and Shrady's "Grant" in Washington is also a great exception. He worked thirteen years on it. He might have worked a lifetime. What Congressional committee would let an artist work a lifetime on a project and perhaps then never get it finished? Modern Sweden, which allowed Ostberg to spend some twenty-five years on the City Hall in Stockholm, has shown that it might be done. The cost for the building was at first estimated at four million, but it cost fifty-two million before Ostberg was through. In Sweden, however, Masonry is a power and the royal family is revered; the Socialists control the vote, cooperatives break the trusts when they won't behave, and the farmers are just too stubborn for words when it comes to horse sense. It takes men with horse sense to trust a great architect and give him all the money and time he needs to do a good job. But an American politician must get things made quickly—for example, war planes that can't fly.

I was never happier than when I at last left that center of blah and noise, cheap shows and Ziegfeld heroines, New York. Let the brown derbies and the Al Smiths have the sidewalks, both on the East Side and the West Side! I left them willingly!

XLV

WHERE THE WEST BEGINS

IN an attempt to wash the stain of New York from my soul
I stopped at the Grand Canyon of the Colorado. A shuddering, abysmal awfulness of mysterious, bottomless space met
my eyes when, from the bright rim of an early morning in November, I looked down into the misty furrow the Colorado has
ground out during countless ages through the mountains. I felt
as if from a beetling height I looked into the monstrous den
where Leviathan, ministered to by Gargantuan behemoths, lived
in infernal gloom. Sunlit slopes flung steeply downward into
fathomless darkness. Interminable passages and caverns overwhelmed the imagination with a vastness the mind could not
grasp. There were bewildering labyrinths, and as I descended
I felt silent hot and cold currents of air and heard weird whis-
perings.

On the back of a temperamental mule, following a guide,
farther and farther I went. An increasing noise met us from
the terrific river that from the rim seemed an anemic little
brook. The descent was over the Bright Angel Trail, the first
that is offered to the tourist. Later I took the two-day trip,
and then my hunger for thrills inspired me to hire an old guide
who claims to have discovered the Canyon and after whom a
trail has been named, to give me a week's camping at the
bottom.

The guide's two daughters accompanied us down to the cave
on the shore of the river chosen for our camp. They returned
to the top with the horses and were to come back for us in a

week. It is futile to try to describe the reactions of an exploration of this crazy and involved place. Up and down and in every direction we found weird temples, steeples, cathedrals and granite formations, like titanic monstrosities from other worlds. Down in the great ditch the outer world becomes small, but the world around you tremendous. The heights seem bigger than mountain tops, and when you drop stones into some of the holes and hear them rattling and echoing down and down until the sounds fade away into depths never explored, you wonder how far those rocks keep on traveling after you no longer can hear them.

I don't remember how many days and nights we had been down there when I was awakened one morning by the most terrific noise I had ever heard. Our camp cave was the space under an overhanging cliff. Jerking my head out from under my blanket, I saw in the dim, bleak dawn huge volumes of water cascading over the cliff, carrying down massive boulders, trees and all manner of débris with fearful clatter, striking the rocky shore of the turbulent river. A hundred hydraulic hammers could not have made a more ear-splitting din. My guide was jumping up and down, yelling at the top of his voice:

"We must get out of here at once. It's raining here but on the rim there is a blizzard raging. The trail will be covered with feet of snow and ice."

And we got out in a hurry. Deluges of rain, sleet and hail blew with murderous force against our aching faces as we got out from the sheltering cliff. Every step was a struggle. For long distances we crept on our hands and knees, feeling with our hands the sometimes only three-foot trail above chasms hundreds, and sometimes thousands, of feet deep. The snow during the last painful ascent was a couple of feet deep. And then at last we found safety and warmth in front of an open fire, with dry clothes and hot drinks. It is in moments like this that even raw "moonshine" is as a nectar of the gods.

After camping on the floor of the canyon, I moved out to a

shack at Desert View, where the Painted Desert spreads out on the right as you look away toward the little Colorado while below you to the left sinks the Canyon. I spent the days from sun-up until night sitting on the outermost point. I used every imaginable mental device to create a synthetic conception of the great chasm. I visualized a single digger with a shovel, digging for countless millions of years, an engineer creating behemoth machinery to dig it out, the dream of a Dante's hell with millions of damned souls dwelling down there. As night came on, the colossal cleft became terrifying. And just before the sun sank, the hole seemed to become bottomless. Only a few nights was I able to stay on after darkness, before terror seized me and I hurried into the shack and barricaded the door. I slept in one of those queer little nests of the cave dwellers, and at night these prehistoric people seemed to be near even here at the View. I am, of course, a thrill seeker, seeking out crooks' nests in every big city, following dangerous paths and seldom finding danger or feeling it even when it has been near.

But here, where there was no danger, I felt nameless fears and tremors. Fear is really a thing of the imagination. During real danger there is no fear because you are so busy fighting the danger. The only fear-emotion comes after the struggle is over, and often, even then, a sense of exultation and of strength comes instead.

But even the most delightful of terrors must have an end, and so, after staying at the Canyon for six weeks, I entrained for Los Angeles.

"We're coming into Los Angeles," some one called. I rushed to look out. No, this could not be it. A nightmare of ugliness. The vaunted mountains were just bigger slag heaps than those I had seen around the Pennsylvania coal mines. The flat floor of the valley was cluttered with ugly monstrosities of architecture, surrounded by sickly looking, ratty palms that resembled stage props. Wizened plots of grass were struggling with the hard adobe soil. Suddenly we were in the city. I went to the best down-town hotel of the period and felt more depressed than I had felt for a long time.

Some one had given me a letter to Harry Chandler, publisher of the Los Angeles *Times*, and I went to see him. The paper was housed in a building constructed in massive imitation Romanesque architecture, so esteemed by the Victorian era in the West. But from the time I entered that atrocity of architecture I became more and more entangled in a chain of events which were anything but Victorian. I feel dizzy to this day when I think of my first experience with Los Angeles publicity. A few years before I had refused to go to the San Francisco World's Fair because of an interview about me, and now I encountered something even worse. In a jiffy I was on the bandwagon and a part of the boom, boom, boom!

In Dallas, Texas, when I was there for dedication of a statue, I had run into an oil boom in which new-made rich men bought pianos by the half-dozen and rugs by the truckload. In restaurants I saw men betting hundred-dollar bills on guesses as to where a fly would alight.

All this seemed colorless compared to the razzle-dazzle of a Los Angeles boom. It seemed for a time as if every one I had met at Naples, St. Moritz, Venice, Rome or Paris was living in Southern California. I was entertained by Henry Huntington, buyer of the famous eight-hundred-thousand-dollar picture, "The Blue Boy." Millions, millions, hundreds of millions seemed to whisper in every breath of the desert air. Easterners like gamblers at Monte Carlo were crowding in to invest in pictures.

In some manner or other I found myself on the Board of Directors of a motion-picture company organized in New York by men that had never seen Los Angeles. Although I never attended a meeting or met the man who put up the money, I was put on a handsome salary to study the business. In the effort to earn my salt honestly, I was soon in a whirl of parties

with the dizziest crowd of humans I had ever known. Gloria
Swanson was at her zenith, and Elinor Glyn, made up in countless jewels, some genuine, some paste, floated around as a mysterious Egyptian princess. Her favorite social stunt was to go
into the silence and tell you about your past incarnations. She
gave me a most gorgeous past through the centuries. I had
been a Chinese prince, Giotto, a favorite of Queen Elizabeth.
And then I displeased her. After that she was not more than
a minute in the silence when she flung at me that I had been
"a horrid, fat old Dutch woman."

A group of high-powered real estate operators or, as they are
now named, realtors, tried to get me to accept five acres in what
is now Westwood. An architect had drawn out the plans for a
palace.

"Here it is, all for your taking. You need not put up a cent.
We build, give you a title, and you move in and achieve a
proper front for your fame."

To their dismay, I refused.

"But the town will be here in a year," they said. "We have
now five hundred thousand and are growing at the rate of a
hundred thousand people a year."

Still I refused and they thought I was mad. Incidentally,
their predictions were correct and that property is now worth
several hundred thousand dollars.

But I was already like a circus rider galloping away on four
crazy steeds to unknown ends. I had left all my sculptures and
personal effects in Europe, and the storage had piled up to a
big amount. I was given a great inducement to send for them
and settle in Los Angeles.

The picture company faded away after having done nothing
save buy an option on a chimpanzee star named "Snooky" and
rent a motion-picture lot at an exorbitant price. The motion-
picture industry put on what it advertised as a "Monroe Cen-
tennial World's Fair." I was made Art Commissioner and

worked myself ragged to carry it through the summer's end after it had gone into the hands of receivers.

Finally I became acclimated and built a modest house in Hollywoodland overlooking Hollywood. At this time the Archbishop of Sweden visited our village and was the chief speaker at a banquet given him. We became friends, and this resulted in an engagement to give a series of lectures at Upsala University, Sweden, under the auspices of the Theological Foundation of "Olaus Petri." He gave me credit for being one of the few truly original philosophers of our day. On the fly-leaf of a copy of his book, *Christian Fellowship,* he inscribed "To the artist, David Edstrom, with thanks to the Highest for the sharing in the Sacrament of spiritual participation of great yearning, sincere and uncompromising truth seeking, and the craving for realities."

And so I went briefly back to Sweden. Giving the lectures was as exciting as attending a Quaker funeral. A funny story I slipped in at my first talk brought a frantic warning from the Archbishop to be serious. At a dinner he gave in my honor our then Minister to Sweden, Robert Bliss, was present. After the dinner the party was invited by the Governor to Upsala Castle where a dinner had been tendered Crown Prince Gustav Adolf and his new wife, Princess Louise. I was happy to meet the Prince again. A group of students sang on the court several hundred feet below the enormous circular medieval tower room. Hundreds of guests were present, most of them decorated with all the Orders of creation. I felt embarrassed because I was not in tails and wearing a white tie. If dear Princess Margaret had been there I would not have felt so mean. Princess Louise looked at me as if I had been something the cat had brought home.

On my way home I was glad to get to London again. I saw Paul Konody and Macfall and lunched once with the Earl of Sandwich. Everybody was depressed and angered at America. I spent the six weeks I was there studying at the British Mu-

"CHILDHOOD"

Bronze bust of granddaughter of ex-Governor Higgins of New York

HARRY CHANDLER

Bust of the Los Angeles *Times* publisher, owned by himself

seum to get proofs of certain postulates I had made about Thugism in the Shiva religion of India. The theologians and philosophers at Upsala had been unable to help me, though they and the Archbishop defended me against the violent attacks of one of the newspapers for my radical views on religion.

Since being Commissioner for the Scandinavian countries in the proposed World's Fair planned for England, I had been deeply interested in the cultural possibilities of these great affairs of modern life and therefore I divided my time between the Museum and the Empire Exhibition at Wembley. Though not elaborate and with no popular glamour, it was the most interesting and valuable fair I had ever seen. Handling of tropical diseases and life in the tropics, mining, farming, and all the hundreds of activities of the great empire, were in a most thorough and comprehensive manner shown for study, not for show or amusement. It was in every way what such an exhibition should be in its influence on the progress of the world. I had bought passage on the Johnson Line to return home via the Panama Canal from Antwerp. I had never visited Belgium and left London in time to visit there for awhile.

After arriving I had a courteous wire from the owner of the line, Axel Axelson Johnson, saying that an artist should not be forced to pay for such a sordid thing as steamship travel, and if I would call at their Antwerp offices I would get a refund.

Strange as it may seem, I was happy to get back to Los Angeles. I decided immediately to get rid of my house on the hill, rent a practical workshop, and drop the social whirl and ballyhoo. At first it seemed a little lonely and sad not to step out. Front means so much out there. But my short fling in Europe had given me back my old ideals. A previous fling in Washington, D. C., had sobered me. During the months I was there, among all the gay affairs I attended, was one of Mrs. Henderson's exclusive Thursday afternoon tea dances. I went to it with the Swedish Minister's wife, Mrs. Wallenberg. Mrs.

Henderson's big attraction that afternoon was a cake-walk competition for two huge cakes. With a young Southern girl I won
the event against a field of young Navy and Army officers and
Washington gallants. My performance became Associated Press
news and I knew something terrible had happened to me when
I kept clippings about it and was more elated than I had ever
been over my artistic success. That was what New York had
begun and Hollywood carried on in me.

To stop my spiritual decay, I sold my house in Hollywood
and rented a cheap studio with miserable living quarters and
really went to work again.

Among interesting people I have met here, the group of
scientists around the California Institute of Technology stands
out above all others. Next to Charlie Chaplin, I believe Robert
Millikan, president of the institute and a Nobel prize winner,
can talk faster and more continuously than any one else I have
ever known. During a Commencement some years ago at the
institute, I happened to visit him. We got into some kind of
discussion of the deeper things of life, art, God, and the ultimate fate of the universe. He took me from one department
to another, and as we progressed from laboratory to laboratory
he demonstrated one apparatus after another. His wife and a
secretary followed with sheaves of papers for him to sign or
pass on. He waved them off with frantic gestures. The secretary, whenever he caught my eye, gave me dirty, venomous
sparks, and his wife appealing ones, as if she would say, "Please,
please, this is Commencement and we need him desperately."

Some time later I was the introductory speaker at a banquet
the Swedish Colony gave Millikan after he received the Nobel
prize. Knowing that Mrs. Millikan would be my table mate, I
prepared a practical joke for her. In her mind I knew I was
catalogued as a windbag, and I knew she would be by this time
wearied to death with banquets and banquet speeches. Before
leaving for the affair I stuck a thick sheaf of typewritten manuscript in my pocket. While we were eating she frankly asked

me if my speech would be a long one and told me how tired she was. I just as frankly told her I could not disappoint the Colony as they very much liked my speeches, and then, knowing both Sweden and America, I could at the same time enlighten her husband about Sweden. As I said this I took out the bunch of typewritten material, and when she saw it she gave a groan and turned away.

I began my talk. When a student in Stockholm, I said, I had come into intimate contact with the great Nobel through his underwear. I told them that besides the many millions he had left he had also left several dozen of the most marvelous suits of underwear, woven from silk and camel's hair. Through a mutual friend of the Nobel heirs who knew of my poverty, these excellent undergarments had been given me and for years I wore the most luxurious underwear ever made.

The Swedish audience was properly shocked, and then I introduced Dr. Millikan. The whole speech took five minutes and forty seconds. And then began the real speeches. Swedes can stand more punishment in the matter of dinner speeches than any people except the Dutch. The more they are bored, the more do they feel they are performing in a proper manner. To do a thing properly means more than entertainment to them.

Romanticist and realist are two curious words freely used but not understood. Young Carl Anderson, who has recently won the Nobel prize in physics, during one of our talks recently criticized Eddington for being a romanticist in science. The late Dr. Michaelson, another Nobel prize winner in physics, who established the speed of light, also pleaded with fierce intensity for realism. During one discussion I had with him, some time before he died, I asked him if he believed in God.

"No," was his answer.

"But do you not believe in an intelligence in nature?"

"No," was his answer; "nature is stupid."

XLVI

OPINIONS

SO there is the story of my life. What have I learned from it? Not even I can tell you clearly.

I believe in no philosophy, not even my own. From childhood I have ardently sought an ultimate rationalized formula and guiding law of life, and I am farther than ever from any such law, philosophy or code. I do believe in art and such philosophers as rise on the wings of the imagination and become poets. They touch the mantle of ultimate wisdom. Among such inspired ones the prophets of the Jews are to me paramount. Jesus as a Jewish prophet separated from the vicious superstitions of paganism and as a carrier of the Jewish code is to me the highest. Buddhism and Hinduism in all their various forms are to me the most pernicious philosophies except for such expressions of them as come from certain poets who diverge from dogma and sing as poets of all lands and creeds sing.

As a sculptor I feel that the art of Greece is the greatest known to man. The peak of that art was manifest during the golden age of Pericles. But the gods of Greece are intellectualized dogmatic conceptions that did not create a lasting moral people. The world knows their stories today only as sagas. The artistic forms alone survive.

But the Judaic people are perhaps more alive today than at any time of their long history because their all in all was a moral code, a law of practical behavior based on common sense. Their code in the writings of all their prophets and singers pulsated with the ecstasy of life and beauty, with the permanence of goodness, with a seeking after and praise of "the good life." What good we have in the world today has its roots in the Mosaic law. What sublimity we have in song has sprung from the singers of Israel, Job, David, Isaiah, the apostles, and all its singers breathe through Dante, Milton, Shakespeare and the other great ones of the Christian era.

One of the great problems of American civilization is crime. It is forbidden to mention the immediate cause, yet many keen thinkers are aware of it. The cause is the emancipation of woman and through that the teaching of boys by women teachers. The rough hardy obstreperous male child gets a sense of hopelessness from being handled by illogical emotional women teachers. Male teachers in military schools cannot even scratch the surface of the evil. They are themselves creatures of American sentimentalism. A woman who is a mother is not just a female of the species but has become a symbol of something superior. The animalistic savage demands of women for jewels, rich gowns, and other creature comforts and securities have become the ultimate good. Our schools from kindergarten to the university have become disorderly institutions to perpetuate a stupid and vicious matriarchal code. It is obvious and natural that thousands of men become criminals.

They are the national overcompensation against the gross materialism of the feminine régime. Our story tellers, poets and artists are not allowed to picture woman or sex in their reality. Only in very recent months have the facts about venereal diseases been allowed to be discussed openly.

No despot of history has fought more bitterly to suppress the truth about himself than the women of America have fought to suppress the truth about woman, her psychology, her abilities and limitations, physically and spiritually. During recent years there has been a growing tendency toward a saner direction, but whether this change will move fast enough to save America from collapse I do not know.

As a fighting people we are inferior to all other peoples. As an economic nation we are inferior to all other peoples. As an inventive people we are behind all other civilized peoples. Artistically, musically we are far in the rear. As organizers and lawmakers we are in a state of infantile puerility. Salves, codes and elixirs cannot help us. The importation and imitation of the geniuses of other peoples cannot help us. We must find and realize the facts about ourselves and build from within. In Italy, Germany or Russia you might not be allowed to discuss any subject that interfered with the ruling code in politics and economics, but you would be allowed to portray in art or literature the basic facts of life. In America we can call each other names, discuss and waste ourselves in misinformation and abuse of each other's pet codes, but we may not be true and basic in our art and literature.

Believe me, however, when I say that, dogmatic as these statements of opinion may seem, I give them only as an artist's picture. I do not know the ultimate good or bad of America or of our code of matriarchalism. It is hateful and ugly to me. Even as a child I hated violently any restriction imposed by a woman. I am an artist and my delight is to formulate life as I see it and feel it, yet reserve the right to change my point of view. As an artist the mood is everything, and the mood of the night is one, the mood of the day another.

In this narrative of my life I have tried as far as possible to reproduce the moods of childhood, youth, maturity, and middle age. I have tried to make not a unified picture but a chaotic sequence of my moods through the years. I have not found cohesion but variation and contradiction. My philosophical digressions have not been made to express ultimate wisdom, but, since I am a moralizer, a generalizer, a chronic preacher, they help to give a picture of an artist with such a handicap. The things of value in my life are those few pieces of sculpture that have merit. My poems and writings are compensations to sur-

vive in a world that has not given me sufficient employment in
my art. All other occupations, adventures and aberrations away
from my sculpture have been hateful to me.

I have never desired wealth or fame, but I have yearned with
an aching heart for the association of creative minds. My misfortune has been that my temperament and my art have not
been necessities to the people of my time. There has been no
real market for my essential talents.

I view with acute joy, however, the fact that I have created
a few pieces of sculpture that are included in permanent collections and am happy in the knowledge that their forms are pioneer forms. That others have copied them has proved that they
are real contributions.

I am not a lover of my fellow man individually. Not my
father nor my mother nor other relatives, friends, or comrades
remain in my memory as being so desirable that I would care
to see or live with them again. The only exception is my second
wife, Cora. In the stillness of the night when the mind is dry
and cold and sees nakedly and microscopically the facts of the
past, I remember her with infinite delight. I do not, however,
long for her. If it were possible to take up life with her in
some other plane of existence I would not desire it. I hate
repetitions. I do not believe in the permanence of any personal relation. We change from day to day, from year to year,
and we can never return. The permanence lies in our memory.

In remembering Cora I am happy that I lived for a time with
a goddess, a very superior person. On her deathbed she sent a
message to me through the lady who was with her. The message was: "Tell him I forgive, that he has been cruel but that
I forgive him." The message left me cold. She no longer
existed in my scheme of things. My memory of her was my
property. I had earned it, won it, and it was mine. What she
was when she died did not concern me. When I walked out of
the door of our home on Rue Tournefort in Paris she was dead

to me. She had made the change and I accepted it. I had to travel on, hurry in my ardent journey to new experiences. I am still traveling and the years stretch out ahead full of mystery and adventure.